A History of Professional Photography in Australia

Paul Curtis

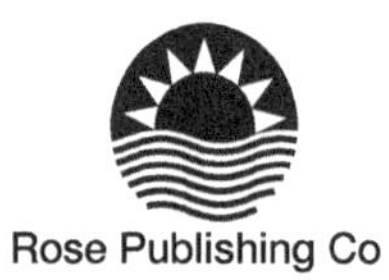

Rose Publishing Co

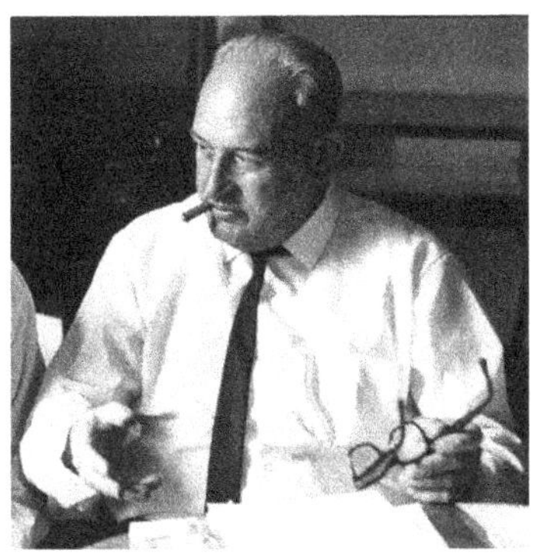

Claude McCarthy OAM
1911-1993

This book is dedicated to the memory of Claude McCarthy, the true father of the Institute as we know it today.

Professional photographers are the visual historians of our times; covering everything from news to fashion, architectural to scientific and from babies to our race to other planets. Australia can lay claim to having one of the highest standards of professional photo creativity in the world. And that didn't happen by accident. It can be attributed to the combination of the photographer's built-in love to achieve, coupled with the educational and motivational work of the Australian Institute of Professional Photography.

This is their story.

Contents

Foreword

The Institute has always been a wonderful catalyst and enthusiasm booster for photographers. It has not only provided constant educational activities and a network of colleagues across the country, but remains a constant source of inspiration. Lifelong friendships have been forged and a helping hand or advice is always just a phone call or email away. As photographers we are very fortunate that we have a purpose, a privileged purpose: enabling unrestrained creativity and in an environment entirely of our own choosing, unencumbered by the normal constraints of human endeavour.

We are indeed privileged because through the AIPP we are able to enjoy the companionship of our peers and we are involved in explaining through photography the mysteries of life which are not available to the average person. Our only limitation is our imagination.

We have reached this 50th anniversary because of the cumulative voluntary efforts of our 24 presidents, and a huge contribution from boards, state councils and members. There is an interesting inevitability about the way an idea becomes a goal and then an unstoppable reality. And so it has been with our history project.

Past president Robert Edwards asked me in July 2011 to begin the AIPP history project with the view to having it completed for our 50th anniversary. Current president Kylie Lyons and the National Board provided an ongoing budget from February 2013. A special committee was formed and nominated me as chair to ensure our remarkable achievement did not go undocumented. My fellow committee members for this project are Greg Hocking and Ian Van der Wolde and we are all deeply indebted to them for their contributions.

We felt the AIPP history was a natural subject for Paul Curtis because he has been a great friend and supporter of the Institute since the 1970's and he has always been passionate about the photographic industry. And so he brings with his journalistic flair a sympathetic philosophy to the project. When at Iris Publishing Paul was editorial director of 7 titles, four of them photographic magazines. For eight years, he was the publisher of the Institute's official magazine, Professional Photography in Australia and afterwards was still closely involved with the Institute through his work as Executive Director of PICA and as Show Director of the annual photo show. Unfailingly courteous, Paul has supported and helped build the Canon APPAs in both its philosophy and in a practical way by overcoming many difficulties and providing the physical space at many exhibition centres. Paul's contribution to our industry has been recognised by the Photo Imaging Council's distinguished service award, The Gold Tripod and he was awarded an Honorary Fellowship of the AIPP in 2007.

This volume celebrates the very essence of what the Institute is about. I find it remarkable the way Paul has taken on the mammoth task, researched all of this information and crafted it into his inimitable and often humorous descriptions of our past endeavours and achievements. If a photograph is worth a thousand words, Paul's tome would amount to a very big stack of ten by eights!

- Richard Bennett M. Photog IV, HFAIPP, FAIPP – Bruny Island, Tasmania , 2013

Preface

Print It or Lose It

We live in fast changing times. And in this new age of digital information, those of us who have an interest in Australia's photographic history are facing some new challenges.

When I researched the first edition of the History of Professional Photography in Australia, I had copies of back issue magazines, books and photographs at my elbow covering the last hundred years. Now, seeking to update this book and cover the photographers' turbulent period of the last six years, I have had nothing for source material but my computer and internet connection. I have had to totally rely on electronic newsletters, websites and social media. Even more tellingly, not a single printed photograph for this period has touched my desk. Welcome to the digital age.

But there is a major problem. Website information is very transient and exists purely at the whim of the website's manager of the moment. I have already experienced what can happen first hand. Before my retirement from the photographic industry I used to be the chief executive officer of the photographic distributor's association, (PICA) an active body that promoted both amateur and professional photography on television, radio and the press and ran an annual photography show for more than twenty consecutive years. I compiled a history of the trade on the association's website and listed all the past presidents and the people who had received awards.

Within three weeks of my leaving, my successor decided not to be bothered with all that old stuff and opted to present a fresh face with no back glancing. So that person trashed it. So, at the click of a mouse, all that work, and history disappeared into the ether.

Which is rather ironic as for that same organisation, the major campaigns that I used to run were to urge people to print their photos.

When I first researched material for a campaign, I proposed the slogan, Print It, or Lose It. Some smart and transient marketing manager on the committee poo-poohed the idea saying it was negative and his agency could come up with something much more sophisticated. And, many thousands of dollars later, they did: it was so sophisticated, consumers couldn't understand it!

Nevertheless, in radio and television interviews I kept talking about Print It or Lose It and the media loved it. Indeed, the idea was adopted by other photo trade associations around the world.

The AIPP has been fortunate in that it has always had good editors keeping information up to date. But in the recent turmoil of change, the Institute's website has also sacrificed much of its historical records.

Fortunately, photographer and publisher, Peter Eastway, continues his excellent digital reportage and maintains a good electronic back copy service. His publications were the main source for this revision. But what happens when Peter retires?

Therefore, at that stage of life when I am heading to be my own digital file in the cloud, I am keeping faith with my Print It or Lose It mantra. So, this book, which has been revised to include new events and the awarding of new honours, will be published in both digital and printed form. Copies will be lodged with the National Library and to protect our history, that is just about as permanent as we can get. That is, unless of course, you print it. And to print it, all you need do is to go to the Amazon Print on Demand files. And where are they? In the digital cloud!

- Paul Curtis Magnetic Island, 2019

Chapter One

Forming the Impossible

How do you get a large group of artistic, strong-willed, competitive and fiercely independent photographers crowded together in one hall to share their secrets in friendship? It seems as likely as us ever seeing a day of civil and intelligent debate in parliament. Fat chance of that. But, without even threatening a single snowflake in hell, this is the miracle the Australian professional photography association has achieved.

For 100 years now, under a few different names, the association has successfully brought together the photographers of the day to share their collective knowledge, experience, creative talent and technical expertise. This ensured a very high standard of photography recorded our Australian way of life. Thanks to their expertise with the camera, those photos of yesterday's young men with trendy side-burns, tight stove-pipe trousers and winkle-picking shoes will provide family amusement for generations.

To follow the path to the formation of today's Australian Institute of Professional Photography, we need to start with the history of photography itself. But rather than beginning our journey with a single footstep, we will move at such a swift trot that true historians will blanch as white as a forgotten print in a tray of Farmer's Reducer. So hold on.

Eventually the camera obscura progressed from a portable tent, seen here being used by Johannes Kepler in the seventieth century,

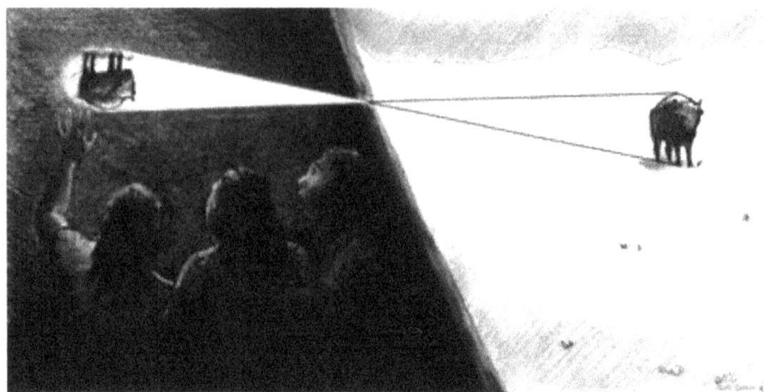

A chink in the side of a dark shelter was observed by early man as the first camera obscura.

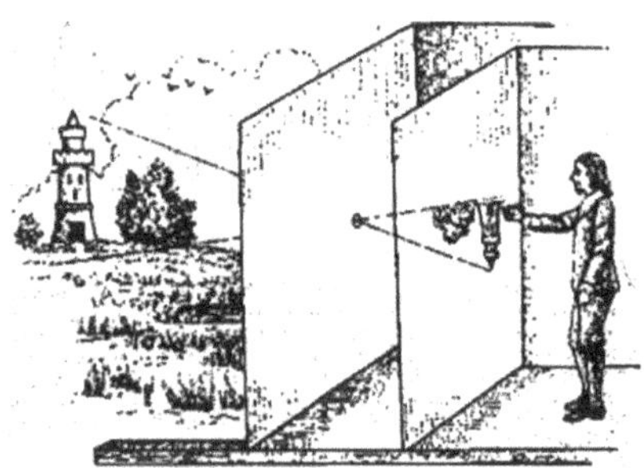

An artist using a camera obscura

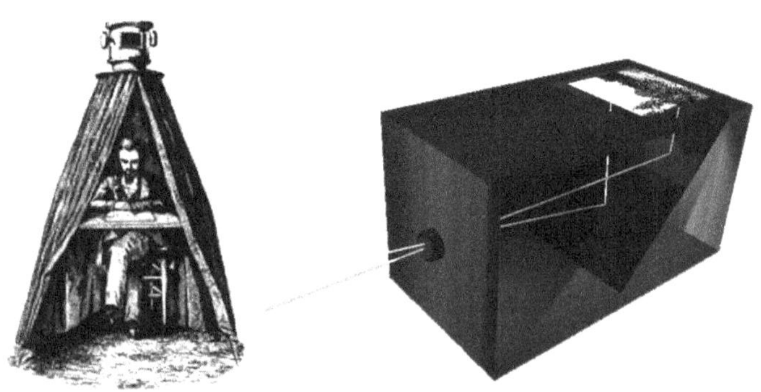

to a simple box working with mirrors in the early 1800s. Up until the 1880s, on location the tent was still being used to wet coat glass plates. Today's professional landscape photographers still use tents, but only as sleeping places waiting for that magic moment when the light is right!

Proclaiming the true inventor of photography is a bit of a challenge as the photo chemical process was more or less abandoned early in the twenty first century. So maybe the proper credit must go to the inventor of the camera itself. We still use those, right?

The camera, however, was more of a discovery than an invention. About 450 years before Christ happened along, at a time when the Athenians and Spartans were going hammer and tongs, the Chinese philosopher Mo-Ti made the first discovered mention of the principles behind the camera obscura. This tiny pearl of information comes courtesy of Wikipedia: and who could doubt that for a source?

Nearly a thousand years later, Aristotle was right into it: experimenting with different types of pinholes and wondering why whatever shape he made the hole, the sun came out round. Still makes you wonder, doesn't it?

The first evidence of a movable form of visual reproduction has been dated to 989 AD when some Arabs camping out in the sands of Saudi Arabia discovered that a pin hole in their tent was projecting an image of life outside onto the back of the tent. "Wow!" they said, looking at upside down images of camels parading past, "There must be some baksheesh in this" So thus, with a heaving stretch of the imagination, we could contend, the first professional image makers came into being.

Fast forward to the early fifteenth century and artists, such as Leonardo da Vinci had discovered another use when painting pictures. To get the perspective right, it was a really nifty trick to trace onto a sheet of paper the image formed from a camera. Doing this in a darkened tent or room had the added advantage of no one else seeing their secret of getting the perspective right.

To this day, the camera obscura is still being used, but mainly as a

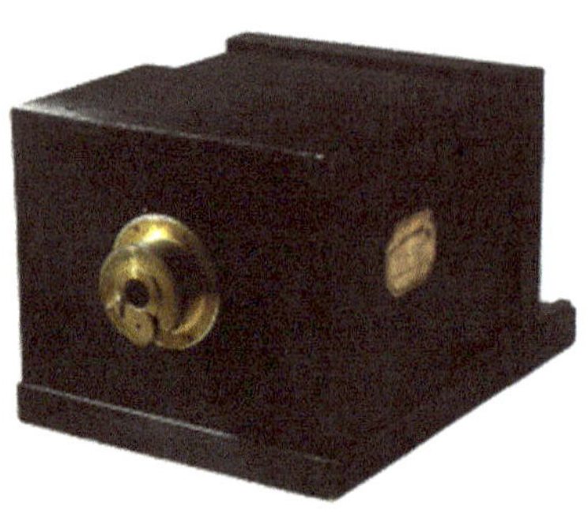

An 1839 Daguerreotype, the first camera to arrive in Australia was brought to Sydney by Captain Lucas in 1841. It was made of painted wood.

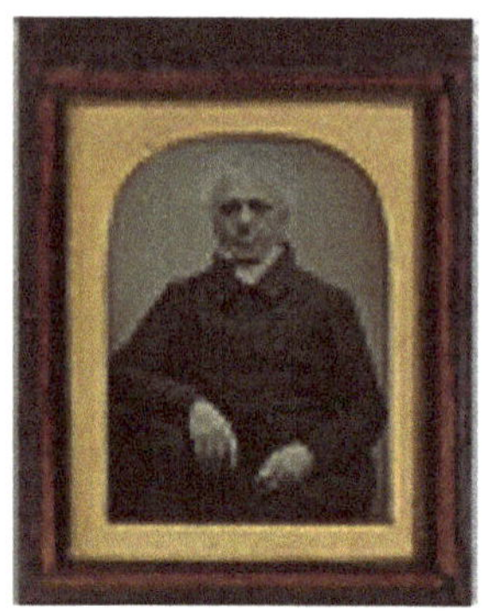

This 1845 Daguerreotype is the earliest known surviving photograph taken in Australia and was photographed by George Goodman in his Sydney Studio. The sitter, Dr William Bland, went from being an ex-convict, to a prominent surgeon, human-itarian, social reformer and inventor. The original photo is in the Mitchell Library collection.

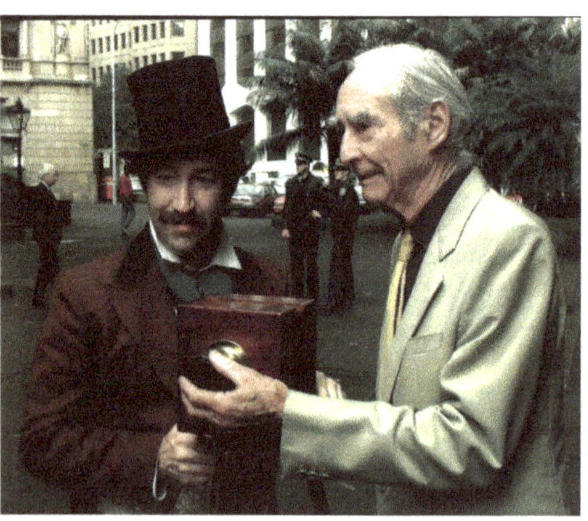

Sandy Barrie (left) re-enacting in 1991 the 150th anniversary of the taking of the first photograph in Australia. On Sandy's right he is aided by none other than legendary photographer Max Dupain. Photo: Peter Rattray.

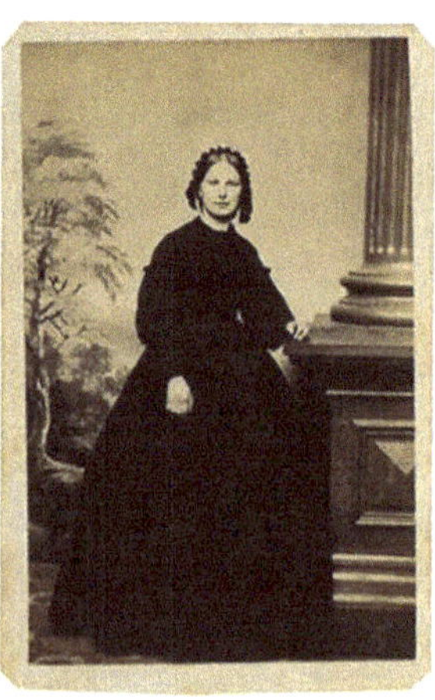

A carte de visite, the must have social calling card in the 1850s, was printed by pho-tographers for their clients.

tourist attraction. There's a very elaborate one located, strangely yet maybe even appropriately, in a Los Angeles Senior Citizens Centre. It's just up the beach from the Santa Monica Pier. Entrance is free: you really should go. Inside, you can rotate an old ship's wheel to operate a roof-top revolving turret to pan the projected image across a darkened wall to see all the activity taking place along the beach front. Last time I was there I overheard a young girl squealing with delight. "Oh look, she cried, it's just like YouTube!"

However, for all its versatility, the camera obscura has one far from obscure failing: the images don't last. Come sunset, they are gone! First in the queue to solve this problem came Frenchman Joseph Niepce. He snapped the first photograph on a fine summer's day in 1827 with an eight hour exposure on a metal plate coated with bitumen. The problem was that the resulting image didn't last any longer than the exposure. Palling up with fellow countryman Louis Daguerre, the two worked together to create a chemical process that after twelve years work reduced the exposure time to a mere 30 minutes and created a so called permanent image. At this point, Niepce died, which was convenient enough for Daguerre to lay sole claim to the naming rights.

Meanwhile, across the channel, Englishman Fox Talbot was working on the same problems. He came up with the negative to positive process that became the true basis of photography. So the idea of Niepce being the father of photography is sometimes challenged by Englishmen with more fervent jingoistic tendencies. But while these three founding fathers were all in on inception, if not conception, a more recent paternity suit could be brought by Steven Sasson, the Kodak electrical engineer who in 1978 invented the digital imaging sensor. Some sour pundits might claim that this was in fact the actual death of photography. Whatever. But it certainly didn't seem to do Kodak any good. Its 1889 advertising call proclaimed 'You Press the Button and We Will Do the Rest'. But alas in 2005, professional photographers found they did not need film and could do the rest quite well without them.

But we are rushing ahead of ourselves. Let's go back to the Niepce family, which on Joseph's death sold its patents to the French Government. It chose to license the patents to professional photographers. Fox Talbot took a very restrictive approach with his process and kept his secrets close to his chest.

After considerable public pressure, he finally allowed amateur photographers to use his process for free. But, and it was a big but, professional photographers had to pay him a commission on every shot. This helped the Niepce Daguerre system, now named Daguerreotypes, to fast gain popularity with the growing group of professional photographers.

On April 13th 1841, the Australian Chronicle reported the taking of the first photograph to be made in Australia. 'The inhabitants of Sydney', it proudly proclaimed, ' will now have the opportunity of witnessing the effects of this very singular invention, one of the instruments having been brought to the colony by Captain Lucas, late commander of the Naval School expedition'.

So historical records would have it that Captain Augustine Lucas, the English captain of a French vessel, was our first amateur, but very keen photographer. It was a view of Sydney's Bridge Street taken from Macquarie Place. While that photograph has now been lost, photo historian, Sandy Barrie re-enacted the event on May thirteenth 1991, exactly 150 years later. Sandy is a Brisbane professional photographer and an Honorary Life Member of the Institute.

Sandy dressed the part in period costume and used an identical Daguerre camera to retake the same scene to create a media event that was commemorated by Australia Post with the release of a special first day cover. Of course, the street scene itself had changed. Horses and carts had been replaced by Holdens and Fords. Sandy also chose to back up his efforts with one of the first digital cameras to be ever be used in Australia, an endeavour in which he was assisted by another highly notable Institute member, Doug Spowart.

Sandy is an incredible character and although now retired, he is as keen and passionate as ever about photography. He devotes his every spare moment to collecting photo memorabilia and has an outstanding collection of both historical photographs and camera equipment. To read a proper history of early Australian photographers there is no better source than his 2001 book Australians Behind the Camera. For the period between 1841 and 1945, this lists 17,000 professional photographers. Since publication and thanks to the Trove Newspaper Digitisation project, Sandy's further research has brought the total number in that period to nearly 20,000. Either way, there were certainly a lot more in those early times than the approximate 5000 professional photographers of today.

Sandy played the part of a photographer in the movie Deluge, the story of the great Brisbane flood of 1893, only, in a cruel twist of fate, to see his own home and a large part of his immensely valuable and historical photo collection fall victim to the Brisbane and Ipswich floods of 2011. As the waters rose, Sandy worked hard to move his enormous collection to the top of his house. But unfortunately, even at the highest storey, the water level rose above shoulder height. In spite of the help of volunteers that later came to help salvage the images, much of the collection was irretrievably damaged. Sandy also lost nearly all his other possessions. But thanks in no small part to Sandy, we know much about our early professional photographers. The year following the commemoration of the first photo ever taken in Australia, he was back in action with the re-enactment of the first day of operation of Australia's first professional studio. This was opened by George Baron Goodman on the twelfth of December in 1842.

So George was the first professional photographer on our Antipodean shores. Arriving from London in 1842, he chose Sydney as the place to open a studio. Convicts were being relocated from New South Wales, mainly to Tasmania, would you believe? So, while east coast cities were becoming more genteel, Tasmania's population was becoming…. larger! But with a population of more than 35,000, Sydney was the big city. Melbourne's population was just under 8000.

For the rights to be the first licensed photographer in Australia, Goodman paid one thousand pounds… a sum that would equate to a few million dollars today. George set up a roof top studio at the

Royal Hotel. On a bright day, with his Daguerreotype camera, he could snap off an exposure in just five seconds. Goodman even advertised that he had chosen his location "so as to be as near the sun as possible", a fact which no doubt impressed prospective clients. It would have to be brighter there, right? There were some odd misconceptions about photography floating around in those days. Many thought bad chemistry was the cause of out of focus pictures and called it 'chemical focus'.

But George was sharp enough and charged a never ending stream of customers one guinea (one pound and one shilling) for one Daguerreotype photo with a frame and case. To put that fee in perspective, that was around a week's wages for an unskilled worker. Alas, not many professional photographers can claim to get that much for a portrait these days.

But a depression soon hit and in order to keep finding new clients, Goodman travelled Australia. Consequently, he is believed to also be the first professional photographer to arrive in Melbourne. In July 1845, the Melbourne Port Phillip Patriot reported: 'We congratulate the public of this District on the arrival of Mr. Goodman from Sydney, with his Daguerreotype machine, whereby such perfect likenesses can be taken in the course of a few seconds. Here is an opportunity for ladies and gentlemen to get their miniatures executed in the most exquisite style, neatly framed in morocco and gold, fit to be presented to those who love them, or transmitted as a memento to their friends at home. As soon as Mr. Goodman has fixed on a place of business he will himself address the public, and announce his readiness to serve them with his magic art.' And sure enough, just two weeks later, he magically opened for business in Flinders Lane.

Goodman did not have the professional photography business to himself for long. Others were quickly arriving from Europe and establishing themselves in each of the colonies and going on road trips to take photos in quite small towns. Prices began falling with newspapers carrying advertising for portraits from ten shillings upwards. One advertisement even proclaimed that "children will be executed between 10.00am and 4.00pm". Oh to have been a photographer in those days.

The first woman professional photographer in Australia is recorded as Thekla Hetzer, who along with her husband William Hetzer, set up a studio in Sydney's Hunter Street in 1850.

The Gold Rush was on and the arrival of carte-de-visite photography in the 1850s lead to a boom for the growing number of portrait studios Through the use of a sliding plate holder and a camera with four lenses, four exposures could be taken on a single 8" x 10" glass wet plate. At this time it was the custom to present one's calling card when making a social visit and one bearing your own photo was very classy indeed. The cards sold for about 15 shillings a dozen. Mass production had arrived.

With more and more people turning to photography, in March 1856, The Melbourne Argus published an advertisement to form a photographic society. This was probably the first bid to set up an association in Australia. Other attempts followed and in 1872 the first amateur photographic society of NSW was formed.

In 1884, the popularity of taking photographs was given a real boost when Thomas Baker greatly simplified the process for Australian photographers. He formed the Austral Plate Company at Abbotsford in Melbourne and began producing dry plates. Up until that time, the glass plates were wet coated just before exposure. Baker was joined by John Rouse in 1887 and the company become Baker and Rouse. In the first decade of the twentieth century the company evolved again to become Kodak Australasia with Baker and Rouse both being foundation Kodak Australasian directors.

The first successful formation of a professional photographers association was in Queensland in 1894. This sowed the seeds for the formation of professional photographers associations in other states, but these early organisations were very much a stop-go affair and worked very much along union guidelines for the ever growing and popular number of street photographers. The idea of forming a national photographic body would have been unthinkable at this time as Australia consisted of six separate British self-governing colonies.

Although the idea of Australian federation was often mooted, it was the subject of fierce and protracted debate. There were those that opposed change and loss of power. Others thought that such driving issues as Chinese immigration, vine diseases, uniform tariff rates and concern about the activities of the Germans and French in New Guinea and the New Hebrides required a national approach. Colony leaders met to discuss issues, but the path to Federation was opposed in particular by New South Wales and New Zealand. Finally, in 1901, New South Wales caved in and the colonies became the Commonwealth of Australia. New Zealand, however, is still holding out!

The very first foundations of what was to finally become the Australian Institute of Professional Photography were laid in 1912 when Harold Cazneaux of Freemans Studio and Sydney Riley came together with other studio owners to form what was to became known as The Professional Photographers' Association of N.S.W. Monte Luke joined this group when he took over from Harold Cazneaux at Freemans in 1920.

In Victoria, in 1913, under the founding presidency of Andrew Barrie, studio employees and some manufacturers and importers began discussions with the State Wages Board in Victoria to cover people employed in the industry. Although it called itself the Photographic Employers Association of Victoria, it was the first organisation that allowed both studio owners and operators to join. It quickly expanded its reach into Geelong and in 1930, in honour of its more catholic approach to membership, renamed itself as the Professional Photographers' Association of Victoria. Ten years later, the association went through another name change and became the Institute of Victorian Photographers. In his last days, Andrew Barrie, reminisced, "Don't gamble: photography has given me two fortunes and I've lost three in mining shares."

Those who didn't lose their money in business gambles were carving out long, successful and highly profitable careers. A new breed of photographers from Europe arrived to help reshape the photographic scene in Australia. Melbourne's Collins Street and areas nearby became the centre for such influential photographers as Arthur Dickenson, Spencer Shier, Athol Shmith, Wolfgang Sievers, Helmut Newton and Henry Talbot. Athol Shmith became president of the Professional Photographers Association and, in 1939, the first president of the Institute of Victorian Photographers.

In September of 1932 the first issue of what was to become the Institute's official magazine was launched under the editorship of Arthur Cattanach. In 1948 it officially became the IAP Journal, taking its initials for the Institute of Australian Photography. Long time contributor Clive Stuart Tompkins became the founding editor and, apart from a few breaks during the Second World War, began an unbroken recording of the history of professional photography in Australia that continues to this very day. Interestingly, in that entire time, there have only been four editors involved. Tompkins has only been succeeded by Neil Murray, Paul Burrows and Peter Eastway. In my time as publisher of the Institute's magazine I was lucky enough to work with the last three and the material in this book could not have been gathered without their assistance.

We will come to hear more of Murray, Burrows and Eastway later on, but Stuart was a key figure in the Institute's early affairs. Institute foundation member Ian Hawthorne described Stuart in later years as 'a fussy, rotund, middle aged Mr Pickwick of a man, of precise character but a fine portrait photographer'. According to Ian, Stuart did everything for the magazine. 'He edited, he largely wrote it, he did the layouts, he sought the subscriptions and he approached the advertisers.' When Neil took over the editorship in 1966, for advertising and distribution management tasks he had the backing of publisher Gordon Hill of the Beaver Group. According to Murray, Stuart also had the 'dubious honour' in 1931 of introducing Mother's Day to Australia.

Born in 1900, Stuart began his photography career at a young age as an assistant to Spencer Shier (1884-1950) one of the well known Collins Street group of photographers. Shier was very much in favour with Melbourne's society scene but used to attend fashion-

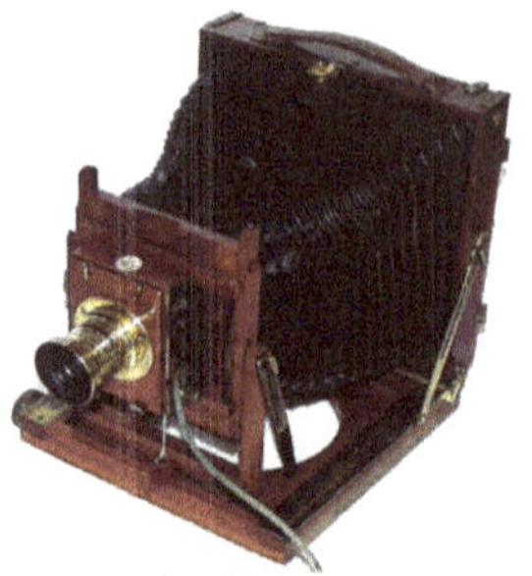

Cameras in the 19th century were often made mostly of lacquered wood rather than covered in leather. This is a Thornton Pickard.

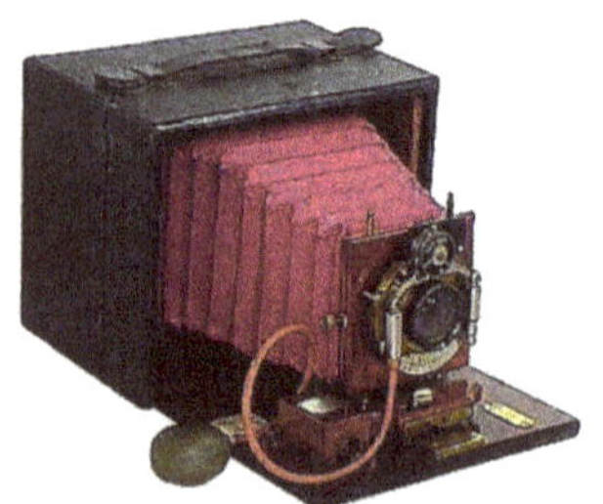

During the 1910s, nickel plated parts become more common than lacquered brass, and red or maroon bellows go out of fashion, such as on this Reko.

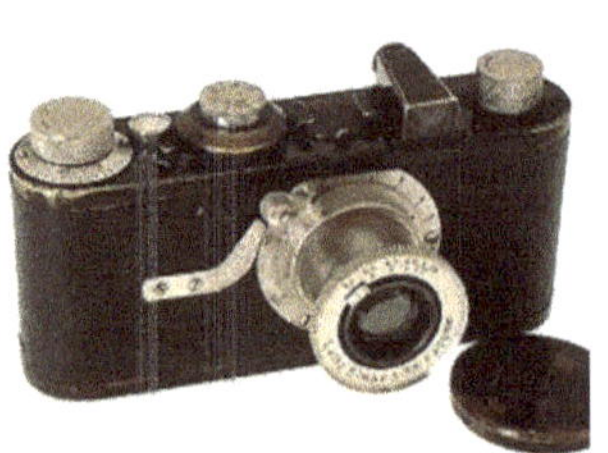

In 1925 the Leica 1 arrives, setting a style trend for satin chrome plated top housings and black covered bodies that held sway for the next forty years.

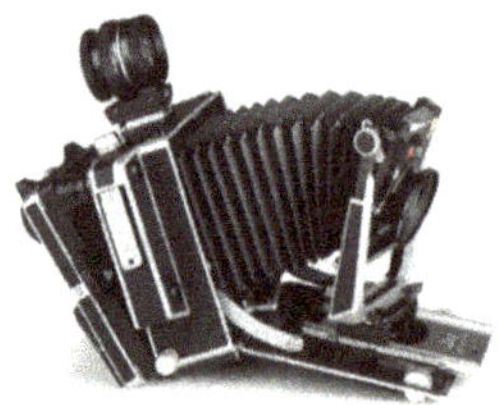

Nikolaus Karpf, joined Linhof in 1934 and designed the first Technika model: the world's first all-metal folding field camera, the same year.

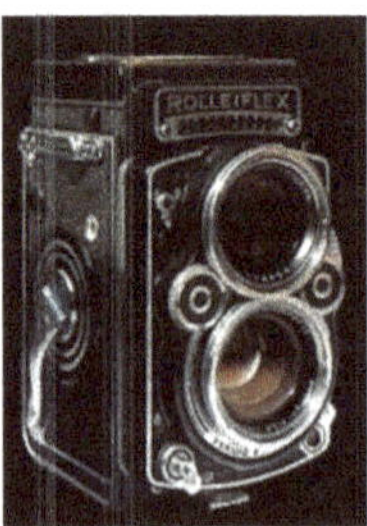

The 1950s saw the Rolleiflex 120 twin lens reflex, with lever wind and a selenium cell light meter, becoming popular with professionals.

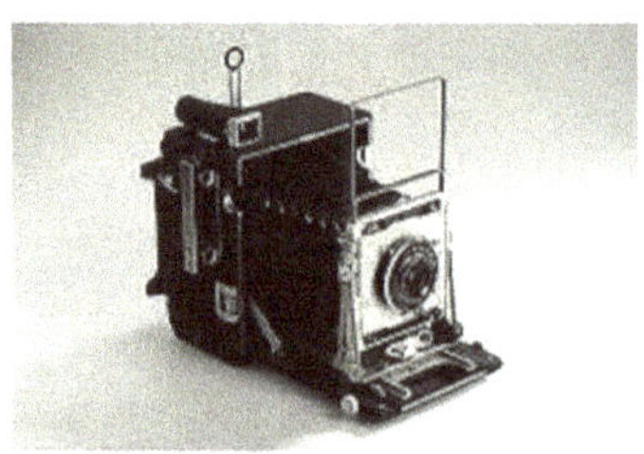

Although the first Speed Graphic cameras were produced in 1912. The milestone camera was the Pacemaker Speed Graphic in 1947. It was still slow and complicated in operation and to be sure they had all the steps right, photographers used to beg for "Just one more". President Harry Truman would introduce the White House photographers as the "Just One More Club."

able weddings on a motorbike with Stuart and all the gear packed into the sidecar.

Weekend weddings were fast and furious affairs and Tompkins later recalled that lunch, if any, was just a block of chocolate. Shier was succeeded at his Collins Street studio by Austin Murcott, who in turn sold it to the legendary Jack Cato. Born in Tasmania in 1889, Jack travelled to London to become a theatre photographer, photographing such celebrities as Melba. Jack wrote, 'In my younger days, Victoria was almost the only important person in her reign who didn't wear whiskers. My age was my chief problem: at seventeen it was considered impertinent for a beardless youth to push himself forward. Today, we are willing to indulge and help the enterprise of youth.'

Back in Australia, Jack Cato joined the PPA of Victoria in the early thirties and became senior vice president in 1938. He later became an Honorary Life Member of the Institute. With Dame Nellie Melba for a patron, Jack's powerful portrait work became enormously successful. But he never lost his irreverent sense of humour and had what was described as immoderate laughter. John Scott Simmonds, who worked with Cato, told the story of this exchange with another famous photographer, Dr Julian Smith, at the opening of a Cato exhibition at Melbourne's Athenaeum Gallery. Noticing the doctor inspecting the exhibits, Cato came up to him. 'Well doctor, how do you like my exhibition?' Dr Julian didn't bother to turn and look round. Still inspecting the prints, beard jutting forward in typical style, he replied briefly. 'Nice frames Cato. Nice frames.'

In later years, Cato sold out to John Warlow to concentrate on his writing. His last major work was in 1955: The Story of the Camera in Australia. Thanks to the support of Institute past president Ian McKenzie, this book is still available today.

The 1940s, according to Geelong studio photographer Laurie Wilson, were the 'Golden Years of Photography'. After first studying and then working with the early Geelong studio photographer, Jack Lockwood, Laurie opened his own studio in the same town in 1945.

He was never a well man, which was not so unusual for photographers of the black and white darkroom era. The various photographic processes produced toxic gases in the confined space of darkrooms built to allow no ingress of light. Consequently, if they were ventilated at all, it was only very poorly. Today's material safety data sheets warn you of the hazards, but up until the 1960s it was given scant consideration.

In my youth, I proudly wore the brown Amidol staining caused by having my right finger immersed in print developer all day as if it were a badge of office. Foolish boy! Sitting on a stool, nose just above a deep tray of print developer, the left hand was carefully kept dry to feed an over growing pile of blank exposed prints into the tray at twenty second intervals. The right hand was deeply immersed in the developer, constantly shuffling the prints one on top of the other. Occasionally, a reluctant highlight on a print would be encouraged with a rubbing of the warm finger, or in more severe cases, the print would be lifted close to the lips and breathed on. Ah those fumes... Heady stuff.

The common small stuffy darkrooms were packed with toxic chemicals: such as developers giving off bromines and sodium bisulphite hydroquinone; stop baths giving off acetic acid and then the fixer solutions: first slowly releasing sulphur dioxide gas and then rapidly increasing as the solution aged and become contaminated with acid from the stop bath.

All this caused damage to organs such liver, kidneys, lungs, stomach gastrointestinal tract, skin and eyes. For this photographer's cocktail of delight, add damage to nasal passages, allergic reactions, ulcerations, eye irritants, depigmentation and then top it all off with an unhealthy but generous dose of carcinogens.

Today those wanting to revisit such arcane processes are warned to ensure good ventilation of the darkroom, with at least, ten air changes per hour. Then they are told they must always wear gloves and goggles; that they should cover all solutions when not in use to prevent evaporation or release of toxic vapours and gases. If a splash does occurs, the affected areas must be immediately flushed with water using an eyewash or safety shower, with fifteen to twenty minutes for eyes. Those days, in our appalling ignorance, sitting at the trays in our normal clothes, we just blinked.

So you can see that living in such times why Laurie was not a healthy man. But recalling the forties in 1970, Laurie said, 'The public image of a photographer was high. People wanted photographs. It was as easy as that. There was no need to leave the studio, either to seek work or to take work. Everyone: from returning servicemen to kids in fancy dress, from girls who simply bought a new outfit, debs, scouts, schoolboys, brides, babies to elderly couples celebrating a golden wedding anniversary: all came or were brought in 'to have their photos taken'.

'Candids', said Laurie, 'were regarded as something nasty and the resulting glossies as cheap rubbish. Studio portraits were very formal and printed on matt surface paper, which was usually sepia toned or hand coloured.

'Six weddings could be handled easily in an afternoon by one operator, assisted by his wife arranging the gowns. There were no weekend casuals equipped with hundreds of dollars worth of equipment! No albums, no electronic flash, no travelling. Just one camera and a handful of half plate double dark slides was all that was needed.'

Laurie also spoke of the long queues of locals that would line up to view every studio change of window. In the late fifties, after school, I was entrusted by my local studio with the job of changing the wedding window photos every Monday afternoon and I recall such days well. When my task was completed I would hide behind the backing of lace curtain to eavesdrop on the mouth watering and juicy tittle-tattle floating through an open fanlight window. The people they had only ever seen before in working corduroy and chequered cloth caps were now all dressed up in hired once-in-a-lifetime finery. As recognition slowly dawned there would come exclamations of astonishment. My favourite, and in my head I can still hear their Hampshire accents, came from two middle-aged, black-dressed war widows leaning over the shopping bag laden handlebars of their ancient bicycles. 'Coorrr blimey! There's our Maureen!' 'Stone me' said the other leaning even closer, 'An' 'er gettin' married in white an' all! ' See… standards were different in those days.

Of course, while still at school, changing the studio window was about all I was allowed to do. I did, however, at age sixteen get to regularly take photos for the local paper, as that sort of assignment was considered beneath the dignity of the studio owner. For this I was equipped with a large and heavy MPP 5x4 camera which used the double dark slide film holder Laurie referred to as 'all that was needed'. These were not slides as we came to know them. The word refers to the sliding back of the light proof sheath that protected the large sheet of negative film from light before it was slid into the camera back. After the picture was taken, the protective sheath was reinserted and then the holder reversed for a picture to be taken on the other side.

For some years after the war, the 5x4 sheet of film was both hard to obtain and very expensive. In my case, I was dispatched on an old 125cc BSA Bantam motorcycle with just the one camera, two household-sized flash globes and one double dark slide film holder. One side was for the single shot of the assignment, the other was in case I encountered some newsworthy event such as an accident on my way to or from the job.

You can imagine the amazement this generation of photographers experienced when they could switch to the new twin lens Rolleiflex that could take twelve pictures on just one roll of film! However, the old 5x4 press camera had one big advantage: its bellows was rolled out on a large and substantial base plate that was ideal for banging on the head of those 35mm toting amateurs that were always running in to kneel in front of you and then pop up right in front of your shot! 'Oh dear,' one would murmur, 'so sorry.'

These were the sort of tricks one learnt from association with other photographers, but there were more important agendas at work as well. By the forties, professional associations had formed in most Australian states. However, two World Wars and the slow methods of communication made for difficult liaison between the various bodies.

In March 1944 the country was experiencing numerous difficulties. Australian Prime Minister John Curtin's health was fading, post war meat rationing had begun, bushfires in Victoria had killed 51 people and the Queensland government was about to return Fred Paterson as the Member for Bowen: the first and only ever communist party member to gain a seat in an Australian parliament. It was into this climate, and before the Liberal Party of Australia had even been formed, that in March 1944, photographers from around Australia first gathered in Sydney to discuss forming a federal body. Under the neutral chairmanship of E.L. (Les) Sharpe, the meeting discussed 'wartime restrictions and Government impositions' and resolved the idea of forming the Professional Photographers Association of Australia to speak as a united voice and to represent the profession throughout the country. It was also resolved to have an annual conference and an annual election.

The first conference of photography was held in 1945 in Sydney with Sidney S Riley being elected as president. Sidney was heavily involved with the association and made strong representations to the federal government on the issue of sales tax. The following year saw the conference being held in Melbourne with Stuart Tompkins elected as president. In the same year, another key player who was going to have such a long term effect on the shape of the association joined the executive: Claude E McCarthy from Brisbane.

The use of first names was not such a normal thing in those days and it took some digging to discover that at the Perth conference in 1947 the federal president that followed and simply recorded as V. Penrose, was actually Victor Penrose. The following year, at the Adelaide conference in 1948, Gilbert Meller from South Australia became president.

Born in 1892, Gilbert started his professional career in South Australia at the age of seventeen. He was the first Australian photographer to use electric lighting: an arc light of a thousand watts which let him capture a portrait without sunlight with just a ten second exposure. If he used his studio for too long, the district would suffer a brown out. South Australia's, The Electric Supply Company, would then hastily dispatch a boy to run down and tell him to please switch the light off.

At the Brisbane conference in 1949, Alva Duryea from Queensland was elected. At a Melbourne conference Gilbert Meller then returned for a second term that ran from 1950 to 1954. At the next conference, again held in Melbourne, R. Brock was elected in a run that lasted until 1957.

The president's position then switched back to New South Wales with Val Waller being elected president through to 1963.

The lengthening terms of the presidents show that with the high cost of interstate travel managing a conference every year was proving difficult. There was a definite loss of momentum and there was considerable discussion about the restrictive practice of only allowing the owners of the studios to attend meetings. This cut out all studio staff and any photographer working for newspapers or the government.

There was a strong division between the studio owners and staff with the key factors being that the some studio owners viewed their staff photographers as future competition and they did not want them privy to all their secrets. Another factor playing a part was that the owners did not want their staff knowing too much about work conditions in other studios or the growing awareness of the health and safety issues of chemical photography.

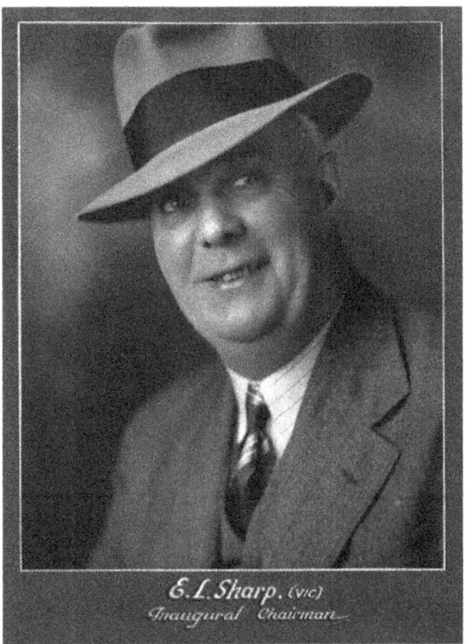

Inaugural Chairman of the Professional Photographers Assoc of Australia (PPAofA)

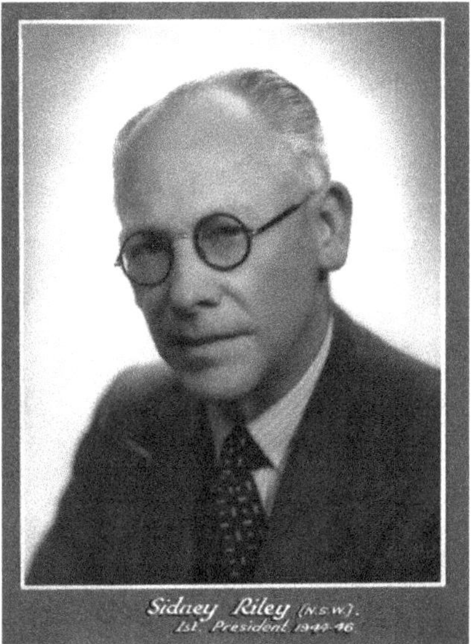

First 'Professional Photographers Assoc of Australia' President 1944-46

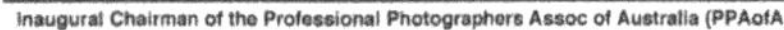

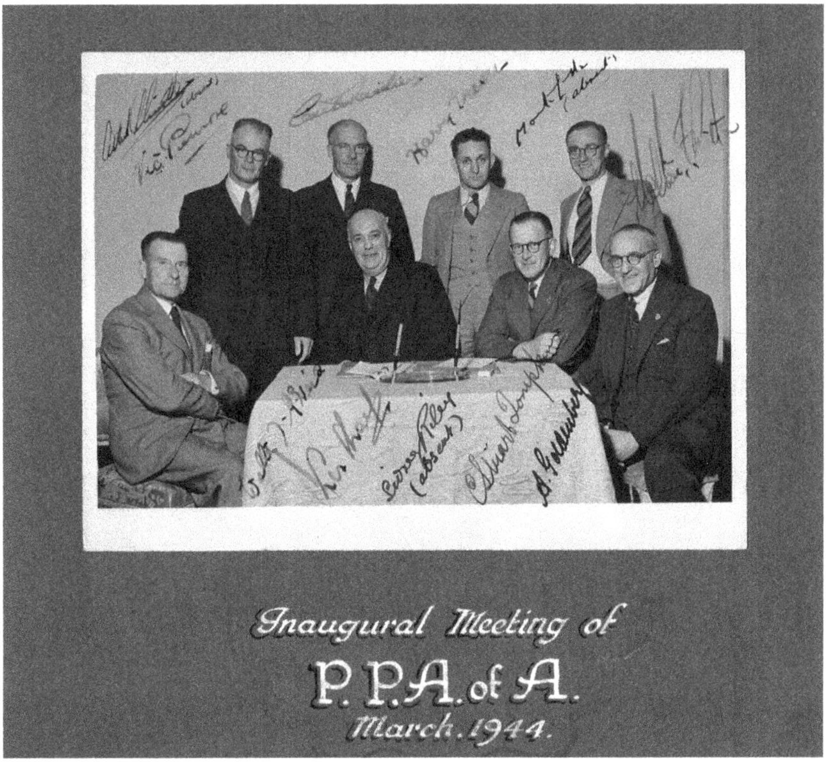

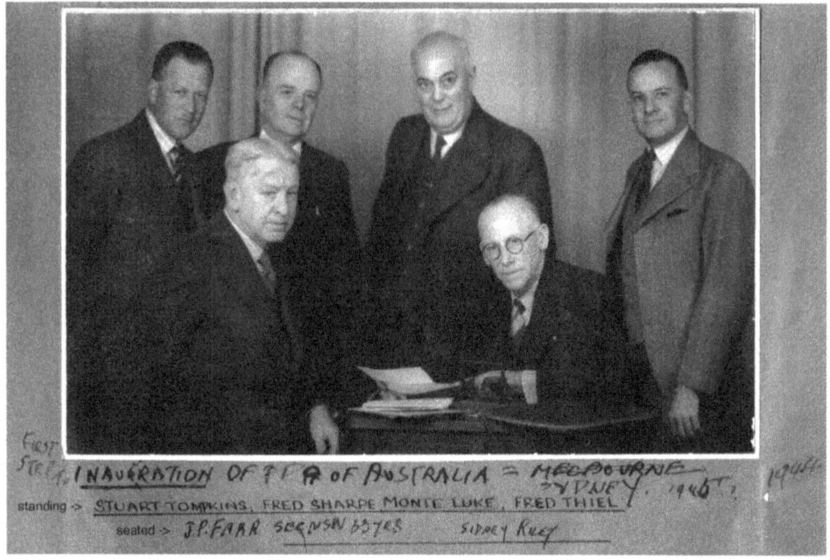
INAUGURATION OF P.P.A. OF AUSTRALIA — MELBOURNE SYDNEY, 1945
standing -> STUART TOMPKINS, FRED SHARPE, MONTE LUKE, FRED THIEL
seated -> J.P.FARR, SORENSEN, BATES, SIDNEY RILEY

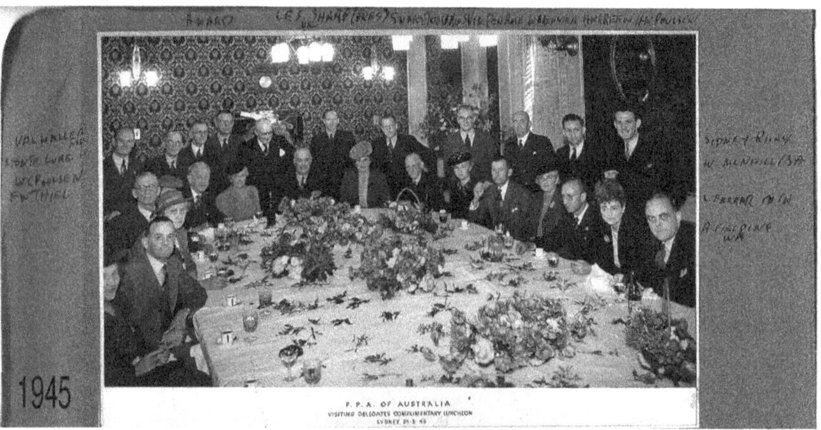
1945
P. P. A. OF AUSTRALIA
VISITING DELEGATES COMPLIMENTARY LUNCHEON
SYDNEY

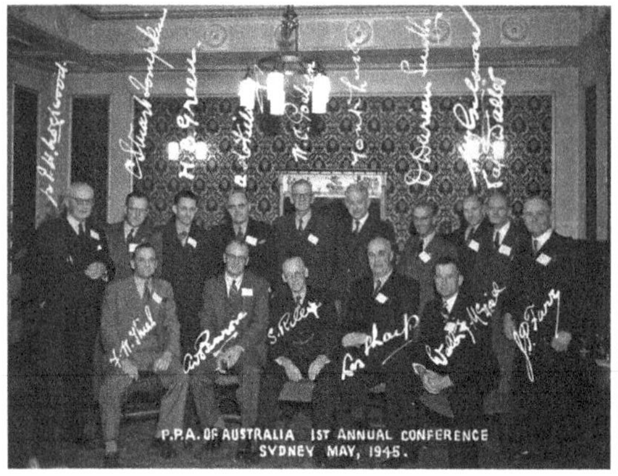
P.P.A. OF AUSTRALIA   1ST ANNUAL CONFERENCE
SYDNEY MAY, 1945.

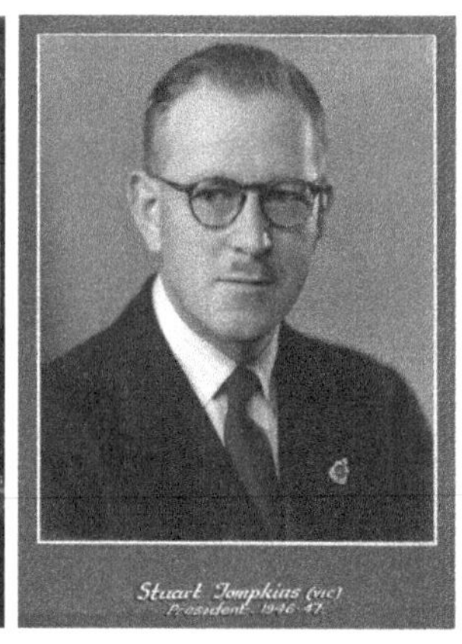
Stuart Tompkins (VIC)
President 1946-47.

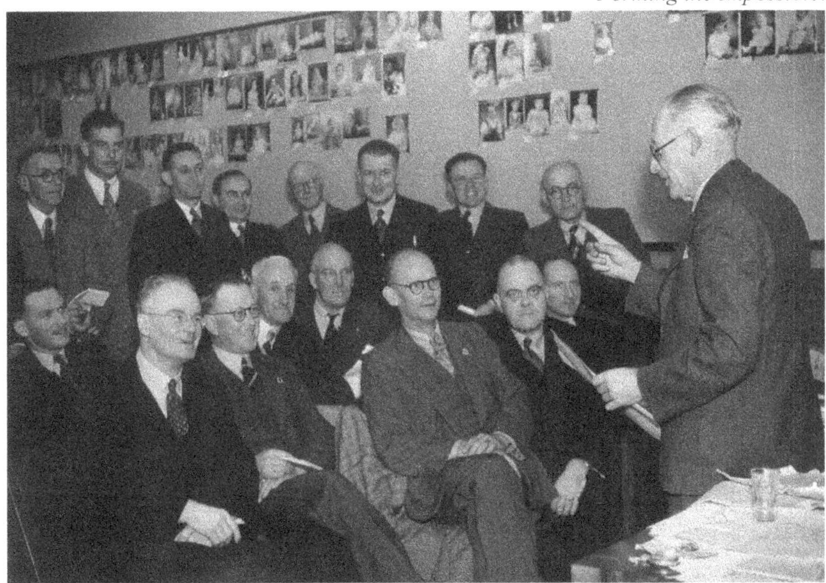

"Sid" in Melbourne 1946 (looks like Sidney Riley talking to the conference delegates)

1946- unknow location

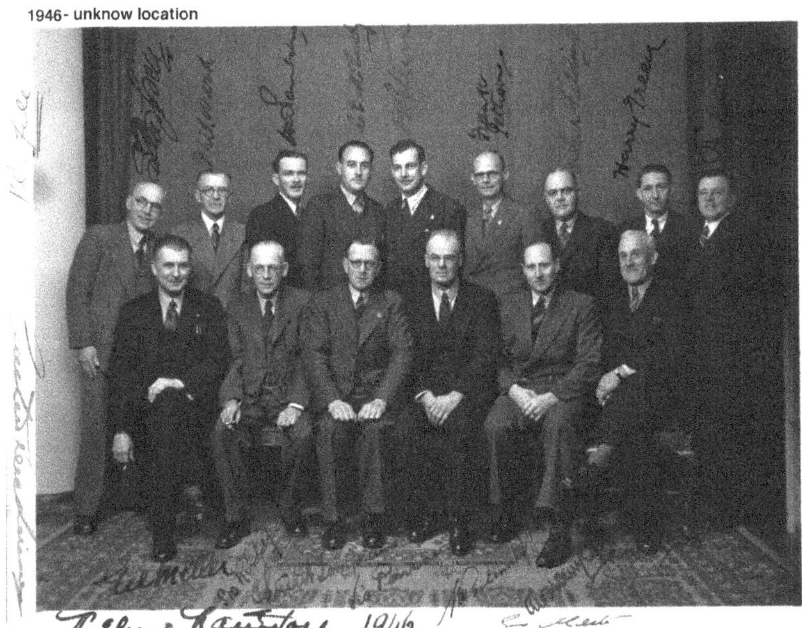

1 ?, 2 Phil Ward, 3 Harry Poulson (Qld), 4 Claude McCarthy (Qld), 5 ?, 6 Frank Peterson, 7 Arthur Fielding (WA), 8 Harry Green (Qld), 9 ?, 10 Gil Muller 11 Sidney Riley (NSW), 12 Stuart Tompkins (Vic), 13 Vic Penrose (WA), 14 ?, 15 Alva Duryea (Qld). *See the TIFF file for identity numbers on the people.*

Photographs: David McCarthy Collection

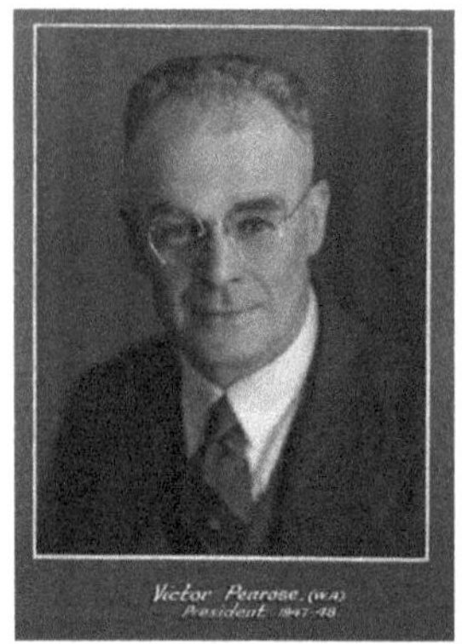

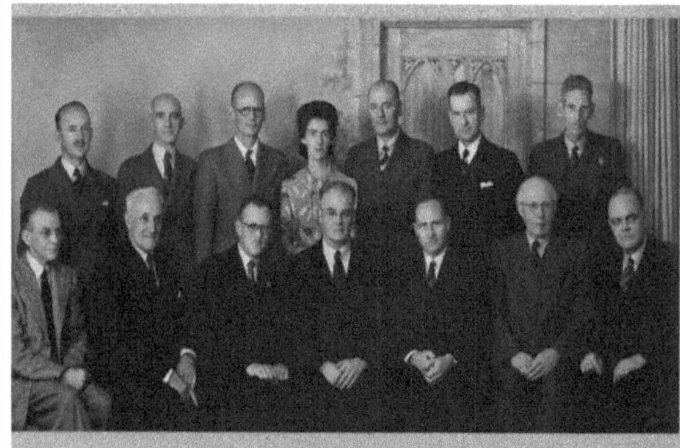

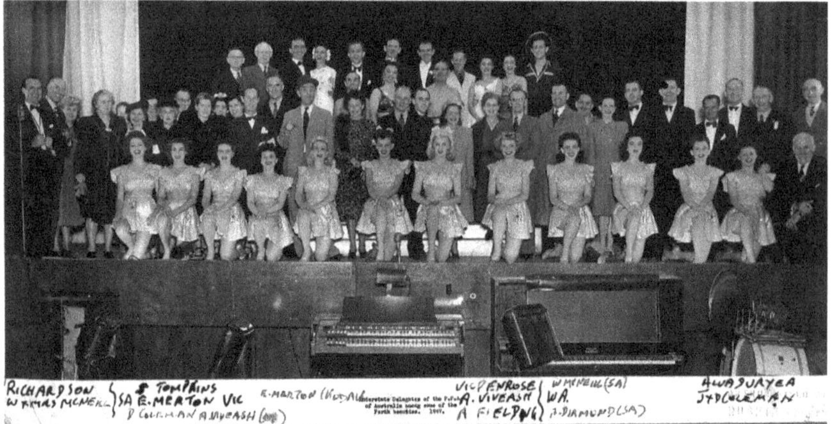

Title says : *"Interstate Delegates of PPA of A among some of the Perth beauties"*.

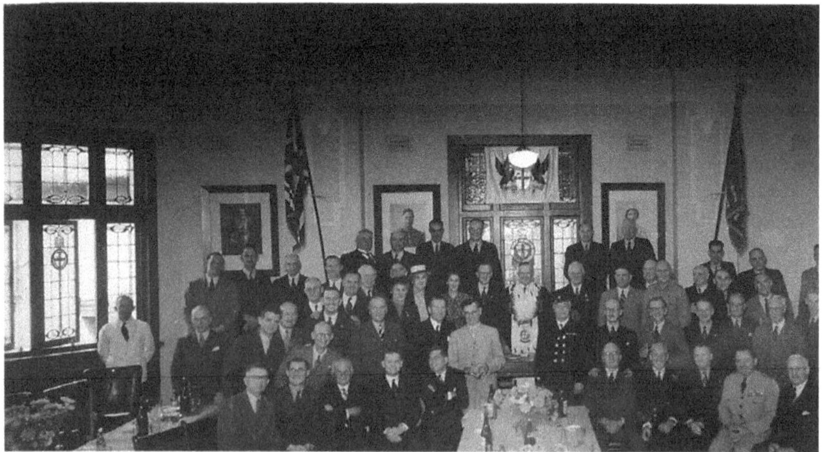

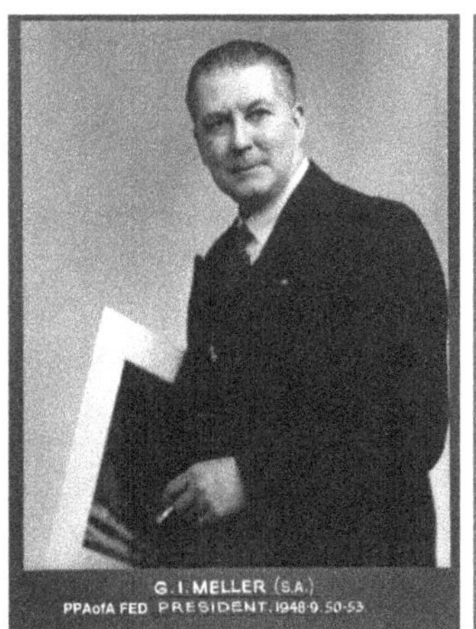

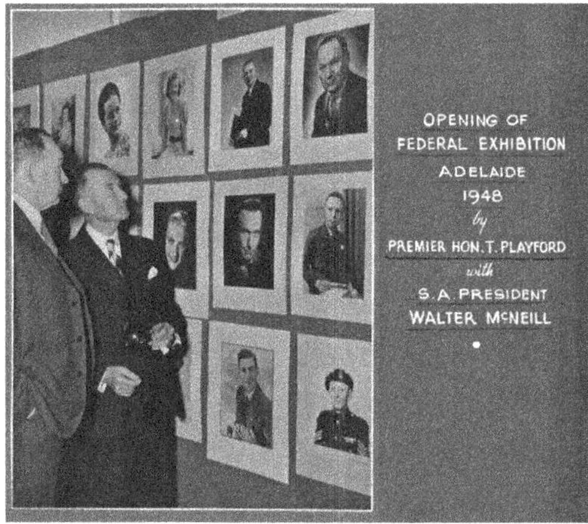

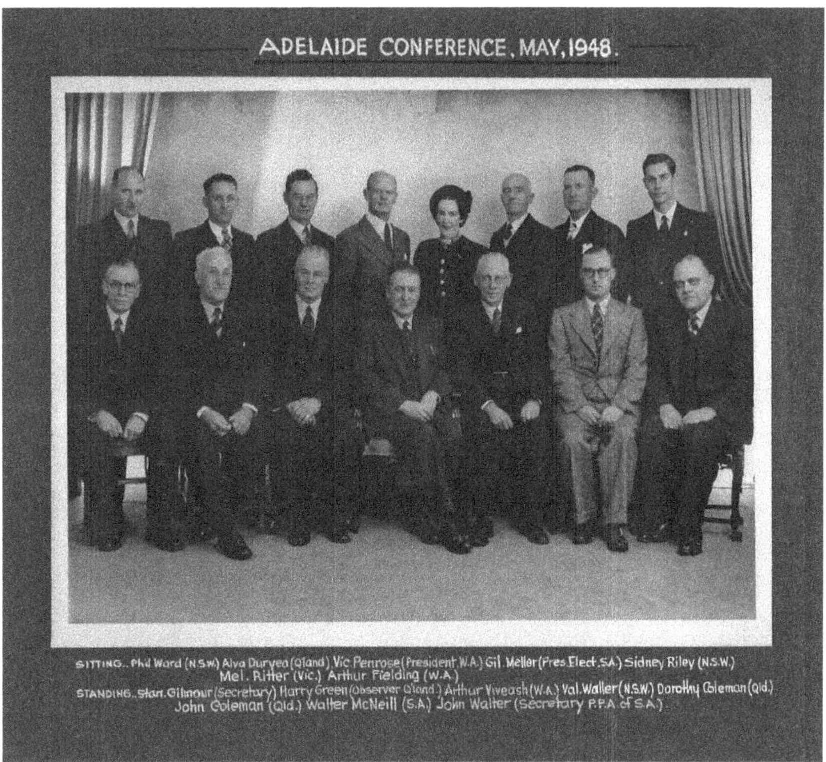

Photographs: David McCarthy Collection

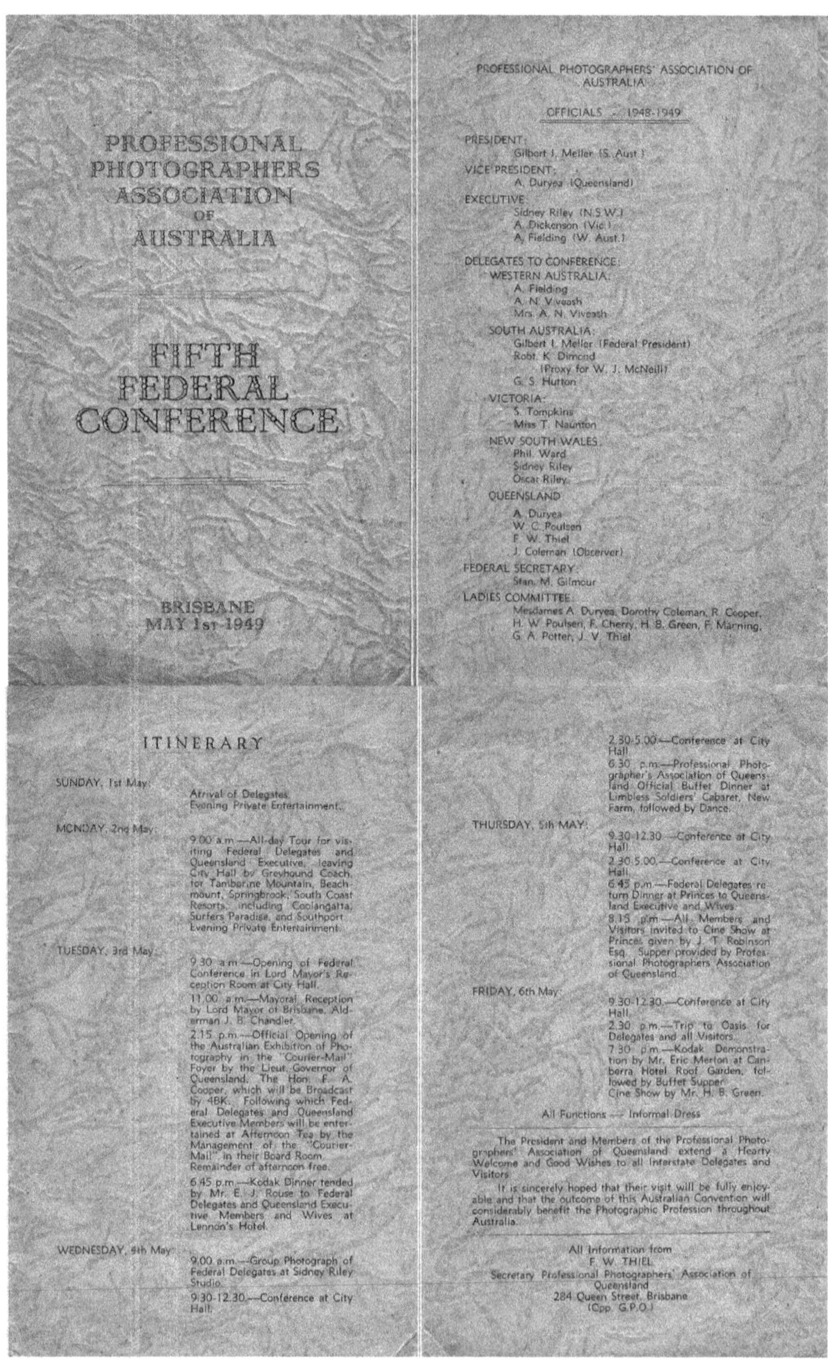

PROFESSIONAL
PHOTOGRAPHERS
ASSOCIATION
OF
AUSTRALIA

FIFTH
FEDERAL
CONFERENCE

BRISBANE
MAY 1st 1949

PROFESSIONAL PHOTOGRAPHERS' ASSOCIATION OF AUSTRALIA

OFFICIALS — 1948-1949

PRESIDENT:
    Gilbert J. Mellor (S. Aust.)
VICE PRESIDENT:
    A. Duryea (Queensland)
EXECUTIVE:
    Sidney Riley (N.S.W.)
    A. Dickenson (Vic.)
    A. Fielding (W. Aust.)

DELEGATES TO CONFERENCE:
    WESTERN AUSTRALIA:
        A. Fielding
        A. N. Viveash
        Mrs. A. N. Viveash
    SOUTH AUSTRALIA:
        Gilbert I. Mellor (Federal President)
        Robt. K. Dimond
            (Proxy for W. J. McNeill)
        G. S. Hutton
    VICTORIA:
        S. Tompkins
        Miss T. Naunton
    NEW SOUTH WALES:
        Phil. Ward
        Sidney Riley
        Oscar Riley
    QUEENSLAND
        A. Duryea
        W. C. Poulsen
        F. W. Thiel
        J. Coleman (Observer)
FEDERAL SECRETARY:
    Stan. M. Gilmour
LADIES COMMITTEE:
    Mesdames A. Duryea, Dorothy Coleman, R. Cooper,
    H. W. Poulsen, F. Cherry, H. B. Green, F. Marning,
    G. A. Potter, J. V. Thiel

ITINERARY

SUNDAY, 1st May:
        Arrival of Delegates.
        Evening Private Entertainment.

MONDAY, 2nd May:
        9.00 a.m.—All-day Tour for vis-
        iting Federal Delegates and
        Queensland Executive, leaving
        City Hall by Greyhound Coach,
        for Tamborine Mountain, Beach-
        mount, Springbrook, South Coast
        Resorts, including Coolangatta,
        Surfers Paradise, and Southport
        Evening Private Entertainment.

TUESDAY, 3rd May:
        9.30 a.m.—Opening of Federal
        Conference in Lord Mayor's Re-
        ception Room at City Hall.
        11.00 a.m.—Mayoral Reception
        by Lord Mayor of Brisbane, Ald-
        erman J. B. Chandler.
        2.15 p.m.—Official Opening of
        the Australian Exhibition of Pho-
        tography in the "Courier-Mail"
        Foyer by the Lieut. Governor of
        Queensland, The Hon. F. A.
        Cooper, which will be Broadcast
        by 4BK. Following which Fed-
        eral Delegates and Queensland
        Executive Members will be enter-
        tained at Afternoon Tea by the
        Management of the "Courier-
        Mail" in their Board Room.
        Remainder of afternoon free.
        6.45 p.m.—Kodak Dinner tended
        by Mr. E. J. Rouse to Federal
        Delegates and Queensland Execu-
        tive Members and Wives at
        Lennon's Hotel.

WEDNESDAY, 4th May:
        9.00 a.m.—Group Photograph of
        Federal Delegates at Sidney Riley
        Studio.
        9.30-12.30.—Conference at City
        Hall.
        2.30-5.00.—Conference at City
        Hall.
        6.30 p.m.—Professional Photo-
        grapher's Association of Queens-
        land Official Buffet Dinner at
        Limbless Soldiers' Cabaret, New
        Farm, followed by Dance.

THURSDAY, 5th MAY:
        9.30-12.30.—Conference at City
        Hall.
        2.30-5.00.—Conference at City
        Hall.
        6.45 p.m.—Federal Delegates re-
        turn Dinner at Princes to Queens-
        land Executive and Wives.
        8.15 p.m.—All Members and
        Visitors invited to Cine Show at
        Princes given by J. T. Robinson
        Esq. Supper provided by Profes-
        sional Photographers Association
        of Queensland.

FRIDAY, 6th May:
        9.30-12.30.—Conference at City
        Hall.
        2.30 p.m.—Trip to Oasis for
        Delegates and all Visitors.
        7.30 p.m.—Kodak Demonstra-
        tion by Mr. Eric Merton at Can-
        berra Hotel Roof Garden, fol-
        lowed by Buffet Supper.
        Cine Show by Mr. H. B. Green.

All Functions — Informal Dress

    The President and Members of the Professional Photo-
graphers' Association of Queensland extend a Hearty
Welcome and Good Wishes to all Interstate Delegates and
Visitors.
    It is sincerely hoped that their visit will be fully enjoy-
able and that the outcome of this Australian Convention will
considerably benefit the Photographic Profession throughout
Australia.

All Information from
F. W. THIEL
Secretary Professional Photographers' Association of
Queensland
284 Queen Street, Brisbane
(Opp. G.P.O.)

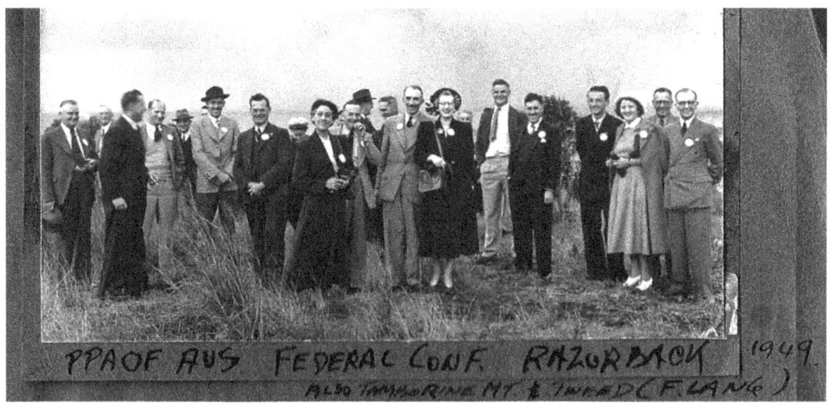

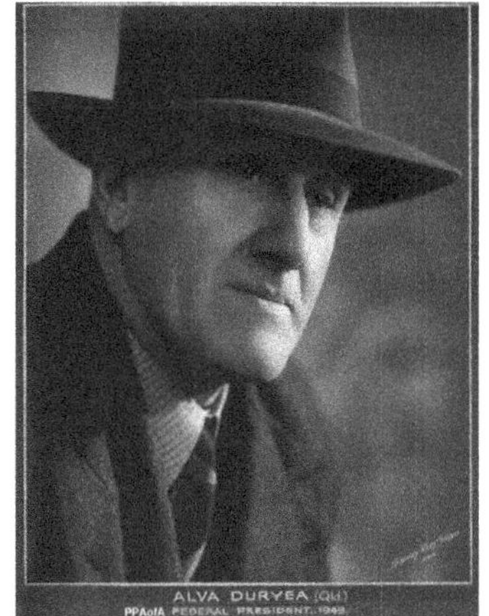

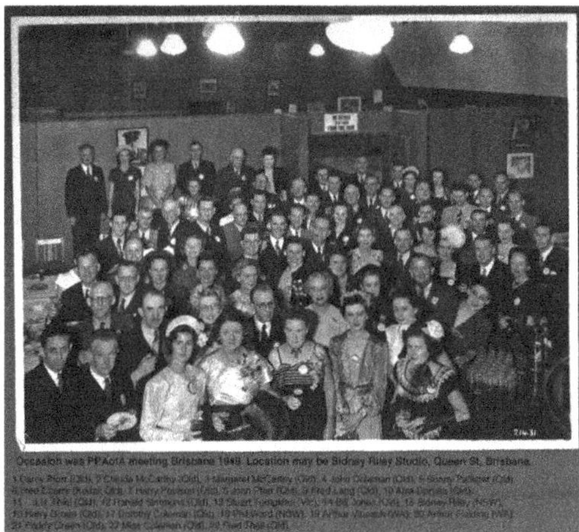

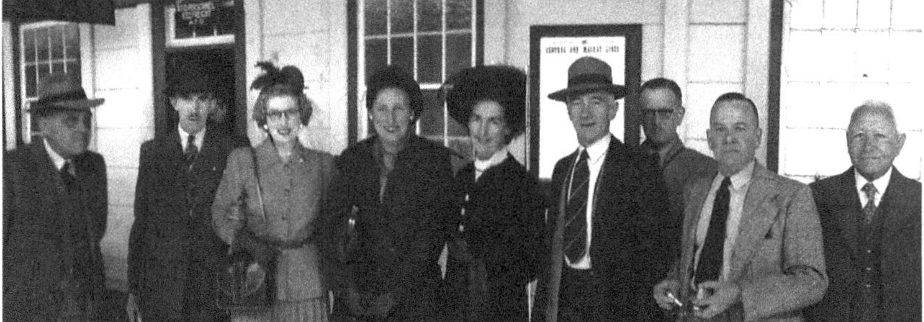

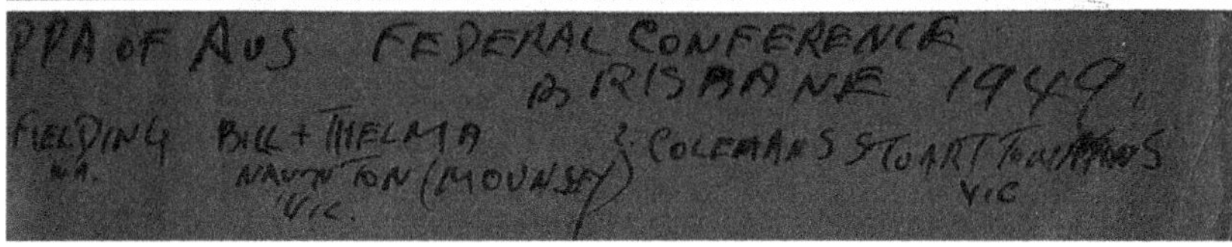

Photographs: David McCarthy Collection

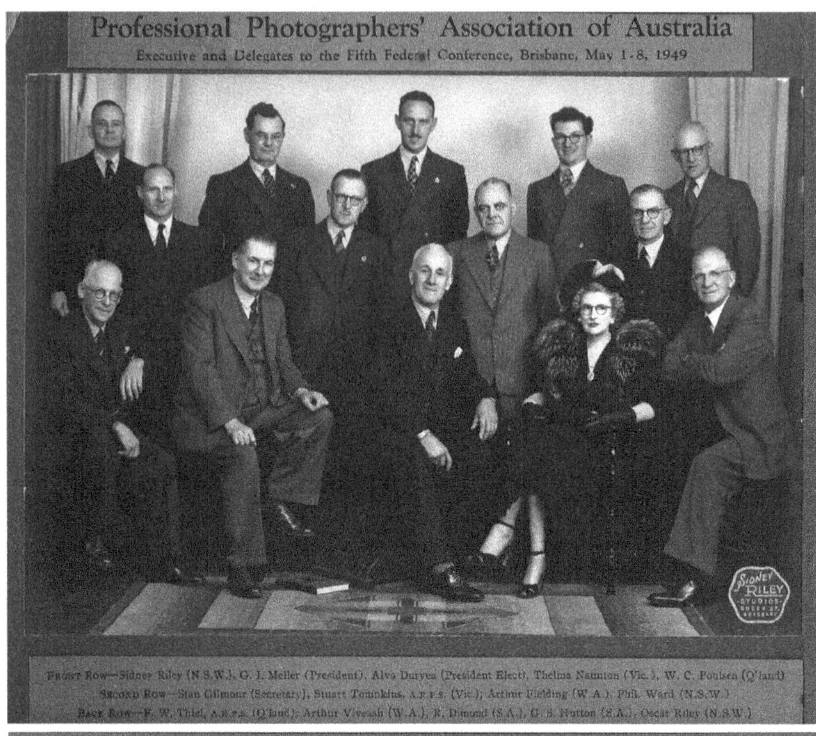

Professional Photographers' Association of Australia
Executive and Delegates to the Fifth Federal Conference, Brisbane, May 1-8, 1949
FRONT ROW—Sidney Riley (N.S.W.), G. I. Meller (President), Alva Duryea (President Elect), Thelma Naunton (Vic.), W. C. Poulsen (Q'land)
SECOND ROW—Stan Gilmour (Secretary), Stuart Tompkins, A.R.P.S. (Vic.); Arthur Fielding (W.A.), Phil. Ward (N.S.W.)
BACK ROW—F. W. Thiel, A.R.P.S. (Q'land); Arthur Viveash (W.A.), R. Dimond (S.A.), G. S. Hutton (S.A.), Oscar Riley (N.S.W.)

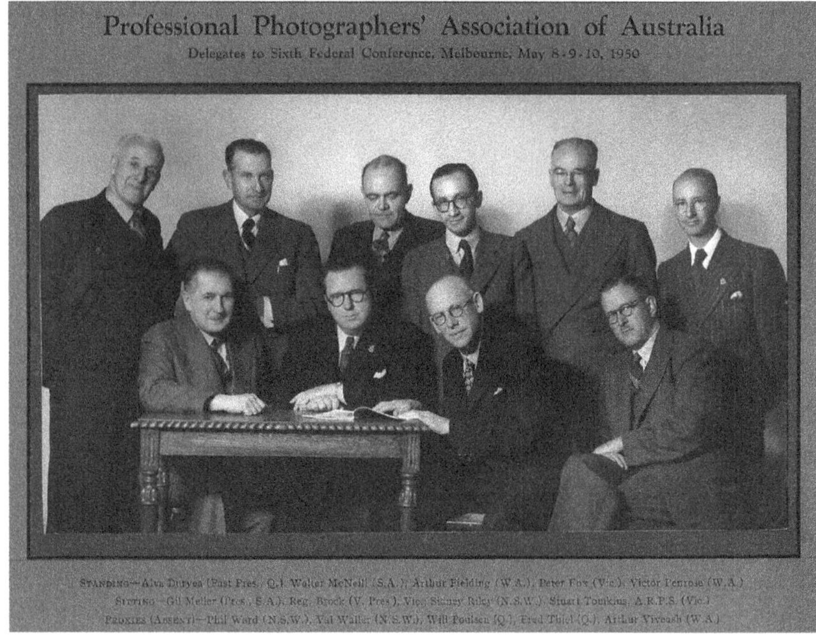

Professional Photographers' Association of Australia
Delegates to Sixth Federal Conference, Melbourne, May 8-9-10, 1950
STANDING—Alva Duryea (Past Pres., Q.), Walter McNeill (S.A.), Arthur Fielding (W.A.), Peter Fox (Vic.), Victor Penrose (W.A.)
SITTING—Gil Meller (Pres., S.A.), Reg. Brock (V. Pres.), Vice Sidney Riley (N.S.W.), Stuart Tompkins, A.R.P.S. (Vic.)
PROXIES (ABSENT)—Phil Ward (N.S.W.), Val Waller (N.S.W.), Will Poulsen (Q.), Fred Thiel (Q.), Arthur Viveash (W.A.)

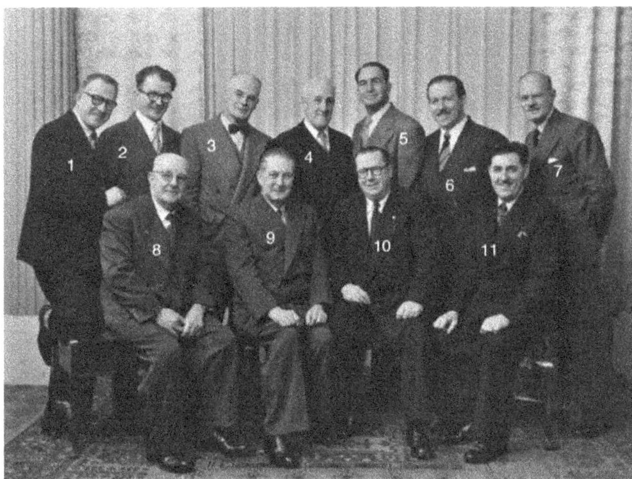

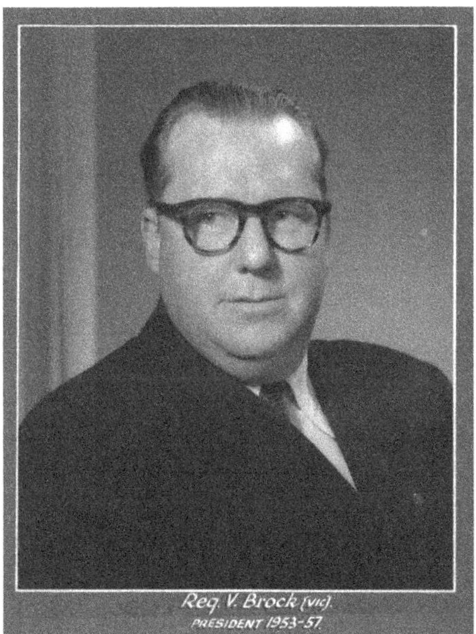

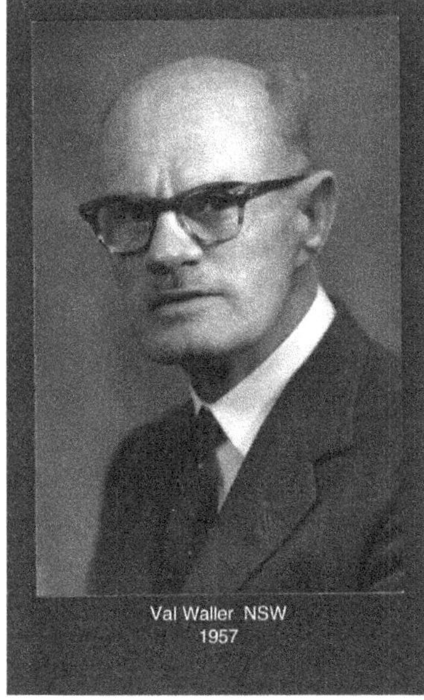

Photographs: David McCarthy Collection

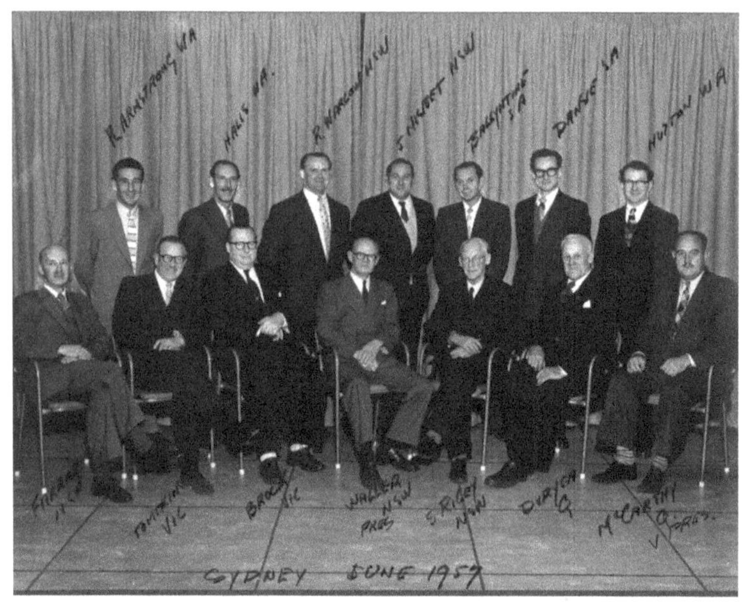

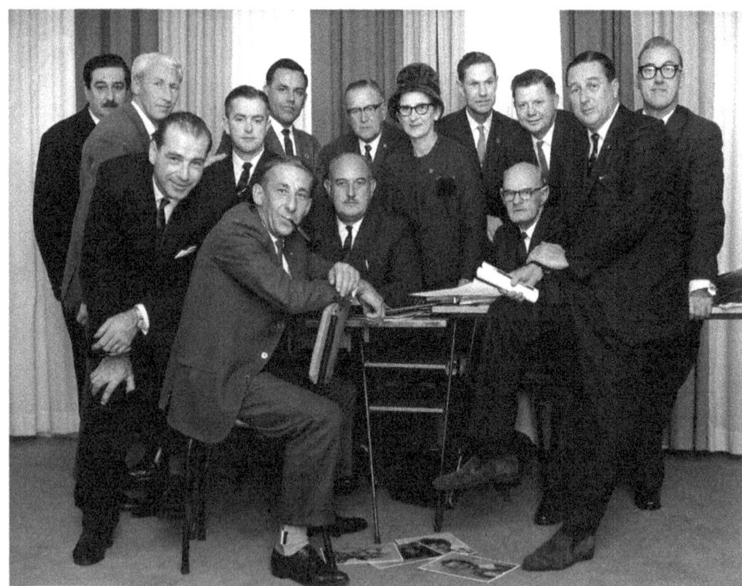

INAUGURAL MEETING IAP - MELBOURNE VIC 1964

Photo: Athol Shmith

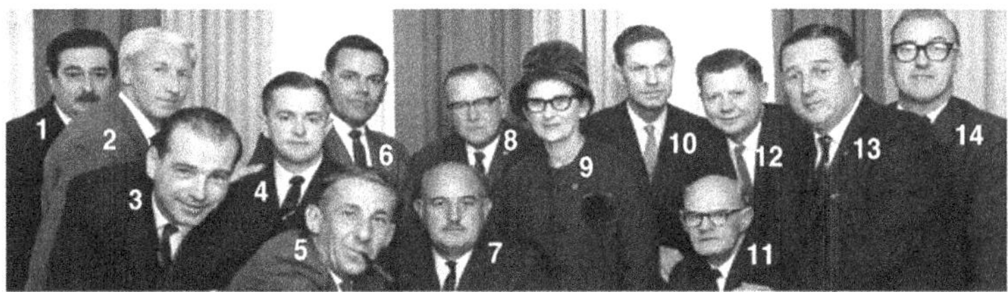

1 Clive Shmith (Vic), 2 Bill Walker (Vic), 3 Fritz Kos (WA), 4 Geoff Cummings (NSW), 5 Ron Armstrong (WA), 6 Max Farrell (SA)
7 Claude McCarthy (Qld), 8 C.Tompkins (Vic), 9 Anna Smith (Qld), 10 John Walters - secretary (SA), 11 Val Waller (NSW),
12 Syd Owen (Qld), 13 John Nisbett (NSW), 14 Darcy Pforr (Qld).

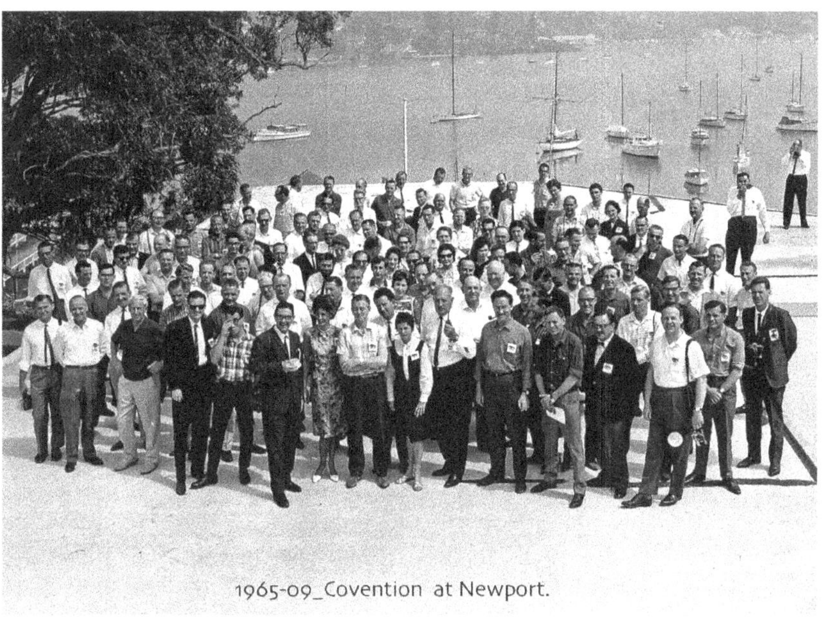

1965-09_Covention at Newport.

Photographs: David McCarthy Collection

41

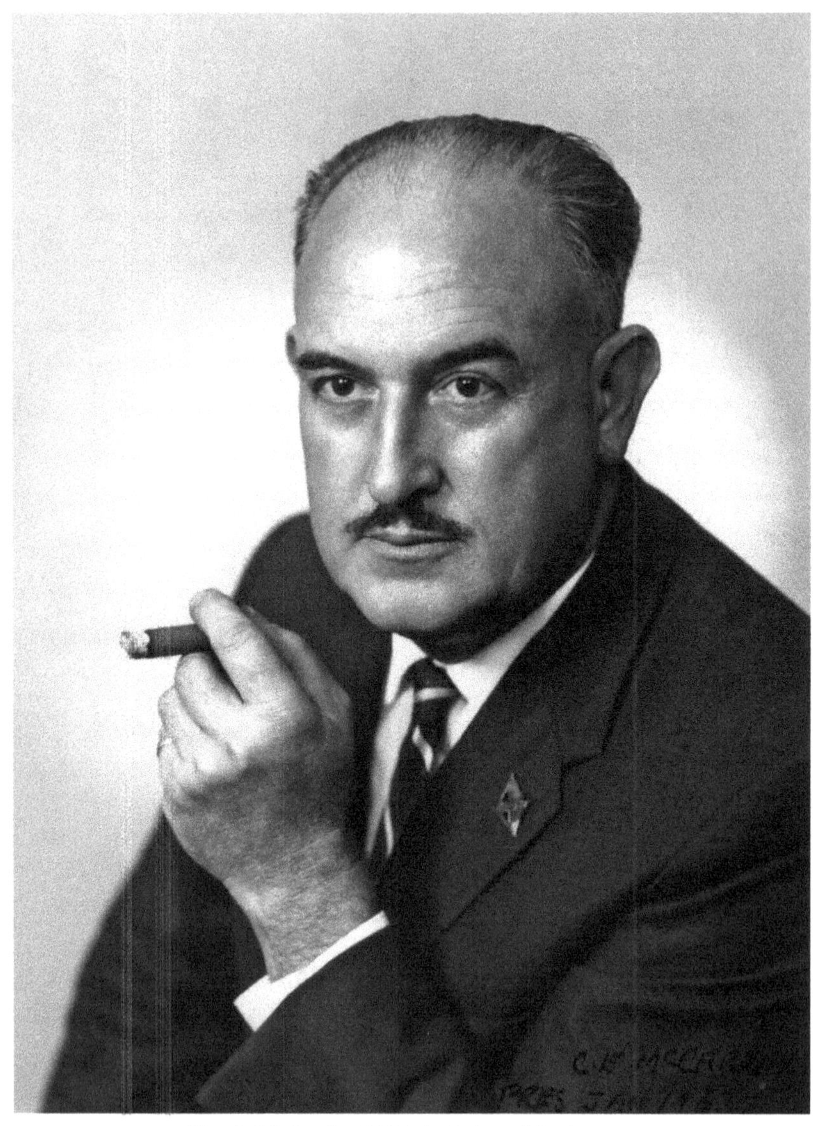

Claude McCarthy OAM, the father of the Institute

Chapter Two

Remembering the Swinging Sixties

Hey Hey, it's the Sixties! Flower-Power and druggie culture burst onto the scene with a proud and youthfully defiant bow. Haight-Ashbury fans: face left. Beatlemania devotees: face right. It was the Swinging Sixties and the old adage was that if you can remember them, you weren't there.

Professional photographers were also keen to strike out in new directions. Val Waller resigned on 1st Jan 1963 and Claude McCarthy from Brisbane was elected president. Supporting him as vice president was D. Dimon from West Australia and as the first federal secretary, John Walter from South Australia.

Claude was a dynamo of a man, a man of the age. He quickly set about the task of revolutionising the flagging association in earnest and became the true father of the association as we know it today. He had been secretary of the Professional Photographers Association (PPA) in Queensland over two periods totalling six years and had served as its president in 1946 and 1954. At the federal level he was vice president from 1957 to 1963 and had acquired all the knowledge needed to get things moving and to make the necessary changes.

'My aim,' Claude told the Institute magazine in February 1963, 'is the protection of the interests of the professional and the promotion of a better understanding of professional photography:

firstly by the general public.'

Remembered leading Melbournian photographer, Val Foreman, "Claude McCarthy was a man who would sit down, have a beer, a cigar, a chat and work out our problems. Not only would he work them out, he would worry them to death!"

Born in Brisbane in 1911, Claude began work in the portrait and commercial studio of Theil Studios in the early 1930s . Claude started his own business in 1934 and as a studio owner was then qualified under the rules of the day to become a member of the Photographic Association of Queensland. By the commencement of the Second World War he was controlling three studios with the emphasis on portrait work. However he enlisted with the RAAF in early 1942 and served in New Guinea in Radar Control, attaining the rank of flight lieutenant. During the war, his wife Margaret took control of the business, but the Services took over the premises of two of the studios.

After the war, Claude returned to his photography business which he operated under the name of Anthony Caton Studio and where he was eventually joined by his son David. The Institute of Australian Photography (IAP) magazine noted at the time: 'Claude looks as a president should. Physically he is a big man, a six footer and solidly built. His voice is deep and carries to the furthest corner of a room. He moves decisively, trailing a thick wake of cigar smoke. The tanned complexion, balding head, and luxuriant moustache are further attributes to a presidential image. As befits a President, Claude is a born organiser who has the organizer's aversion for untidiness and poor planning.'

One of his first objectives for the profession was to admit non-owner members to membership and rename the association. Claude promoted the concept of changing the title of the Professional Photographers Association of Australia to the Institute of Australian Photographers (IAP). The object of the name change was to bring greater recognition as the name 'Institute' was in use overseas and in Victoria. A postal ballot held on the first of July 1963, officially sanctioned the name change. In the same month, the West Australian division was formed and joined New South Wales, Victoria, Queensland and South Australia in becoming state divisions of the Institute. Thus Claude McCarthy became the first president of the Institute.

The ninth conference, held over three days beginning on May 25th 1964 at 120 Collins Street Melbourne, was the first to be held under the new name. The full details of how the Institute would function had yet to be determined and the occasion was the first opportunity for all the state association to sit down and discuss future directions. It was to be a long process. Representing the Photographic Association of Queensland were the state president Claude E. McCarthy, Darcy Pforr, Sidney Owen and Anna Smith. The Professional Photographers Association of New South Wales was represented by Geoff Cummings, Val Waller and John Nisbett. While the Institute of Professional Photographers of Victoria was represented by W. Wailer, Athol Shmith and Clive Stuart Tompkins. The Professional Photographers Association of South Australia sent Max Farrell, John Walter and G. Mitchell and the Professional Photographers Association of Western Australia sent Fritz Kos and Ron Armstrong.

Claude McCarthy opened the conference by commenting, 'It appears that from the 1950s onwards, the initiative of the earlier pioneers in forming this association was somewhat countered by the existing conditions of the times. During this period portraiture commenced its decline, commercial photography started to gain favour and many of the old stalwarts of the profession gave way to a younger generation not yet in the profession long enough to assess the need for association activities. I sincerely trust that the delegates meeting here will succeed in formulating a program for the future administration of this institute to build upon the foundation already existing, so that the Institute will become recognised as the guiding light and authority for the profession in Australia.'

With a balance sheet showing £1041 (pounds) and with a sometimes spirited debate, the conference addressed the reconstruction and future development of the Institute. Anna Smith played a key role in these discussions and was a remarkable person. She was the first woman to become a president of a professional association, the

PPA of Queensland. In 1978 she travelled to England where Her Majesty the Queen presented her with an OBE for services to the community and photography. She lived to the age of 104, dying in 2011.

Included in the proposals was the concept of opening up membership to not only both employers and employees, but to the representatives of photographic importing and manufacturing companies and others with associated interests in the profession. It also suggested that the states would become divisions with an agreed level of autonomy. The change in association name also led to a review of the honours system and the PPAA life memberships, granted to S.Riley, V.Penrose, C.Stuart Tompkins, G.Meller, R.Brock, A.Duryea and V.Waller, were transferred to the Institute.

After months of perusal by the state divisions, the first official IAP Convention and meetings of state and other invited associations was held on the 26th Sept 1965 at Newport, NSW. This time the various bodies formally accepted the new articles of association. They were subsequently and finally ratified on 26th Jan 1966 at a Federal Council meeting in Sydney with Queensland, New South Wales, Victoria, and South Australia agreeing to the new structure. Later in the same year, in July, the Australian Capital Territory signed up and Tasmania finally followed on the first of January 1973.

On the second of November in 1971, a minor name change was made by replacing the word Photographers with the more embracing word Photography to become the Institute of Australian Photography. One more change was to come. After a proposal from the Western Australia division, through its delegate Richard Syme, in 1990 the association finally became the Australian Institute of Professional Photography (AIPP).

David McCarthy, a son set to follow in his father's footsteps and also to become an Institute president said, "We would not have had an association without Claude. I think one of the reasons for his success was that he habitually arose at 3.00am to potter about in the garden, finishing off in time to prepare breakfast for the rest of the family before heading off to the studio. He believed that one must be early to work, preferably before the staff, in order to get things done. He was also a man who loved to throw a party, a man who loved to go home each night, turn on TV, throw up his feet, settle back and fall asleep snoring!"

During Claude's six year presidency, he presided over the establishment of a national conference program to see that it was held every two years, the introduction of the honours system, raising the standards of technical training and established an editorial committee aimed at improving the magazine's coverage. Claude retired as president at the end of 1968 and at the conference in 1970 he became the first person to be awarded an Honorary Fellowship of the Institute.

The second president was Geoff Cummings from Sydney. Aged 34, Geoff was the managing director of Group Colour, a pioneer of professional colour film and print processing. These were the days when professional photo-finishing houses began playing a major role in the business of photography. With consumers demanding everything from weddings and portraits to advertising and fashion to be shot in colour, the average professional photographer had a problem. They neither had the funds, the necessary volume of work, or the ability to tackle the difficulties of producing either colour transparencies or colour prints. Their mastery over the whole process was over. They had to wait another forty years before they could get it back! They could mostly shoot colour, but that was it. Processing had to be left to experts.

This in itself lead to another problem: the expert processors could not produce a good image unless the photographs had been exposed and lit properly in the first place. Thus began decades of the professional photofinishers trying to educate their clients on how to take the best printable image. First the labs tackled the issues of technical education of photographers and then moved on into areas of everything from posing to business management.

The whole colour process was so exacting it was deemed too much for any one photographer to tackle alone. In the early sixties I was working with a team of three other photographers and our employer, in a foolish moment, sent me on a special course in Europe to master the black art of early colour processing. I came back with the knowledge that the whole secret revolved around doing every step of an eight bath process to the second. This of course had to be done in total darkness. The fear factor was considerable, as the costs of prints and chemicals at this time meant that any mistake with a single print immediately forced you into a potential loss and threats of redundancy!

On my return, I discussed the difficulty of the situation with my colleagues as we all had to be able to process the films in exactly the same way and at any time. We took ourselves a little drink and pondered the situation. We then took another drink and another ponder. This led us to ponder some more and drink some more. Then one of us hit on a brilliant solution. I am sure it wasn't me. As consistency in the process was the key to the success, we decided to set up a reel-to-reel tape recorder and tape our processing actions by giving a commentary of the shaking of film reels and all the dipping and dunking required to develop colour negative films. That way, all we had to do for future batches, was play the tape back and follow the commentary and we would have it right to the very second. Brilliant.

So emboldened by fearsome quantities of rum and coke, we stationed one of our team outside the darkroom with a stop watch and embarked on laying down our master tape. Unfortunately, by that time, we were all a little the worse for wear. The tape took on a very convivial air with merry little bursts of song, much chanting of the dips and dunks and numerous clinks of glasses being refilled in total darkness. (In those days, if you couldn't pour drinks in total darkness you could never be a proper professional.)

It was all great fun: at the time. But believe me, after having to play back that damned tape, day after day, month after month, it began to lose its charm. Eight months later, sometimes playing it as early as a very sober 6.00am, it was a total nightmare. To this day, that wretched tape still rings in my ears: 'Give the films a little shake, shake, shake, have a little drink, drink, drink, give the films a little shake…'Oh horror, horror, horror.

So you can see how important a proper professional film processor became to the photographer? Geoff Cummings was running both a major lab and a busy wedding studio and played a significant role in the amalgamation of the Professional Photographers Association into the Institute. First he served from 1961 to 1962 as the president of the PPA New South Wales and then became the founding president of the NSW Division of the new Institute. He was also the organiser of the 1966 first annual convention held under the Institute's new banner.

The convention was held at the Newport Inn Motel on Sydney's northern beaches and was conceived as a very ambitious undertaking. Writing at the time, Geoff said, 'A tortoise does not start to move until it sticks its neck out . . . and stick our necks out we did.

'We had no precedent, no money, no crystallised ideas, but we did have enthusiasm and a conviction that there was an urgent need for such a convention in Australia. In the light of subsequent events our initial programme was rather ambitious. We were going to hold a National Photography Week supported by thousands of posters and photographic displays in the City of Sydney to coincide with the convention, a trade exhibition, photography exhibition, model of the year competition, a newspaper quest for the Photograph of the Year and a lot of other gimmicks.

'We had meetings and discussions with Kodak, Hanimex, Ilford and some of the other suppliers, but the consensus of opinion was that our programme was too ambitious to promote in the few months available for organising. Our final programme was reduced to the convention, trade exhibit, photography exhibition and model of the year competition. We had a convention programme designed and printed in a matter of a week or more, together with a convention letterhead. In all about 1500 individuals, firms and organisations were circularised.

'We needed 100 delegates to fill the motel, we hoped to get between 150 and 180 delegates in total at the convention, and our final figure was 170. Some indication of the quality of the speakers could be gauged from the average attendance at all lectures which was

The professionals by Pentax:

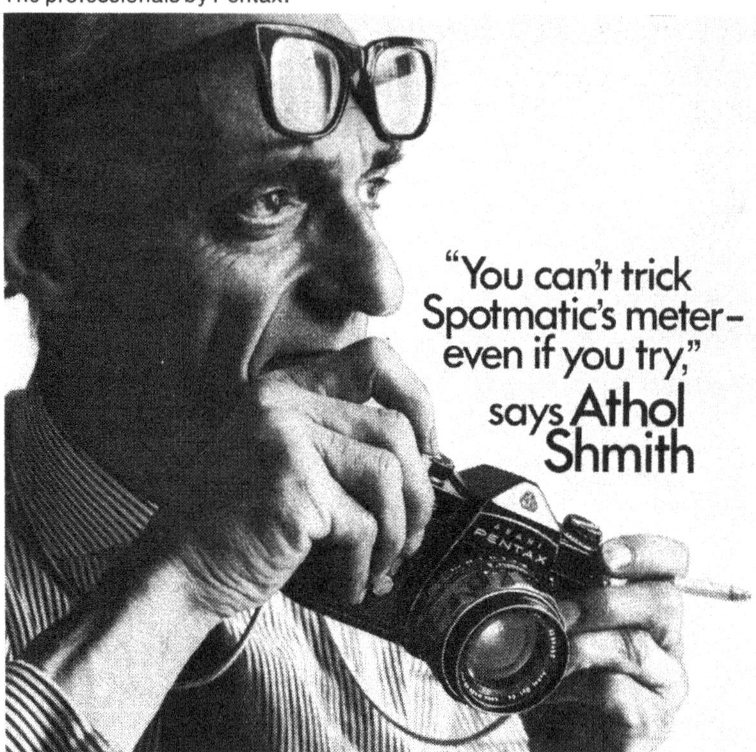

Shmith — one of the greats of Australian photography — has always combined a love of innovation with sternly disciplined technical quality. "Until I started using Pentax", he says, "I would never have trusted an in-built TTL meter. Now, having tried Spotmatic under all possible conditions — and some impossible ones as well — I'd always back its judgement". High praise indeed from such a remarkable talent.

The compact, lightweight Spotmatic has not just one but two highly sensitive CDS cells positioned for optimum accuracy on either side of the ground glass screen. This gives the completely reliable results the amateur wants and the professional demands. (Incidentally, drop us a line if you'd like a free copy of the Pentax book, giving the facts of competitive TTL meter systems.) With 23 superb Takumar interchangeable lenses and an infinitely flexible accessory range, Pentax is the world's most admired SLR camera. What more could any amateur want than the thoroughly professional Pentax?

PENTAX INTERNATIONAL GUARANTEE

By purchasing your Pentax camera in Australia, before going overseas, you may obtain free service under warranty in 34 countries throughout the world! Cameras purchased in duty free ports are not eligible for free service. Ask about the Pentax International Guarantee where you buy your Pentax.

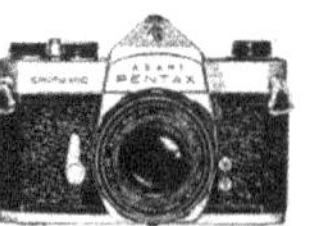

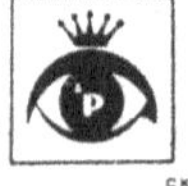

C. R. Kennedy Sales Pty. Ltd.,
P.O. Box 75, Carlton South, Vic. 3053.

CK22

This is the first known use of an Australian professional photographer used to promote an internationally known brand of 35mm camera.

more than 160. One delegate remarked "I'd love to sneak away and have a game of golf, but I can't afford to miss any of these lectures."

The success of the convention gave the new organisation a flying start and photographers were filled with a new confidence in their association. However there were a few studio owners, particularly in New South Wales, who felt that their voice as business owners was being lost. So some members of the PPA of NSW held out and remained an employers' only organization trading under that name.

Six years after the adoption of the Institute's new name, the PPA of NSW sought to establish itself as a national body of studio owners and changed its name to the one abandoned by the Institute. But although it renamed itself the PPA of Australia, it was in fact a new association. It registered itself as an industrial union of employers. Leading the drive was New South Wales chairman Paul Trenoweth, who used the offices of industrial arbitration specialists L.W. Farrar & Associates in Sydney's York Street, to pursue the case for studio owners with government. LW Farrar had also been providing secretarial services to the Institute.

Writing at the time in an issue of the Institute's magazine, Trenoweth said, 'The [new] PPA recognises the need for two photographic organisations and the IAP provides a very important voice for employees in all facets of the industry as well as freelance photographers and studio owners. However, it is necessary to retain a body able to represent the employers in the arbitrations courts.'

In 2013, it was impossible to trace any form of a national PPA body. However there were a few members of the PPA of Queensland and the PPA of Western Australia, which list a combined membership of fewer than 40 photographers, many of whom also belong to the more than three thousand strong members of the Institute.

The second convention held under the Institutes' name, was called Hypo'67 and held in Melbourne. Members were invited to register for three full days at a cost of $37 or, if they chose to live in the hotel, an all inclusive price of $79.

The Hypo bi-annual conventions were often the lynchpin for resolving industry issues. In the year Armstrong became the man in

ENLARGERS
by LEITZ
give you greater precision and convenience that shows out in your prints

Give or take a few dollars, all top quality enlargers cost the same, BUT with LEITZ FOCOMATS you get optical performance, rugged life-long precision and operation convenience you've never had before.

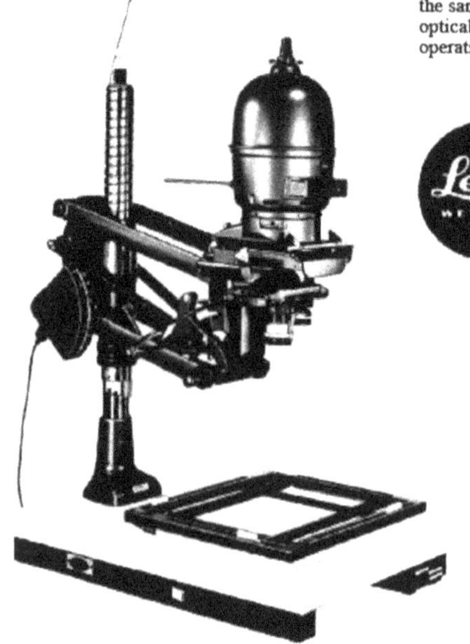

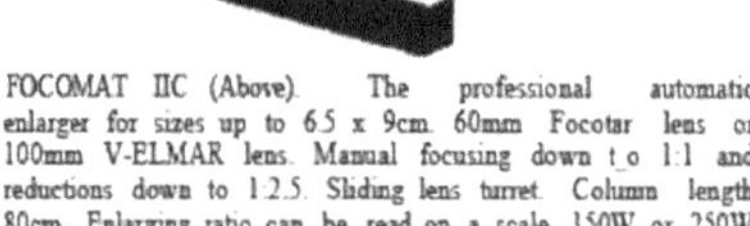

FOCOMAT IIC (Above). The professional automatic enlarger for sizes up to 6.5 x 9cm. 60mm Focotar lens or 100mm V-ELMAR lens. Manual focusing down t.o 1:1 and reductions down to 1:2.5. Sliding lens turret. Column length 80cm. Enlarging ratio can be read on a scale. 150W or 250W enlarger lamp.

FOCOMAT IC (Right). 50mm Focotar enlarging lens. Automatic focusing range 2 to 10 diameters. Manual focusing to approximately 24 diameters. Interchangeable film guides from 8 x 11mm to 4 x 4cm. 53 x 61Y. em baseboard. 120cm column. 150 or 250 Watt.

*In the Seventies, photographers had not moved out
of the darkroom and into the Lightroom!*

the moon, the October Hypo'69 held in Canberra featured Gordon De'Lisle, FRPS, FRSA, EFIAP as a guest speaker. Gordon was a highly successful photographer that shook his delegates to the core with a stirring address which had the Institute's journal editor Neil Murray salivating over the copy as he prepared it for publication. Here is a slightly abridged version of what a very discontent Gordon had to say:

'I, unhappily, have little but melancholy to impart. The individual Australian photographer is involved in a sad, sick, depressed profession. It is a profession that has sunk so low in dignity and public esteem as to be accorded a status basement perhaps unique for photography in all the world!

'This is a profession that is chronically crowded and where buyers of photography are totally undiscerning and content with any old result. The available pie, in consequence, is being cut into so many bite-size chunks that nobody gets a square meal.

'It is a profession that has abased itself to such a degree that some of its biggest businesses will slash their prices by half, like back-alley garment sweat-shops, to get 'machine-filler' work: where one firm quotes $4.25 to industry for a copy negative and 67 cents to government for the same job! This is a profession where a photographer with a lifetime of training and with plant worth $20,000 finishes with exactly the same money for taking a fashion photograph, processing it, retouching it, packing it and delivering a ten-by-eight print as does his model: whose plant is a bra, panties, and a pair of false eyelashes.

'This is a profession whose ideas are pillaged consistently and blatantly by art directors of advertising agencies; who pay the photographers' meagre fees, with luck and after endless dispute, in five months. Above all, this is a weak-kneed, spineless profession, whose members wallow in apathy and self-adoration; while those trades and professions about them get on with the task.

'Do any of you really feel any concern for your image? Are you content to be made to look like bumbling congenital idiots on television? Are you content to do more and more, yet accept less and less?

Are you content to slash the ground from under your contemporaries by every known price-cutting device?

'And here's something of particular importance to your wives and children! Do you know what the community thinks of you? The Sociology Department of the University of New South Wales does! It finds you enjoying precisely the same esteem in the eyes of your fellow citizens as do beekeepers, bank clerks, surgical boot makers, cotton growers, electricians, enamellers, house repairers, entertainers, furniture removalists, laboratory assistants, trainee nurses, magicians, models, pipe fitters, sugar cane growers and sanitary plumbers.

'Now these doubtless are worthy folk. But are they specialist masters of the most potent dynamic, exciting, visual art of the space age? Indeed they are not. And you, as and representing the nation's great photographers, should resent a demeaning status with your every fibre in your every waking minute!

'Man blasts to the moon! Do you think man knows of man on the moon? Wrong! Man knows only the photography of man on the moon. A president is felled by an assassin's bullet! Does man know his death throes and their impact on history? Wrong. Man knows only the photography of such dread and horror.

'An unknown photographer in South Africa has his wife's girl friends model nude for his camera; and into being come some of the most beautiful physical images ever recorded: Sam Haskins' books, proudly erotic, through photography. In my home I have the greatest art since man rose from the swamps. I have the Tate Gallery, the Prado, the Louvre, the Leningrad and a whole host of others: through photography. We belong to a profession whose history holds nothing but honour; a profession that we know to be more of a vocation than a profession. And yet only the paparazzi of Rome or the porno-photographers of Kowloon abase it more deeply than do we Australians!

'Can I urge and beg you to get enough iron in your spines and bellies to go out and meet this abasement head-on? Sacrifice your stupid much-cherished individuality: act together. Don't ask for a reasonable return for your standards and talents; demand it! This is no more than your due. Refuse adamantly to work for advertising agencies who withhold acknowledgement of your name on your work.

'Refuse point blank to ever do a job of work for anyone, particularly those in public relations, who say to you there's no money in it, but plenty of great publicity. Even refuse point-blank to do free photography for simpering new models. When they attain even minimal success you'll find that they can't quite recall your name!

'Refuse to carry on your books million dollar businesses wanting credit for months. Many of them have deliberate fiscal policies that involve using the money that belongs to your wife, your children, and the Taxation Commissioner, as interest-free floating capital. After thirty days, warn them; after forty days, threaten them; and after sixty days, within 48 hours have a process server drop a summons on the desk of the chief accountant; just as your suppliers do with you.

'Refuse to work nights and weekends at normal rates for the promise of continuity of work. And above all demand the respect that you earn.

'Now, since we are met together in Canberra, let me say something of quite considerable importance about the attitude of government to photography. The Australian government, through its constituent departments and sub departments, treats this profession generally, this Institute particularly, and photographers individually, with total contempt. Whether this contempt is deliberate, or whether it comes about through ignorance, is broadly immaterial. The government recognises no specialist skills, so that every specialist photographer who has broken his back and blown his mind in an effort to become great in his specialist sphere is chucked mentally into an amorphous group of amoebic, lumpen snappers.

'When government wants photography it says 'get a photographer', meaning any old damned photographer, and the whole thing is put up for public tender in exactly the same way that the army buys 'goldfish and dog biscuits'.

'To show you how public tendering on a price basis could work with professions, let me pose you a couple of hypotheses: the Prime

Minister of Australia strolls out to his VIP jet at Fairbairn airport; off electioneering. He happens to look at the flight-deck window, and sees an unfamiliar face. To the public service protocol officer strolling with him he remarks that the pilot looks strange. Whereupon this worthy replies that the post of pilot went up for public tender; but since jet captains cost so much money it had been decided that the job should go to a fantastically well skilled Woolloomooloo bus driver! Ridiculous and illogical?

'Of course it is, but let's try another one: the Prime Minister of the Commonwealth has a 21-gun VIP as his guest at The Lodge. The guest complains of some slight eye trouble, and the Prime Minister asks the public service to get a doctor. After some days of treatment, by which time the guest is bumping into doors and feeling his way along passages, the Prime Minister asks about the qualifications of the doctor. The public service replies that actually, they had found that they could get a gynaecologist, great with ovaries, for two-thirds off! Outlandish? Certainly; but no more outlandish than the way in which government uses photographers.

'Let the long fight back for photography begin today, in this room. Much needs to be done; but let these be some starting points.

1. More unified and militant action by photographers degraded in terms of status and money.

2. An immediate demand by specialist photographers in and out of government to be regarded as specialists by government.

3. An immediate end to the practice of creative photographic work being put up for public tender to the detriment of the country's overseas image.

4. Immediate appointment of a rotating adviser or advisory panel from within this profession to consult with government on all photography and photographic design for overseas exhibition; and

5. An immediate search for industry sponsors sufficiently interested in the future of Australian photography to establish grants for contemporary Australian photographers to study

overseas in aesthetics or technique, and lecture on return. Let's start the great move forward. Now! Today!'

Following Gordon's address, slightly startled delegates took an extended tea and coffee break.

Later, Geoff Cummings commented, 'Hypo '69 seemed to me to be a combination of acid wit and quiet lucid exposition of fact. To the thinking photographer, both are necessary to inspire a higher degree of professionalism. An awareness of our own shortcomings as a profession as exposed by some speakers must not, however, be allowed to dominate our resolve to improve both individually and collectively as an Institute.'

Incidentally, the status of Gordon's 'unknown photographer in South Africa' undertook a dramatic change when at the next Hypo, Ian McKenzie brought Sam Haskins to Australia as the keynote speaker. This began a long association between Sam Haskins and the Institute. This was strengthened even further some years later when Ian sponsored this iconic photographer's move from London to Don Bradman's old home town of Bowral in New South Wales.

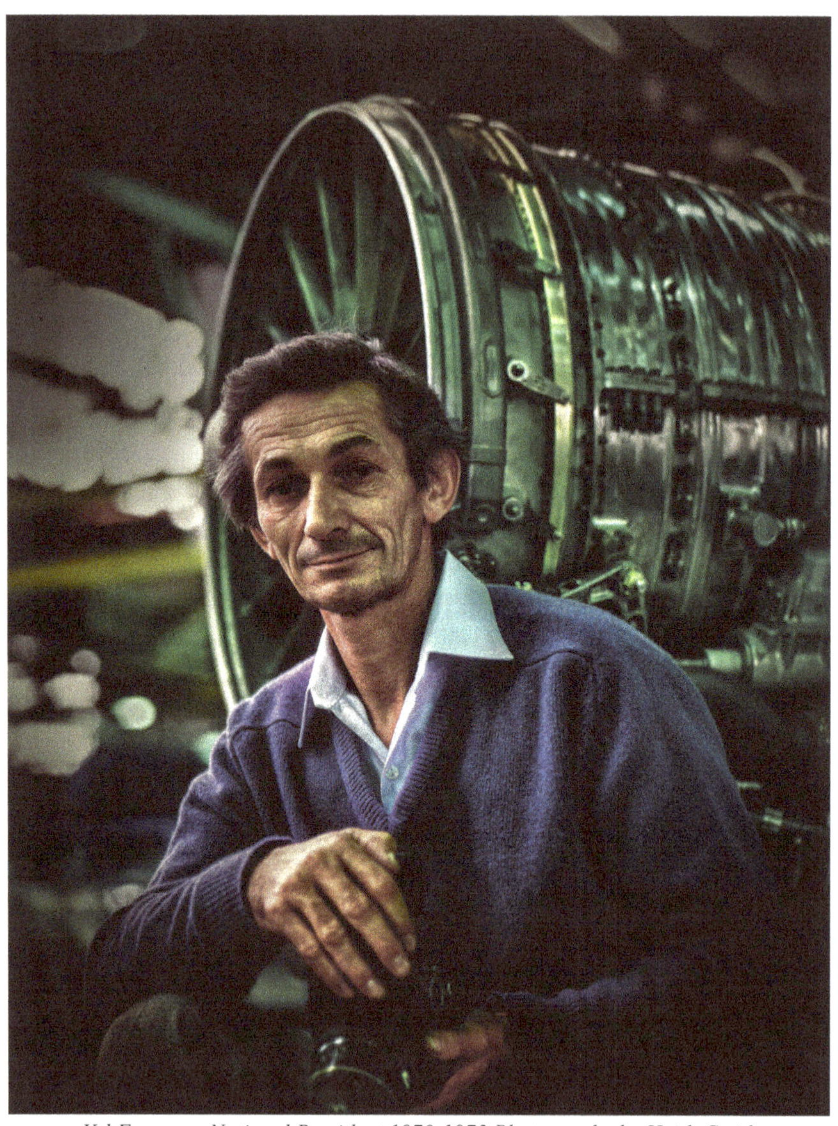

Val Foreman, National President 1970-1973 Photography by Heide Smith

Chapter Three

Striding into the Seventies

Striding into the seventies came infamous fashion model Twiggy, still in her wonderful miniskirts of the sixties, but now marching on platform shoes. Australian men dropped their flared trousers, keen to follow South Australian Premier Don Dunstan's lead by jumping into safari suits. This was the true photographer's ultimate garb. You didn't need a gadget bag in those days, just a safari suit. Ah, all those pockets! Fashion designers, please, please, bring them back right now.

Internationally, the Israeli war with Syria and Egypt was in full swing. Oil rich Arab countries, not liking the United States and its Allies support of Israel, threatened to stop supplying fuel. Suddenly, in Australia, oil became a scarce resource. Petrol prices shockingly soared to more than twenty cents a litre. Ah, If only we had all filled up then.

On the national political front things weren't going so smoothly. The Vietnam War had degenerated into a total shambles and Gough Whitlam was calling our troops home. Just three years later, Governor-General John Kerr sent Whitlam home. While Gough is the only prime minister to ever be sacked by the Queen's representative, there have been occasions when some Australians wished the Queen's representative would please, pretty please, perform an encore. But even worse was in store: Ray Illingworth's English test team stole the Ashes.

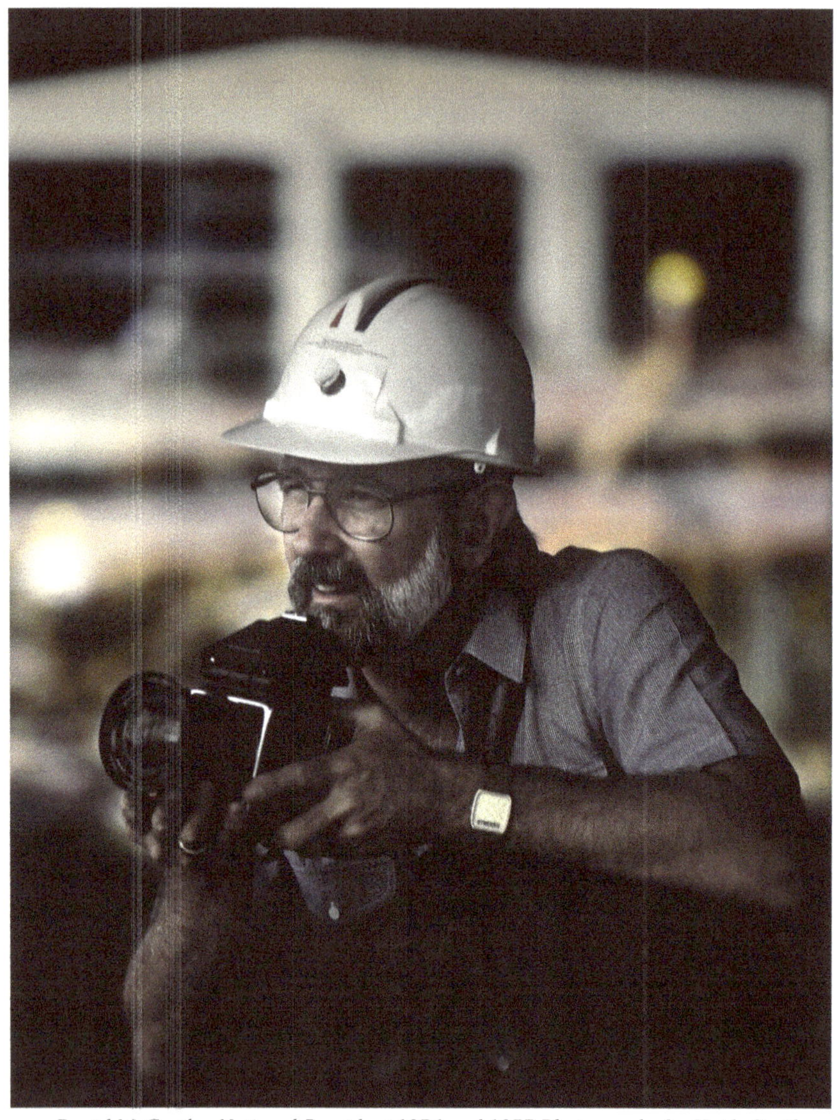

David McCarthy, National President 1976 and 1977 Photography by Heide Smith

It was onto this seventies stage that Val Foreman entered the arena as third president of the Institute. A commercial photographer, Val was a wiry, short, intense character with a mop of wavy dark hair and a tremendous passion for the Institute. He was to make a contribution that extended to the eighties. At the end of his first year, in 1971, Val oversaw the minor name change that replaced the name of Institute of Australian Photographers with the name Institute of Australian Photography. A subtle change that didn't even affect the initials of the Institute, but one that was of great significance in indicating the direction the Institute wished to pursue.

As president, Val dealt with ailing Institute funds, copyright issues and lobbying the government over its too low depreciation rates of photographic equipment. He also had to contend with the problems of Australia's change to metric measurements. Although our currency was decimalised in 1966, we were still working in feet and inches. Wishing to keep in step with what it thought would be the way of the new world, in 1970, parliament passed the Metric Conversion Act. With this single stroke of the bureaucratic pen, we were overnight propitiously propelled into centimeters and grams. It was all reminiscent of the fabled army call for volunteers: Australia, Britain and the Americans were standing at full attention in line. The sergeant called for volunteers to step forward and turned his back. Both the USA and UK shuffled backwards; thus leaving Australia out front and alone! All these decades later, we are still waiting for them to come into line.

But metrication in Australia was absolute law and the nation's police were forced to issue descriptions of wanted men, with a height, say, of 170.8 centimeters and weighing 82.5 kilos. From such descriptions, no criminals were caught for decades. The public didn't know if it was looking for a fat giant or a thin dwarf. And just as suddenly it was the same for photographers. No longer could they talk to their customers of whole, half or quarter plates. Overnight a 12x10 became a 30.5 x 25.4. Catchy wasn't it?

Photographers were faced with specific problems adapting and in August 1972, the Metric Conversion Board formed its Photo-

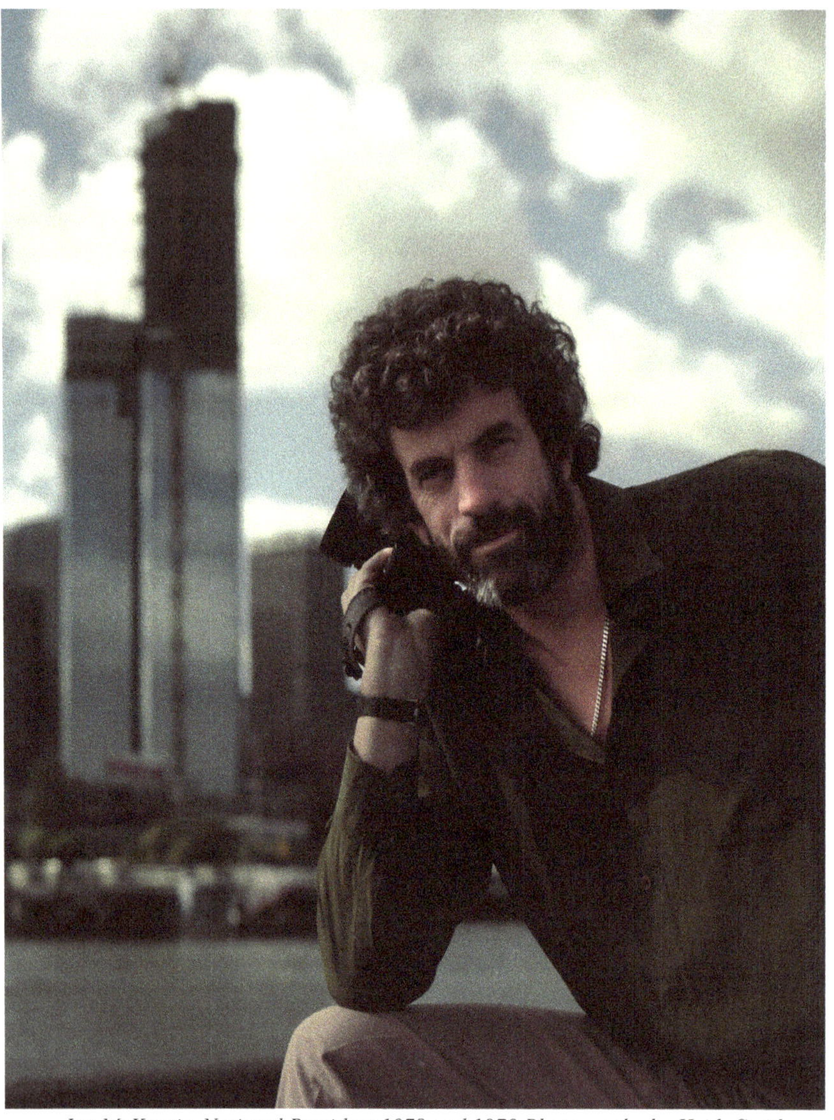

Ian McKenzie, National President 1978 and 1979 Photography by Heide Smith

graphic Sector Committee to begin a more consultative approach.

Any transgressions in the commercial world from the new standard were being aggressively pursued by an all powerful metrication board, vigilant in punishing any transgressors straying from the metricated path of righteousness. As the publisher of a magazine I received a threatening letter from the Metrication Board for having the temerity to refer in print to a ten by eight camera. Still at a youthfully stroppy age, which I think possibly now I have grown out of, I fired off a missive invoking poles, perches rods and roods and every other imperial measurement I could think of. In a fierce defense of civil liberties and freedom of speech, I was not, I proclaimed, a grocer and would not give an inch to such government bullying. I wouldn't touch it with a ten foot barge pole and I would walk a country mile before losing the freedom to say what I wanted and how I wanted. I would fight across gallons of seas and oceans, I would fight on acres of beaches, I would fight on furlongs of fields, yards of streets, on foot across the hills and would never surrender!

Alas, it was published and I mentally began preparing for the jail sentence I had been threatened with. But the Metrication Board had the last laugh. They simply ignored me.

However, Val Foreman and his committee were more cooperative and worked with the Metrication Board to introduce new terminology and the new sizes for print making.

Val was a tireless worker for the Institute and at his instigation the board reviewed the three year terms then being served by the elected president and reduced it to a two year period. This would allow the elected president to take less time from his own business and give the Institute the possible advantage of a more frequent renewal of a fresh and revitalised president.

Accordingly, vice president Max Farrell was elected for the years 1974 and '75.

Based in South Australia and after his discharge from the Royal Australian Navy, Max started as a wedding photographer and began long term freelancing for the Australian Women's Weekly covering everything from royal tours to more mundane social events. On the

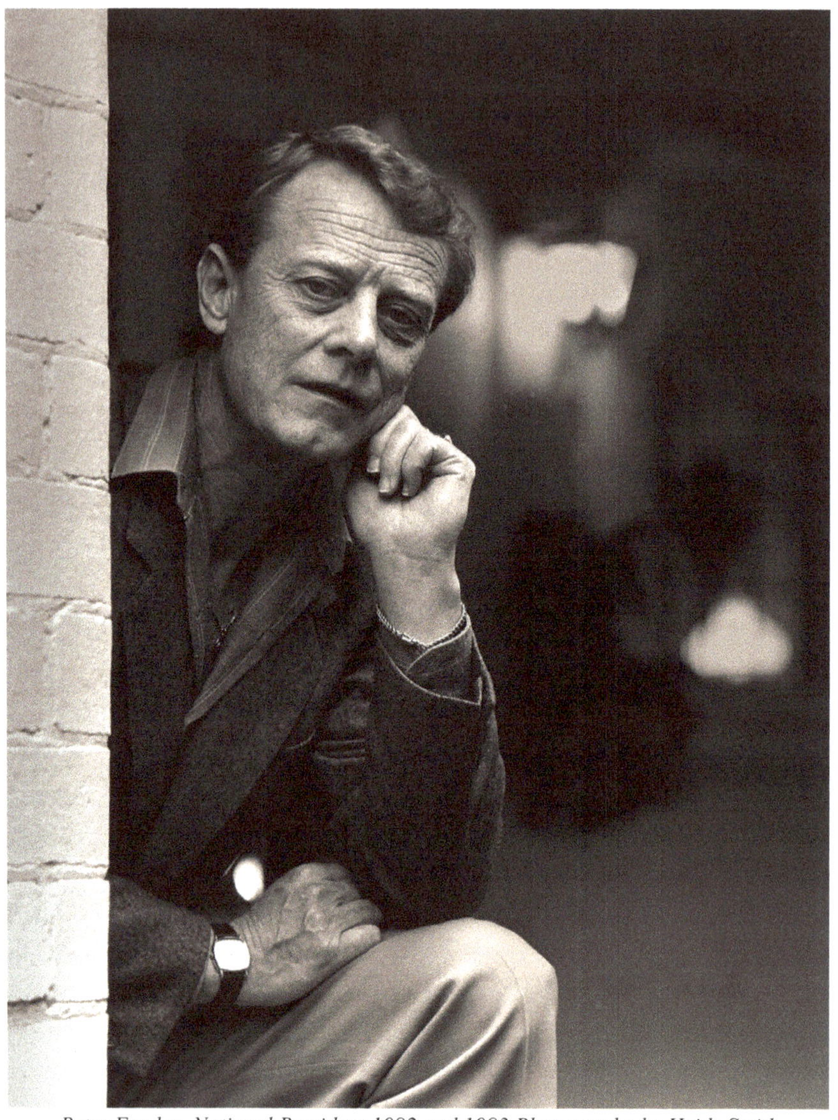

Peter Foeden, National President 1982 and 1983 Photography by Heide Smith

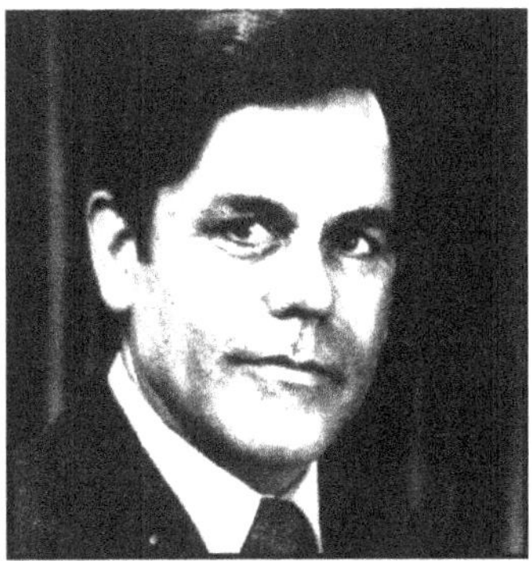

Max Farrell, National President 1974 and 1975

commercial and advertising front, Max handled throughout South Australia and Northern Territory assignments for clients such as BHP, Chrysler (later Mitsubishi) and the Adelaide Steamship Co.

In 1952 Max joined The Professional Photographers Association in South Australia and served on its executive for many years. In 1964 he was elected president of the South Australian Division of the PPA. He went on to become a key player in the transformation of the association from a loose amalgamation of state bodies to an adhesive national organisation.

At the end of Max's term and at the beginning of 1976, the Institute went back to the future and elected David McCarthy as president, the son of the founder of the new Institute and the youngest person to ever take this role. David was born and raised into the industry. He was undoubtedly a chip off the old block in terms of energy, commitment, passion and orderly decision making. But he also brought with him a deftness of touch and a delightful sense of humour that made him a very powerful persuader and a great entertainer. David could easily have swapped his camera for a microphone in show business. As an emcee at the industry's annual dinners he was without peer. His whimsical asides and observations of his fellows in the industry not only brought pride to the photographer's heart but tears of laughter to the eyes.

During his term, David also dealt with a problematic issue first raised by future Institute president Peter Foeden in 1970. Peter had broached the idea of introducing an awards system to recognise outstanding professional photography. Although it was in use by professional bodies overseas, the idea was controversial with many members protesting that they were not a camera club. Years of debate went back and forth, but in 1977, David steered the concept into reality.

He was also the first offspring of a president to become a president, a trick only repeated by Alice Bennett in 2008. Like his venerable own father, Claude, David too became a father of the profession. Said David McCarthy 'Our professional organisation didn't get to where it is today just by people whingeing when things weren't going to well. It grew to the strong force it is today because of the people who have dedicated their own personal time and effort to promoting something which without, most of us would be wandering in a professional wilderness.'

Like Claude, David too was honoured with the Order of Australia for his services to professional photography.

In 1978 the presidential baton was passed to Ian McKenzie. Tall, slim, athletic, articulate and highly intelligent, the perpetually all in black and casually dressed McKenzie cut a dynamic figure across the Australian photography stage for four decades. Indeed, his influence is still felt strongly to this day. Born in Melbourne in 1939 Ian spent two years in chartered accountancy before becoming a professional photographer in 1958. Basing his business in Melbourne, he specialised in architectural and industrial photography and also shot aerial and illustrative pictures for company reports.

He joined the Institute of Victorian Photographers in 1959 and became a member of the Institute at its inception. In 1966 Ian began a four year program designing and overseeing the construction of

educational facilities and diploma photography course at Prahran College in Melbourne. He was department head for two years and the diploma course Ian introduced was later reclassified as a degree.

In 1973, he returned to private practice and became the convener of the Institute's national conference. Such was the success of the program, Ian was asked to perform this voluntary task for the next four conventions up until 1981. Ian has also had a long association with the Awards, joining the National Awards Committee in 1976 and then serving as a judge and panel chairman until 2012.

Venturing into publishing with Attila Kiraly and Val Foreman, Ian republished Jack Cato's The Story of the Camera in Australia under the Institute's imprint. He went on to publish the Contemporary Photographer Series. This consisted of monographs by photographers such as David Moore., Athol Shmith, Lewis Morley, Wolfgang Sievers, Graham McCarter, Ian Dodd and Michael Coyne.

Up until the end of Ian's term as president, the national conventions were held every second year and were known as Hypos, followed by the last two digits of the year they fell in: thus Hypo '77, Hypo 79, etc. The state divisions were encouraged to hold a division convention in the off year.

At the Hypos a trade display would be held in conjunction with the convention which would only operate during conference lunch and coffee breaks. This trade participation was important to the success of the convention as the revenue was mostly responsible for keeping the convention finances in the black.

For some years this worked well until the trade suppliers felt that because of the escalating costs of mounting displays they needed to expand the show and attract larger audiences. This led to a new body, called the Australian Photo Industry Council, which was made up of delegates from all the various associations representing photo dealers, consumer and professional distributors, photo laboratories and, of course, professional photographers. Ian McKenzie was elected to represent the Institute and at his instigation it was agreed that the distributors rather than the Institute would fund the costs of overseas photographers to lecture at the Institute's conventions.

Still continuing his service, in 2006 Ian McKenzie established and chaired the AIPP Commercial Group and became a member of the Institute's Policy and Planning Committee. In 2010 he developed the structure and syllabus course materials for the AIPP National Mentoring scheme and managed the scheme nationally. It is hard to think of many who have made such a long and sustained contribution to the Institute.

Ian was also actively involved in the first moves to bring to Australia internationally respected photographers to give lectures to photographers and help lift the standards of the profession. Following Sam Haskins, Monte Zucker made his first Australian visit for Hypo 73 and set off a new slavishly copied fashion in portrait lighting and posing. In 1979 the famous British Vogue photographer Norman Parkinson made his first visit to Australia for the Institute to share his fashion secrets. While checking his lighting balance with a Polaroid SX-70, he recounted the time when working on a fashion shoot with David Bailey they had gone through cartons of the instant self-developing pictures. As the shots would spit out, the creative director, lighting, makeup artist, model and client would quickly crowd the photographer to see the result.

According to Parkinson, in a break in proceedings Bailey took the SX-70 and retired to the men's room. There he dropped his pants and captured a close-up of his pride and glory. Bailey then fed the exposed print back into the film pack in the camera and returned to the set. Soon there was a call for another lighting check and everyone flocked around the photographer to see a fully developed print whirring out. They were all in for a big surprise.

The tide of international lecturing photographers eventually lead to a reverse wave of Australia's leading photographers travelling to Europe and the States to in turn share their knowledge and experience. I hate to think of some of the stories they may have told.

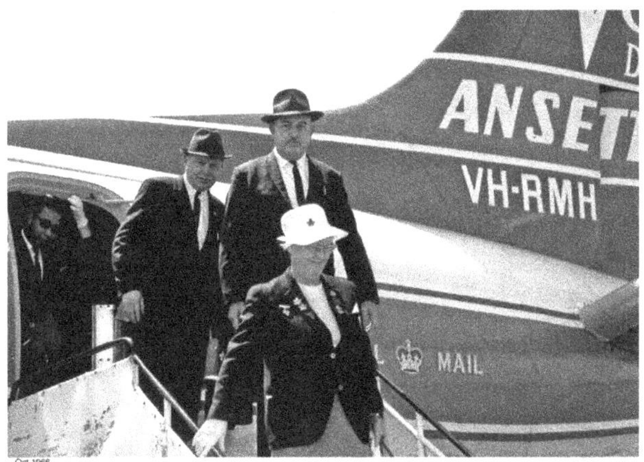

Oct 1966
Syd Owen (Qld) & Claude McCarthy (Qld) Fed Pres arrive in ACT. Photo made the local press.

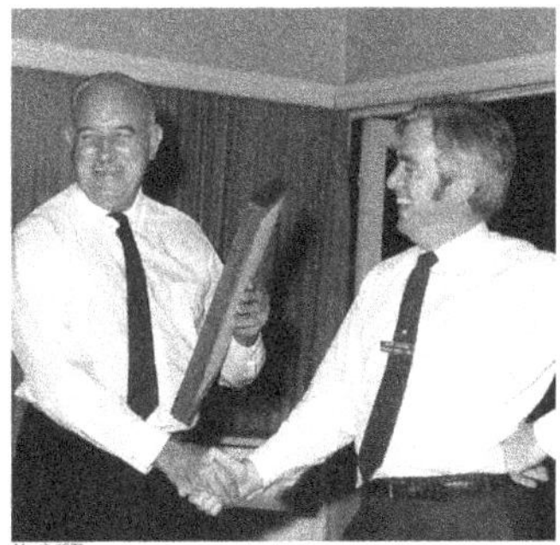

March 1970
Claude McCarthy (Qld) hands over something important to Geoff Cummings (NSW)
(or McCarthy receives something from Cummings!)

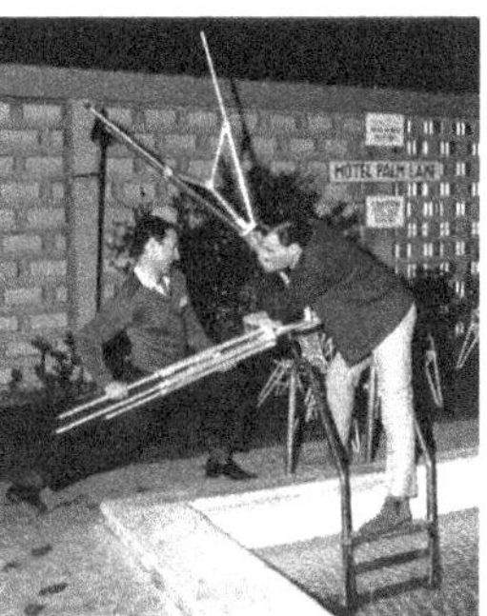

LtoR: David McCarthy(Qld) & Max Williams(Vic) dueling over a disagreement

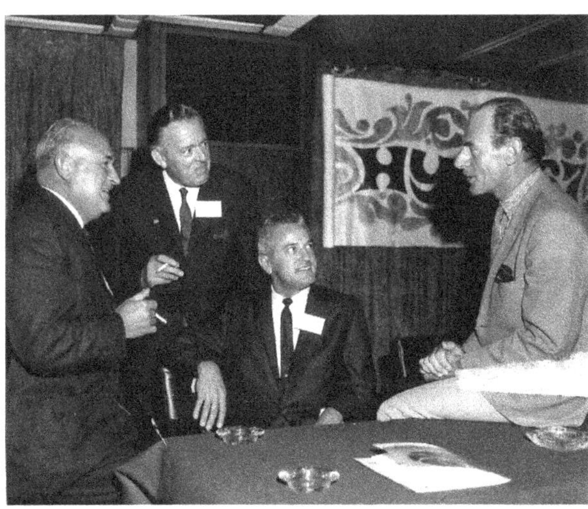

LtoR: Claude McCarthy (Qld), (?), (visiting American?), Dacre Stubbs (VIC) at HYPO 67.

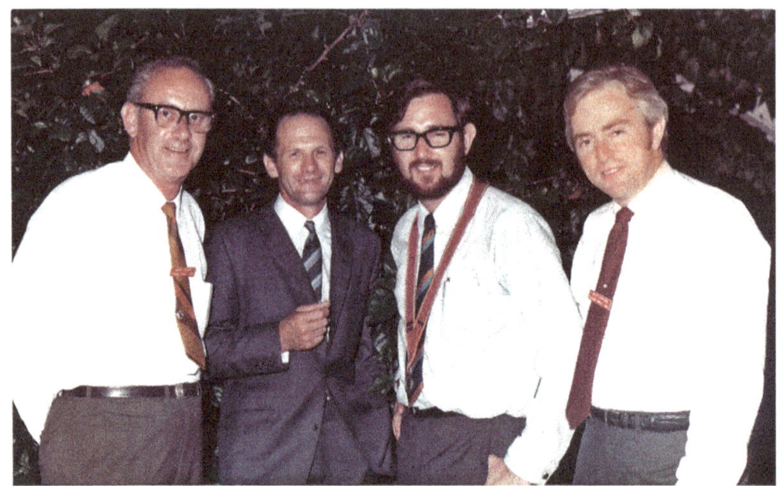

LtoR: (?), Ian Hawthorne (Vic), David McCarthy (Qld Pres), Geoff Cummings (NSW).

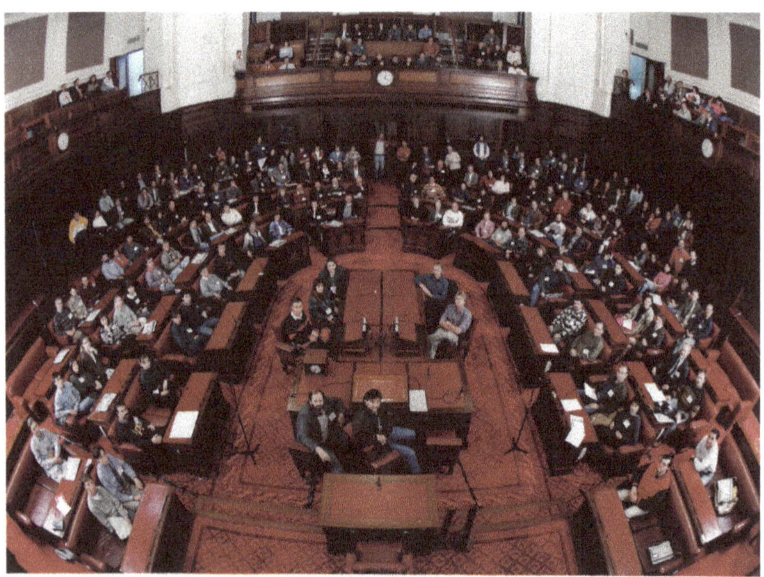

70

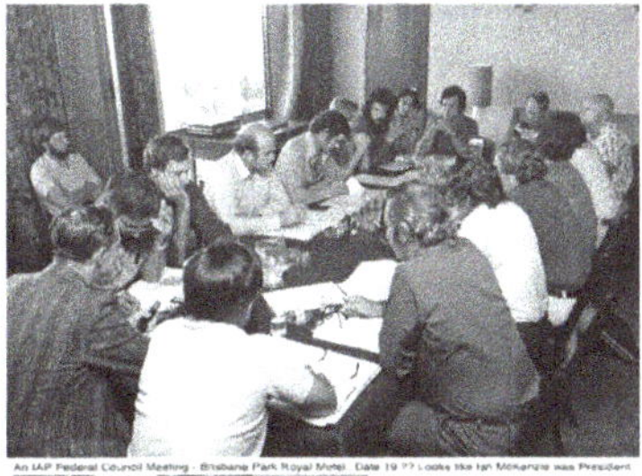

An IAP Federal Council Meeting - Brisbane Park Royal Motel. Date 19 ?? Looks like Ian McKenzie was President

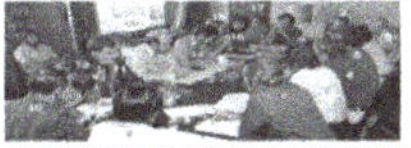

1 Peter Whyte (WA) 2 (?) 3 Norman Danvers (NSW) 4 Alan Mortimer (NSW) 5 Mike Kealy (ACT) 6 (?) (ACT) 7 ?? (?) 8 ?? (?) 9 Max Farrell (SA) 10 John Walter (Sec-SA) 11 Al Higgs (QLD) 12 David McCarthy (QLD) 13 Jim Nisbet (TAS) 14 John Leeming (Tas) 15 Peter Foeldon (VIC) 16 Ian McKenzie (VIC) 17 Val Foreman (Vic) 18 Will Street (Qld)

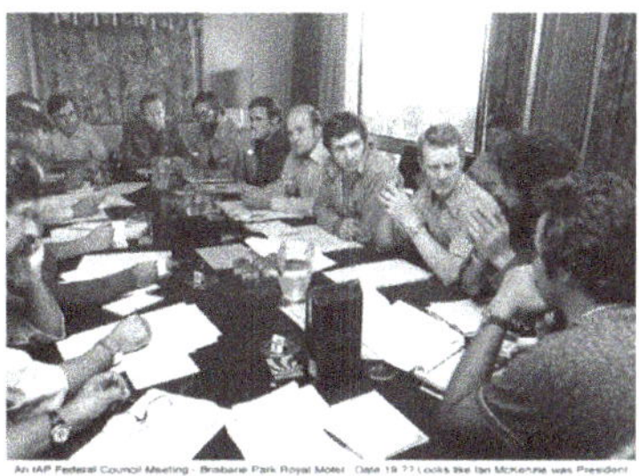

An IAP Federal Council Meeting - Brisbane Park Royal Motel. Date 19 ?? Looks like Ian McKenzie was President

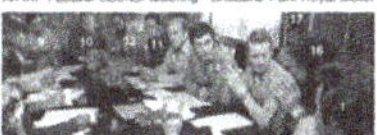

1 Peter Whyte (WA) 2 (?) 3 Norman Danvers (NSW) 4 Alan Mortimer (NSW) 5 Mike Kealy (ACT) 6 (?) (ACT) 7 ?? (?) 8 ?? (?) 9 Max Farrell (SA) 10 John Walter (Sec-SA) 11 Al Higgs (QLD) 12 David McCarthy (QLD) 13 Jim Nisbet (TAS) 14 John Leeming (Tas) 15 Peter Foeldon (VIC) 16 Ian McKenzie (VIC) 17 Val Foreman (Vic) 18 Will Street (Qld)

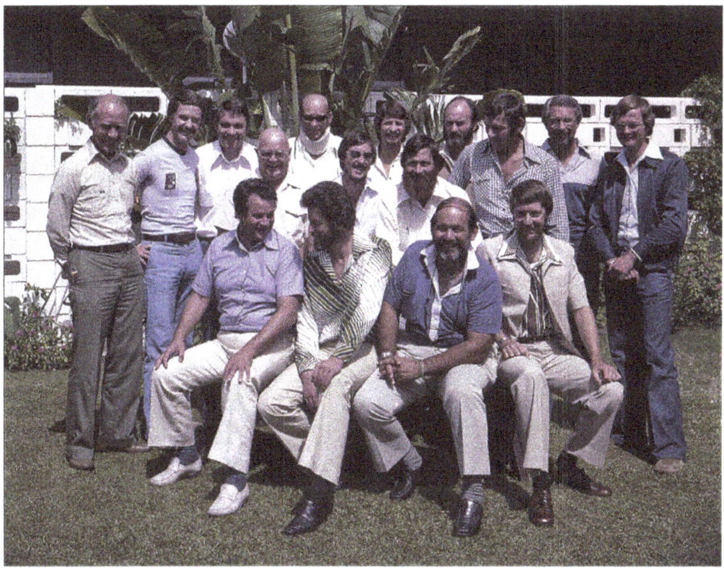

FEDERAL COUNCIL MEETING (Brisane Park Royal Motel - when ?)
Standing LtoR: Brian Barrow (WA), John Venus (SA), John Atkins (SA), Norman Danvers (NSW), Alan ??-neck brace), (Unknown-sunglasses), Rick Sherwyn (NSW),Richard Bennett (Tas), Attila Kiraly (?) (ACT),John Leeming (Tas), David McCarthy (Qld), Mike Wood (Vic),
Seated LtoR: Peter Whyte (WA), Ian McKenzie (Vic), Don Taylor (Qld), Will Street (Qld).

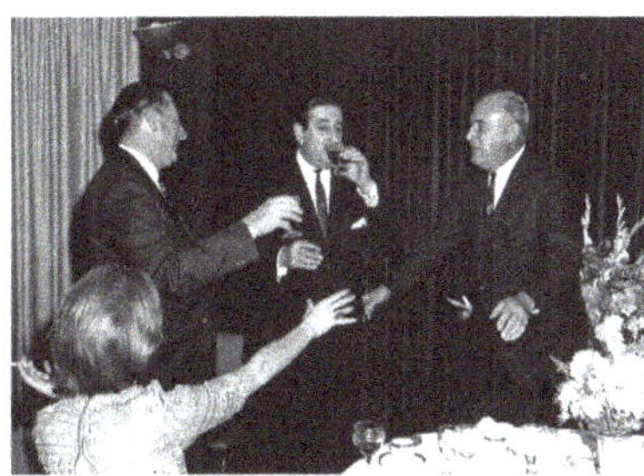

LtoR: (foreground back unknown) John Nisbett (NSW), Clive Shmith (VIC), Claude McCarthy (Qld)

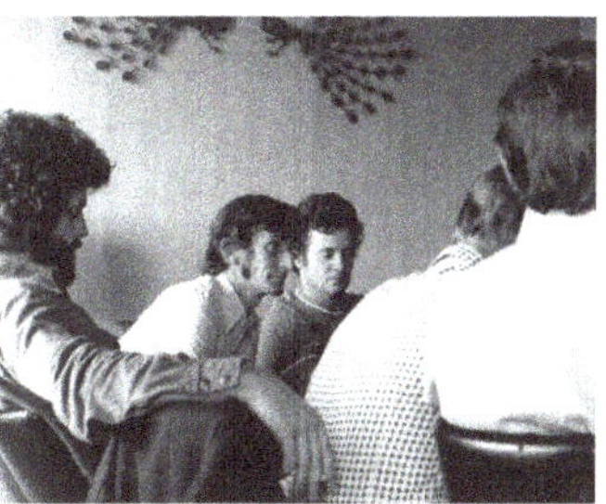

LtoR: Ian McKenzie (Vic), Val Foreman (Vic), Peter Whyte (WA) at a Federal Council meeting

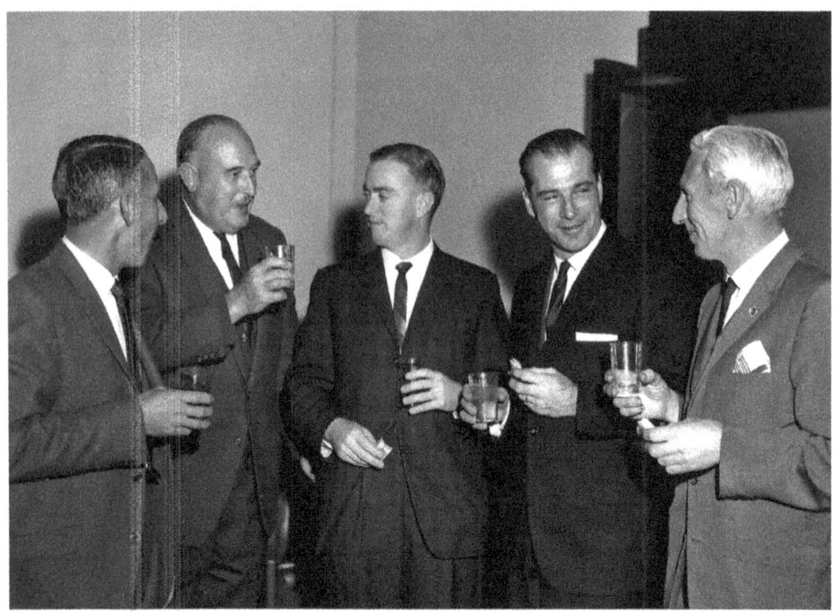

Melbourne 1964. LtoR: Ron Armstrong (WA), Claude McCarthy (Qld), Geoff Cummings (NSW), Fritz Kos (WA), Bill Waller (Vic)

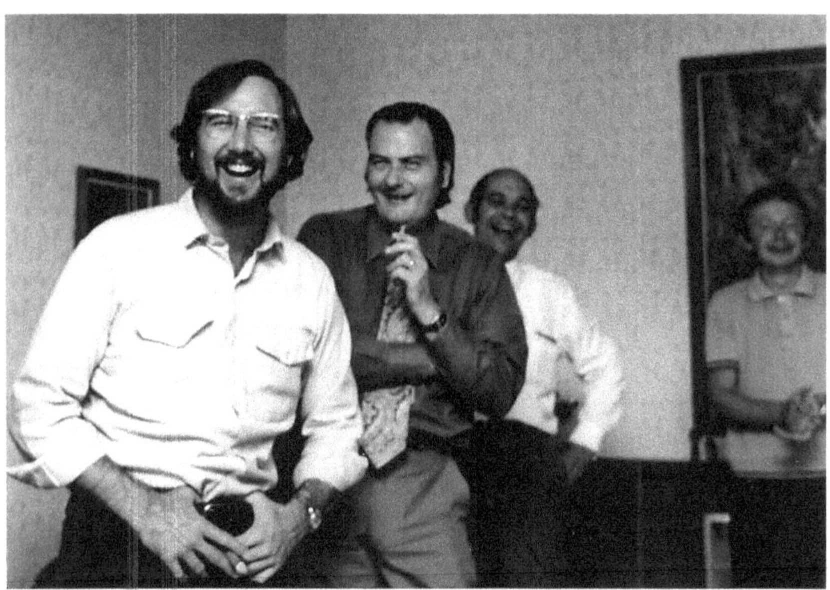

LtoR: David McCarthy (Qld), Max Williams (Vic), Don Taylor (Qld), Ivan Fox (ACT)

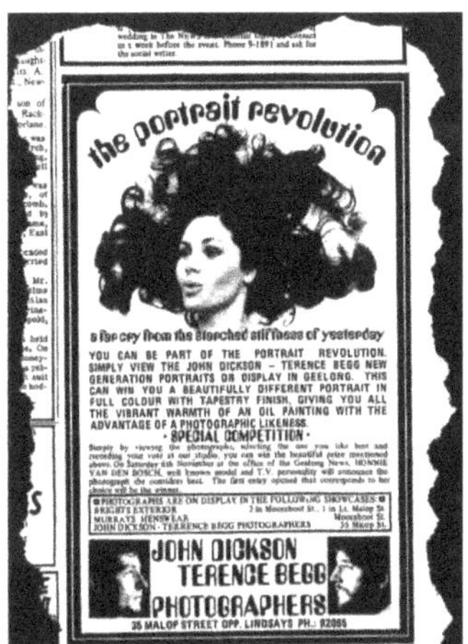

1972, the 'Portrait Revolution' arrives!

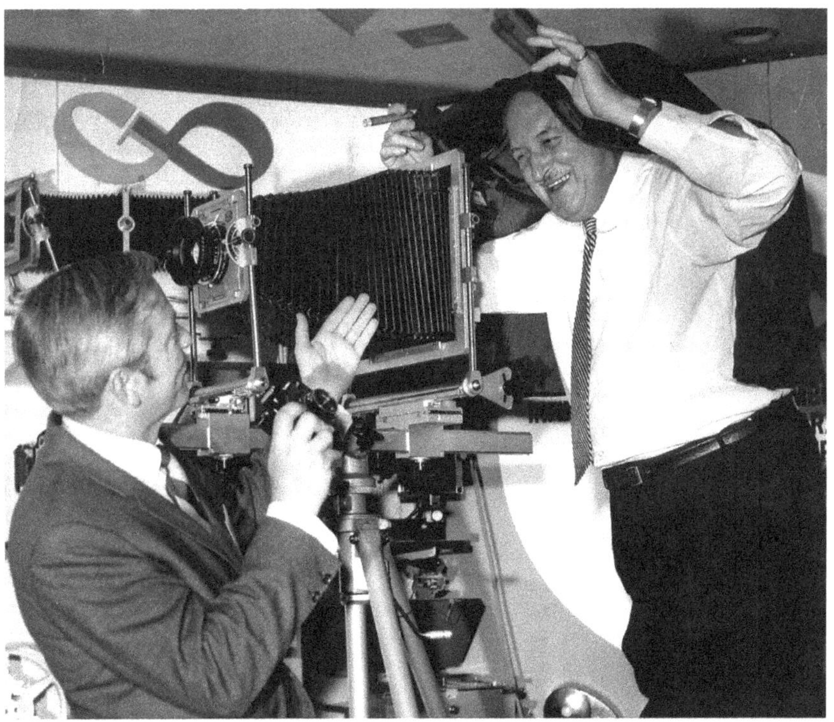

Geoff Cummings (NSW) and Claude McCarthy (Qld).

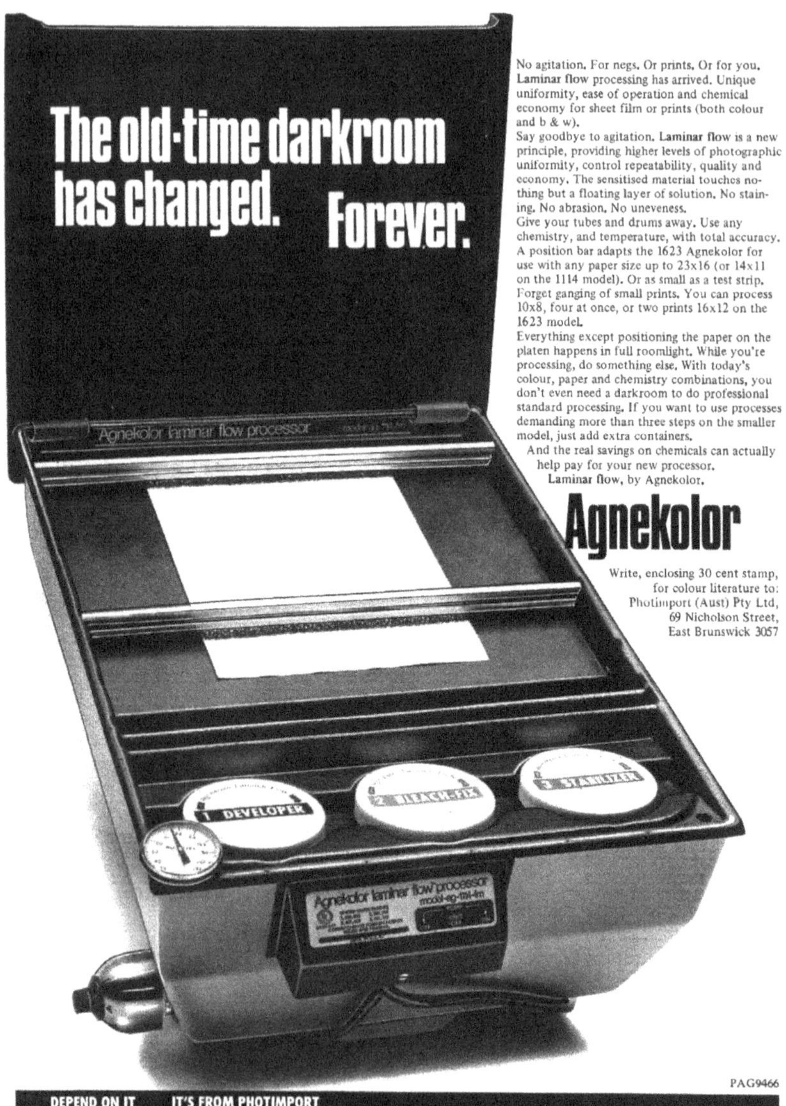

Later in the Seventies photographers wishing to spend less time in the dark began to toy with contraptions like this. But they never did take off!

Chapter Four

The Exotic Eighties: The Disappearing Studios

The Australian economy got off to a roaring start in the 1980's. This led to increased spending by consumers welcoming a glitzy, showy and glamorous life-style which became referred to as the 'Me' decade. In London, Prince Charles and Diana tied the knot before the world's largest television audience. Later Charles was to decide it wasn't 'Me'. And it was tears for the entire world in 1987 when stock markets crashed and Australia went into economic recession.

In commercial photography, the use of grain had become unusually fashionable with the major advertising agencies. In portraiture, a new informal style was gaining popularity with photographers escaping their studio backdrops for more natural settings in the great outdoors. At last photography in the park had become respectable!

Professional Photography Magazine, the Institute's official organ, was discussing the high cost of running studios and asking whether or not a wedding portrait photographer even needed to own a studio anymore. This prompted some comments on the fees being charged for portraiture with Canberra's Heide Smith proclaiming, 'For good portraits you should charge a high fee –it's not a pixie photo'. The magazine's inclusion of this comment leads to the threat of legal proceedings by pixie against the publisher! Alas, that publisher was me!

Meeting, meetings, meetings are an essential part of running an organisation; all time consuming but essential to find consensus. I should know, for in my capacity as executive director of the industry association for 25 years, I've seen more than my fair share. I used to complain about their frequency but one day I witnessed a magic and very special moment that made it all worthwhile.

It was in the 1980's and the Photographic Industry Council was meeting in the imposing, timber-panelled boardroom of Kodak's head office. Representing such major brands as Agfa, Ilford, Kodak, Canon and Fujifilm, there were about two dozen managing directors. These were more formal days, so they were immaculately suited, slightly wary of each other and studiously polite. I had been asked a week earlier by one of our more passionate country based professional photographers if he could address the group to start an industry promotion. I had thought it would do my directors good to hear direct from a working photographer for a change and allocated him a ten minute spot.

At the appointed time, there was a knock at the door and in he came. I introduced him to the group and asked him to begin, but please keep to his allocated time. Standing up, he pulled out a cassette recorder, placed it in the middle of the board room table and asked if it was okay. It was a bit unusual, but I shrugged my shoulders and said 'Sure, it's your presentation.' So he picked up his notes and off he went. Well, he started ok, but, maybe due to the effect of all the silent suits, the loud ticking of the clock, the oppressive sombreness of the oak walls, or maybe because he became too swayed by his own conviction, his voice started to get quicker and louder.

He was getting more excited and passionate with every sentence. Eventually, faintly reminiscent of Hitler addressing a Nuremburg rally, he worked himself up to full volume, threw down his notes, pointed his finger and thundered that they were a bunch of apathetic bastards and the time had come for everyone to get of their fat asses and do something! The directors sat there: silent and ashen faced. It really was quite the most splendid presentation I've ever seen! Checking my watch, I thanked him for his time and escorted him to the door while politely murmuring something about how grateful we were to hear such an energetic address and we would get back to him regarding his proposal in a few days.

After closing the door, I made my way back to the table wondering how I was going to explain all this. The directors were just sitting there, opened mouthed and as cloudy eyed as yesterday's catch at the fishmongers'. Somehow, I didn't think they were quite used to hearing such forthright presentations!

I shuffled some papers and fidgeted a bit. After a long pause, one ventured a faintly derogatory comment. Emboldened, the others, one by one, joined in, topping each other until they eventually were saying in no uncertain terms exactly what they thought of the proposal, him personally, the questionable identity of his parentage and whether or not giving him a one-way overseas plane ticket would not be the best investment.

A few minutes later, there was a knock on the door. I opened it and there was our photographer. 'So sorry,' he said, bustling into the room and approaching the centre of the board room table. 'I forgot this'. Totally silent, we watched him pick up his still running tape recorder and sweep from the room.

Of course, I had to disgrace myself even further. I just dissolved into hysterical laughter. At some of the countless meetings I have had to attend since, there have been tedious times, when in order to gain the strength to carry on, I've had to privately revive and treasure that memory. That one moment has made my entire industry career worthwhile.

I hasten to say that this gentleman was never one of the presidents of the Institute, although I think maybe he should have been!

Due to the heavy commitment of time that had to be made by a president, in 1980 and 1981 the Institute elected its presidents for one year only. For the first time the board elected for its president a West Australian: Peter Whyte. Peter founded Churchill Colour Laboratories in Subiaco, Western Australia in 1977 and, with his wife Lyn, built the business into one of Australia's leading E6 and Cibachrome labs.

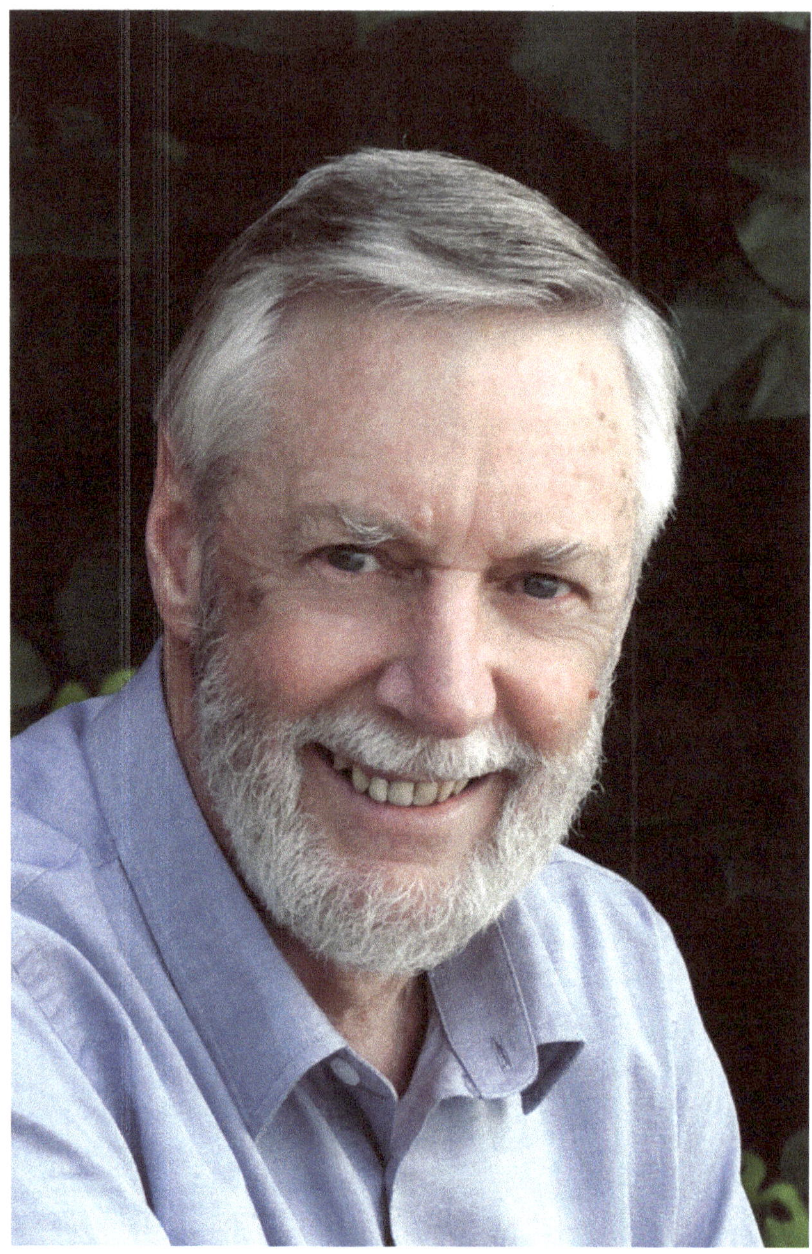

Will Street, National President 1984 and 1985

Peter's great photographic passion was aerial photography and he both designed and built several special purpose aerial cameras. The trade organised the 1981 equipment show and called it Photina. Outside the exhibition area and in the foyer of the Sydney Hilton, there was a display of portraiture by photographers from across Australia. All the portraits were similar in style to that of previous visiting lecturer Monte Luke and the comment was made that it was 'plastic portraiture' and they appeared to have all been taken by the same photographer. Peter said that one of the overseas speakers had told him that they all looked like fine examples of the embalming trade!

The following year, veteran Sydney photographer Norman L. Danvers was elected president. Norman began his career with a short spell as a commercial artist before becoming a newspaper photographer. Two years later, this was brought to a sudden end by the arrival of World War Two. Quipped Norman, 'My budding career was interrupted by a compulsory government-paid, clothing and accommodation provided holiday in the Southwest Pacific. I never did get used to people shooting at me. It gives you the feeling that you are not wanted.'

After the war, Norman began business as an advertising, architectural and industrial photographer. For twelve years, he also did all the photography for the Australian Broadcasting Commission in Sydney. Norman said this beautiful friendship ended when the ABC decided that for three hours work on a Saturday with only two hours notice, his fee of three pounds and three shillings was just too much! They put a photographer on permanent staff.

By the time he was elected president of the Institute, the bald, bespectacled and boisterous Norman had more than thirty years experience as a photographer under his belt and had won his Associateship of the Institute for his photographic skills. Norman said, 'Forget about the old days: any time you have a day or two to spare I will tell you how good they were!'

Norman claimed he would give anything to be 30 years younger and thus able to learn like young people can from the procession of great lecturers now so willing to share all their secrets. Influenced by American motivator Napoleon Hill, Norman advocated, 'Get in there now and do it with enthusiasm. Tomorrow will be too late.'

After presidents Peter Whyte and Norman Danvers, the Institute's board took the view that in order to get a full agenda carried through, it was desirable that the elected president's term would run for to two years.

Accordingly, in 1982, Melbourne photographer Peter Foeden took the president's role until the end of 1983. In these days, the president's terms used to run on the calendar rather than the financial year. Born in Holland in 1930, Peter's first job was as a physical education teacher. He started his professional photography career when he turned thirty and was originally mentored by Val Foreman. He joined the Institute in 1967 and he spent two decades lecturing and sharing his secrets of success within the profession.

Quietly spoken but extremely articulate, a tall trim figure immaculately dressed in grey, Peter influenced a whole generation of photographers. He sold his studio in 1985 to concentrate on his partnership in Nulab, a professional colour processing laboratory. He also formed a company, Albums Australia, to supply quality wedding albums exclusively to professional photographers. He sold out of Nulab in 1990 and then sold Albums Australia in 2002, but Peter is still doing some occasional consultancy work.

Probably the most lasting contribution Peter made to the Institute was the introduction of the Awards system to recognise professional photography at its highest level. At the annual conventions, it was the custom to have a small exhibition of professional photographs. In addition to making a decorative display and creating a talking point, the exhibition gave visitors a yardstick with which to compare their own photography standards. But there was definitely no judging or public critiquing. Oh no! So when at a 1970 federal council meeting Peter Foeden first mooted the idea of an awards system for the photographs displayed, there was some shuffling of uneasy feet. Indeed one sniffed, 'we are not a camera club!'

But Peter pressed his case citing the successful annual USA Professional Photographers Association's annual awards which proved not to pitch individual members against each other. Melbourne pro lab owner Max Townsend also liked the idea and fought vigorously to keep the issue on the agenda. Others progressively came round and in 1977 the first National Print Judging was held at Hypo '77 on the Gold Coast. Seventy one members submitted 268 prints. Commented Peter Foeden, 'With the American system as our guide, we have developed a system to suit the Australian temperament.

The effect of the introduction of the Awards on the Institute was revolutionary. The combination of the critiques and the competition fuelled creativity and innovation in Australian photography. By the mid 1990s the Awards were attracting 2000 entries and had an operational budget of $100,000. Foeden's commitment to the program extended until 1983 when he passed over the chairmanship of the Awards committee to Geelong photographer Ian Hawthorne. As chair, he worked with the team, initially composed of dedicated Victorian members to run the National Print Awards. As a photographer, Ian wrote numerous articles for the Institute's journal and had an inexhaustible depth of knowledge he shared lecturing to fellow photographers.

The consolidation of the event into a key part of the Institute's calendar can be largely attributed to another Melbourne photographer, David Puddefoot and a co chair with Ian. David was the enduring strength of the Awards. The Committee continued to formulate, develop and document the Awards process during his involvement from 1979-2004, enabling the Awards judging process to move forward and from state to state.

He was an extremely efficient organiser and with his dedicated team handled the ever growing task of coordinating the judging process at the annual photography show with calmness and assurance.

This talent has been inherited by subsequent coordinators including David Paterson, Craig Bassett and the incumbent at the time of this publication: Sue Lewis.

The role of chairman of the Awards Committee has been held by only a few. Ian was chair until 1990 and then succeeded by Doug

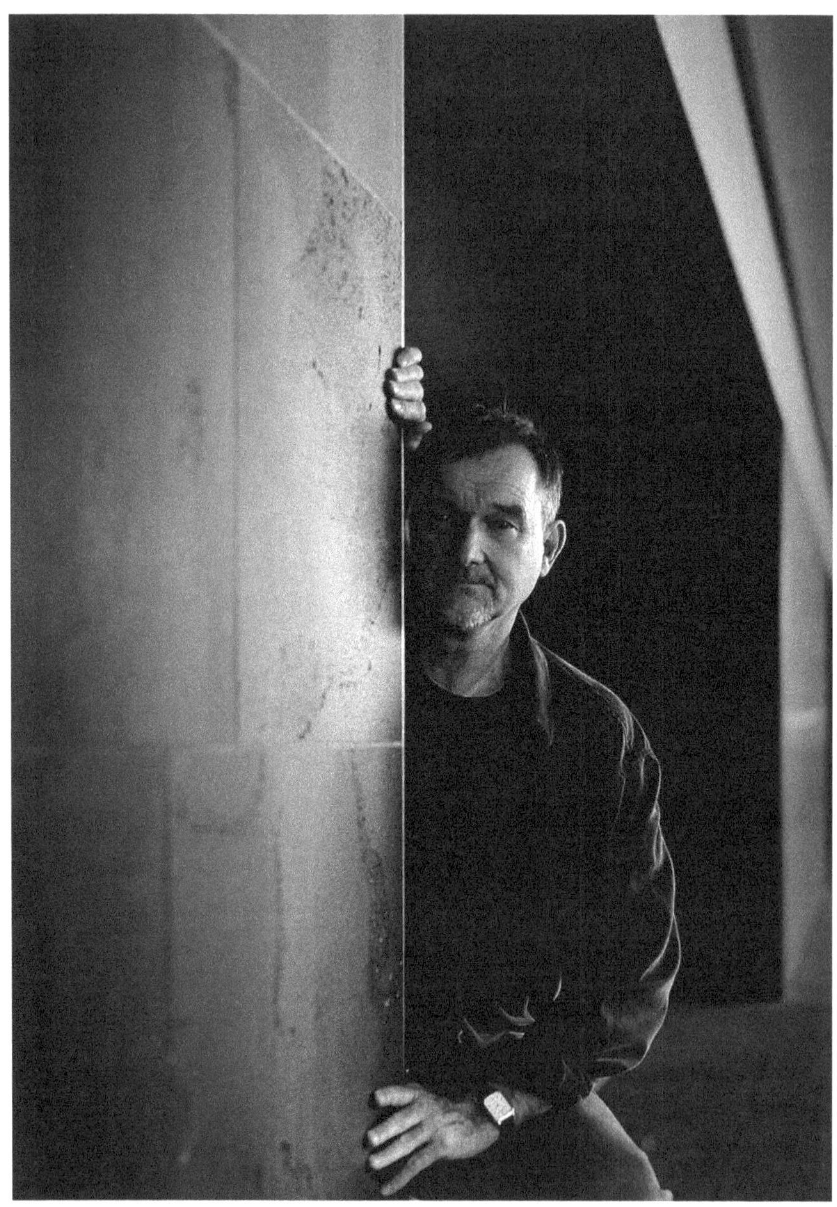

Kevin O'Daly, National President 1988 -1991 Photography by Heide Smith

Spowart from Queensland, who took over until 1999. He was followed by former institute president Richard Bennett who occupied the chair until 2005 before handing over to Peter Eastway who in turn handed over to the current chair, David Paterson, in 2010.

The judging process is a great occasion and in the past has been supported by such celebrities as Lord Lichfield and Lord Snowdon. But you can be a commoner too and indeed it can be viewed by anyone visiting one of the three theatres at the annual photo show. The atmosphere is electric as each picture is displayed anonymously and commented on by the panel of judges. The judges are dedicated professional image makers selected by the committee for their experience and who spend hours and days each year at the forefront of the process.

While usually a hushed environment, some judging comments bring cheers; other times a sharp intake of breath: such as on one occasion when the long established judge Peter Adams found a photo of a cute kitten just too much chocolate box for his taste. His opening remarks began with 'This is a f...ing picture, of a f... ing ugly cat, in a f...ing ugly pair of slippers '. Emboldened by such remarks, another judge began, 'This itty, shitty little kitty...' And it got worse after that!

On another occasion, celebrated photographer Graham McCarter had his judging audience in tears of laughter when slightly miffed with the high number of vignetted prints and wondering if vignetting was just used for the sake of it rather than helping the image, he dryly remarked,' To me, vignetting is a bit of a dodgy thing.'

Richard Bennett, the famous Tasmanian yachting photographer and also long time chair of the Awards, also experienced the possible vagaries of the judging process.

Entering a photograph of his that had just won the media's Sports Photograph of the Year Award, he was surprised to find it only earned thirteenth place in the Institute's own editorial category! So no benefit for the chairman there!

Through the Awards program an Institute member could accumulate points towards achieving higher levels of membership of Associateship then Master of Photography. A silver awarded print was one point and gold two etc. In later years, entrants could also aspire to become category winners, sponsored by individual trade companies and ultimately to the prestigious title of Professional Photographer of the Year. Those with a Master of Photography could more recently, gain further recognition through the Awards, to the level of Grand Master.

Throughout all these years, Peter Foeden has maintained a keen interest in the Awards which have been his legacy. While he believes the Awards are maintaining the highest standards, he does question the growing number of photographers gaining the Grand Master level. Indeed, he is slightly uncomfortable with the word itself and wonders what other terminology will be introduced as photographers reach new heights.

The exhibition of the awards and the display of photographic equipment was becoming of increasing importance to the industry. In 1980, in a move instigated by Don Hogarth, then chairman of Kodak, a new body was formed called the Australian Photo Industry Association. The objective was to bring together the all too numerous individual photographic associations. The objective was to explore common goals. Great idea? Sure, but you try throwing together all the competing aspects of the industry altogether in the same room to achieve a common goal and see what you come up with! It's not easy! I should know: I was a part of it.

The organisations represented were the Institute, (AIPP) the consumer distributor's association, the Photo Industry Council, (PIC) the professional photo industry distributors association, (PIMA), the photo dealers association (PMA), the Australian Photographic Educators Association (APEA) and the Australian Professional Colour Laboratories Association (APCLA). All these organisations came together to form the Australian Photographic Industry Association: the APIA. All that was missing from this veritable alphabetical soup of associations was Old McDonald and his EIEIO!

Somewhat shell shocked by the temerity of the mere idea of us being crowded together in one small room, for hours at a time we all anxiously peered through the vile, pea-soup smog emanating from the pipe of moderator Carsten Petersen. Ah yes, there was an organisational white board there. With the great Australian wave normally reserved for persistent flies, we could see clearly now! Nevertheless, with Ian McKenzie leading the representations for professional photographers, we thrashed out a new era of cooperation between the different areas of interest which lead to the organisation of a new show called Photographics '83.

Eventually the professional and consumers associations were merged and although the formal structure of the industry wide council was discontinued, it formed the guiding principles for my own twenty five year tenure of running the combined industry's annual shows. For much of that period, Ian actively represented the Institute. Although we all worked in harmony, Ian was always a forceful and persuasive presenter and we all enjoyed a drink together after meetings.

After Peter Foeden retired from his position as president in 1983, on the office management front, Tim O'Daly succeeded Ian Howell, who resigned as executive director in order to relocate to New Zealand to manage a commercial photography business. Will Street took the reins as president in 1984.

First studying professional photography in the United States, Will Street started his professional photography life on Queensland's Gold Coast, and operated studios there and in Brisbane until 1993 when he became Queensland Director of Townsend Colour Laboratory. He joined the Institute in 1971 and served as Queensland Divisional Secretary from 1977 - 1984. He was also the convenor of the photographers' convention on the Gold Coast.

The Exotic Eighties: The Disappearing Studios

As the publisher of the Institute's magazine at the time, I know that as president, Will Street was a strong negotiator. In 1985, keen to set up a permanent record of the winning award entries for each year, Will persuaded our team at Iris Publishing to produce a special Professional Photographer's Handbook. Although this was a soft cover annual for some years, this was the forerunner of the high

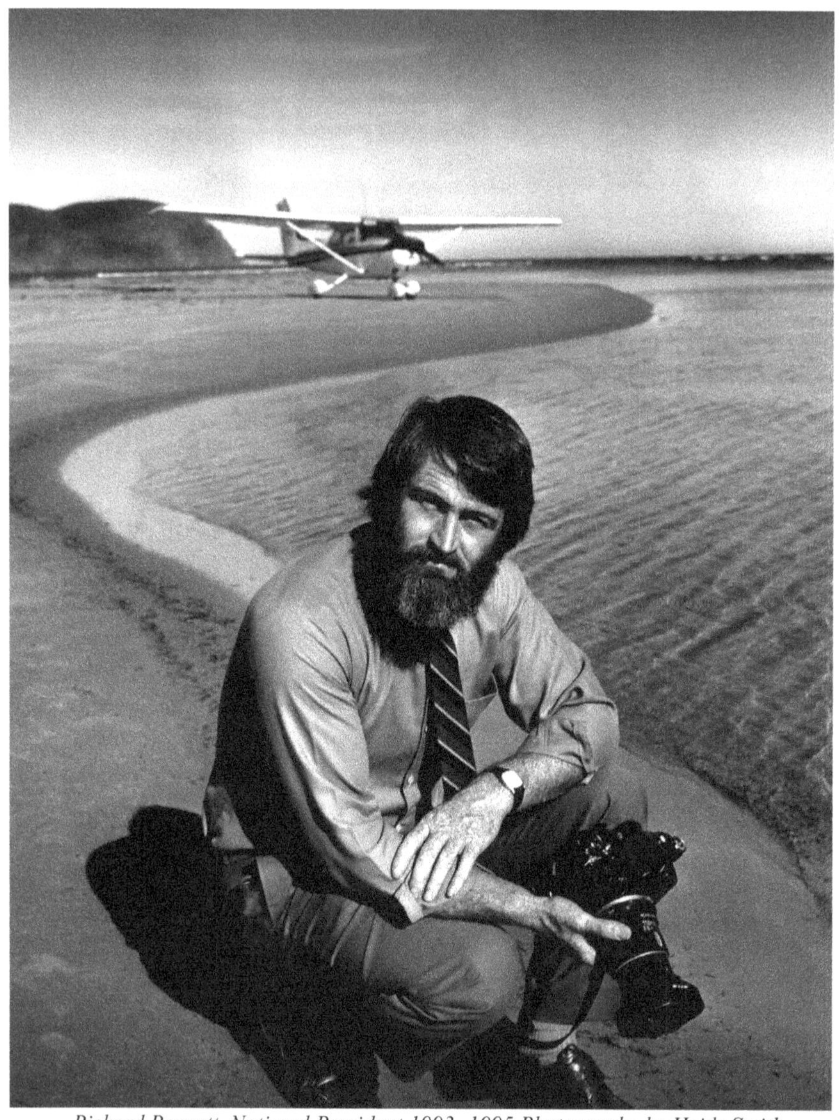

Richard Bennett, National President 1993 -1995 Photography by Heide Smith

quality annual awards book published since.

During Will's term, future president Robert Gray began campaigning to restructure the Institute. At that time the various States were a group of unincorporated divisions with each sending a representative to elect The Federal Council. With Will's support, Kevin O'Daly, Malcolm Mathieson and Peter Eastway set about the task of keeping the incorporation on the agenda, Kevin O'Daly had the job of getting it done when he became President and the AIPP hired the legal firm of Corrs in Melbourne to help redraft the Articles and get the Institute into one incorporated national body. This naturally led to a fear by some States that they could lose autonomy, but after many long and heated meetings, the advantages of incorporation began to be understood.

Kevin O'Daly put it very simply to the membership saying, 'Let's take an oversimplified example: the New South Wales division exhibits some prints and a visitor has a sheet of glass fall on her foot. She sues us for one million dollars.

If we are incorporated, the Institute is sued. If we are an unincorporated body, the Institute can't be sued (it's not a 'legal entity') but the council members (possibly state and federal) at the time can be! Sure, if there's an insurance policy we're okay, but what if it was for a maximum of $500,000? It is the committee who becomes responsible. Of course, becoming incorporated also makes it easier for us to sue someone else. And it puts the Institute on a more professional footing within the industry — something the federal body is very keen to do.' The Institute finally became an officially incorporated body in early 1991.

Towards the end of Will's term, the idea of incorporation won through, but Will was feeling the Institute was still at a crossroads and so commissioned a survey to help determine how the Institute could play a stronger role. He also commenced a campaign to attract new members from the government photographer market segment, and the Federal Council considered a suggested name change brought to it by Richard Syme on behalf of the West Australian Division.

Said Will in his end of term report, 'I think it was a turning point to introduce the word 'professional' into our name to make us the Australian Institute of Professional Photography. However, I do not believe that we are yet a truly professional organisation. Our membership numbers are static while the total number of potential members is increasing.'

Taking over as president from the quietly spoken Will Street came the booming voice of Robert Gray in 1986. Rob is a stocky, impressive figure and his incisive questioning and very direct manner quickly gets to the heart of any issue. He has been acknowledged as a true visionary of the Institute.

He began his career in 1969 as a cadet with the Melbourne Age. Robert recalls working with everything from 4x5 cameras to 35mm. At the Melbourne Age, at a time when most press photographers were using twin lens reflex 120 cameras, Robert witnessed press photography veteran John Lamb unpacking the first 35mm camera to be used at the paper. It was a Nikon F and because of its small size by most it was not initially well received! At The Age, Robert's career blossomed and after winning Best Sports Photograph of the Year a couple of times he rose to the position of Picture Editor of the Sunday Press. He spent most of 1976 travelling in Queensland for a monthly magazine before moving to Hong Kong and working around Asia in partnership with Dinshaw Balsara on fashion, advertising and corporate work. Three years later he returned to Melbourne and in 1980 with Ian McKenzie he formed McKenzie Gray and Associates.

In 1987 Robert decided on a change of lifestyle and took advantage of the then North Queensland tourism boom to base his business in Cairns. There he remained until 2001 when he retired and moved to Brisbane.

His capacity to see the way ahead clearly on an almost visionary scale lead the AIPP to make some revolutionary changes which contributed to its gathering strength as an effective national body. His development of the professional photography awards included introducing the Professional Photographer of the Year award into the

Awards structure. The Professional Photographer of the Year Award was initially introduced by the West Australian Division and Roger Garwood in Perth in 1983, but even with the help and backing of people as influential as Lord Snowdon, it became apparent that it needed to move east and gather the Institute's wholehearted support to continue. Dr Ted Eakins travelled from Perth to present an outline of PPY to the Federal Council which was adopted and Robert drove this project into its now indelible spot on the Institute's Award judging program.

With the help of Kevin O'Daly and Malcolm Mathieson, Robert also managed to winkle the Awards judging out of it normal place in Melbourne and take it on the road to other major cities. Until 1984 the awards were annually judged in Melbourne and for the first time in 1985, moved to Sydney. This was a momentous move as those who knew how the system worked were based in Melbourne. However, the move was a success and since then the Awards judging has mainly followed the annual industry shows which have in recent years mainly alternated between Sydney and Melbourne with occasional visits to Brisbane.

In another move, Robert raised the bar for conventions by hiring both the Sydney Opera House and presenter leading illustrative photographer Dean Collins from the USA. Robert made a substantial profit that enabled the groundwork for future conventions to start and Tony Reade commenced negotiations with Vice President of Kodak USA Ray De Moulin to come to Australia to the Ayers Rock Convention.

In his president's report in 1987, Robert recalled the foundation stones of the Institute. 'We now mark the 75th Anniversary of the beginnings of what is now the Australian Institute of Professional Photography, whose aims are as they were in 1912: to promote the status of its members as true professionals in the eyes of the general public, governments and business, using a strong code of professional conduct, workshops and seminars, a bi-annual national convention and the magazine Professional Photography in Australia as its means.'

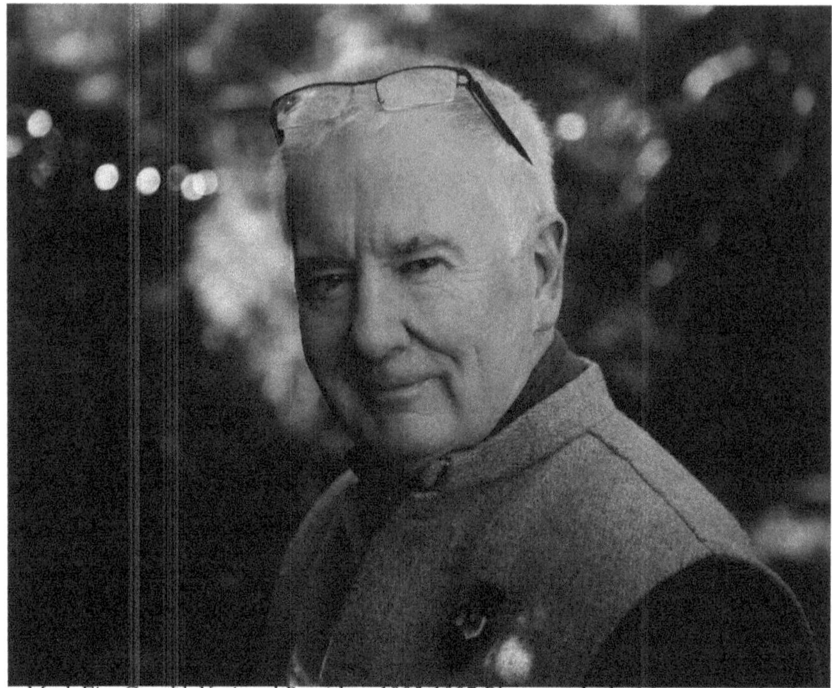

Mark Fitz-Gerald, National President 1995-1997 Photography by Margaret Ambridge

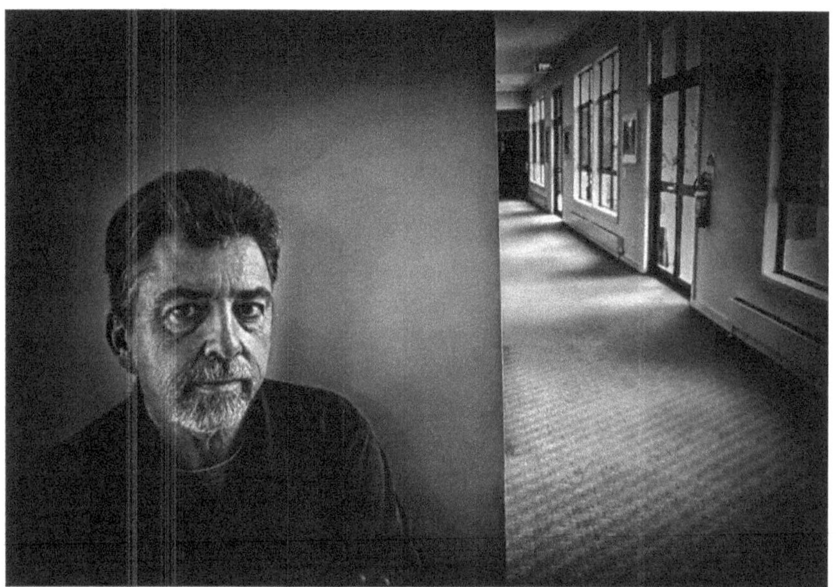

Greg Hocking, National President 1997-1999 Photography by Heide Smith

South Australia's Kevin O'Daly took over as president in July 1988. Kevin first worked in The National Bank and then at the Weapons Research Establishment in Adelaide but asked to change his job from clerical to become an assistant in the photographic department after 3 months. That meant a lower pay grade, and signing a form titled 'Reduction by Consent'. However, he received a good grounding in photography in what was the largest photographic establishment in the Southern Hemisphere with a staff of 24 and shooting anything from Passports to Rocket Launches as well as all the photography for the RAAF Edinburgh before the establishment of their own photographic section. This knowledge gained over an eleven year period, Kevin later put to designing and building one of the best photographic studios in Australia and setting himself up in private practice.

His mild and somewhat whimsical approach to life tends to disguise a persistent determination to get things done. On the management committee his constant voice of reason and level-headedness was a key catalyst to reaching consensus in what was sometimes an emotional atmosphere. The board also decided to stop referring to itself as a 'federal' body and instead opted to use the word 'national.' So after Ian, there were no more federal presidents... only national ones.

Kevin's persistence and a three year sponsorship by Fuji saw the Awards book dramatically upgraded to a thick, hardcover collector's piece. Kevin also launched a new revamped insurance package to save money for members and introduced new contracts for advertising and commercial photographers.

Kevin was keen for the Institute to do more in the education arena to promote the professionalism of photography and the education of students to fulfil the needs of the industry and in 1989 the Awards were adapted to introduce a National Student of the Year Award. Said Kevin, 'The Institute knows that its future lies in the youth of today and in the fact that photography students accept the challenges of the future.'

However, the O'Daly era was to continue. Tim O'Daly handed

over the federal secretary role to his brother in law, Bryan Pascal. With Kevin successively serving as federal treasurer, vice president, president and chair, altogether, the family created an unbroken thirteen year term of involvement with the management of the Institute.

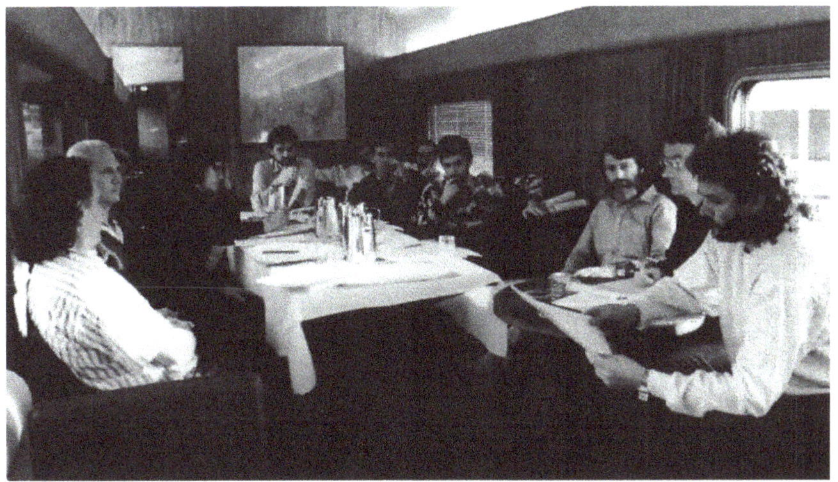

The longest ever meeting of the Federal Executive... On the train from Adelaide to Alice Springs. At the time it was suggested that this was the first time the federal executive had all travelled together in the same direction! 1989.

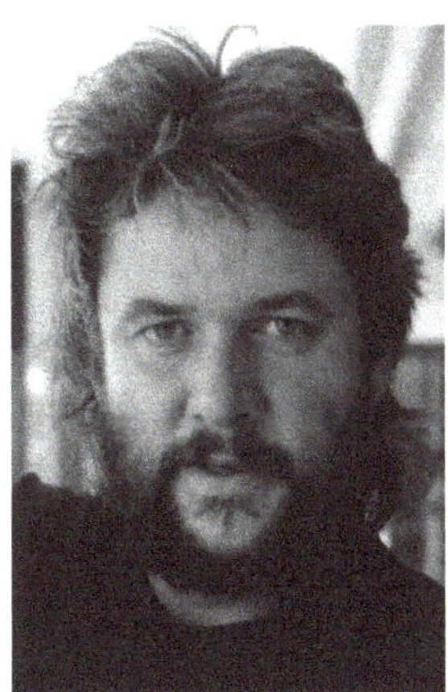

Robert Gray, National President 1986 and 1987

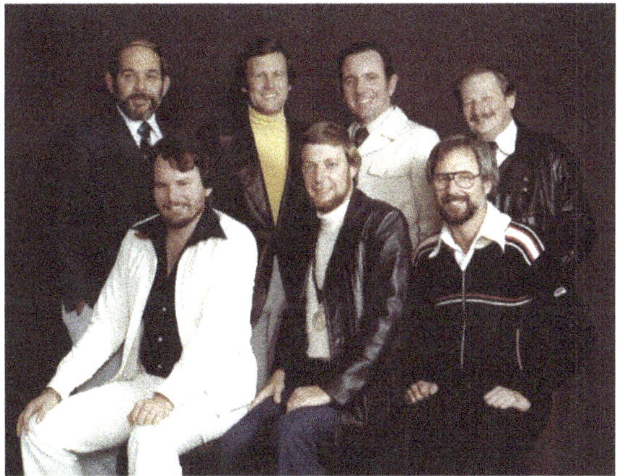

The 1980s Queensland Divisional Council: Sitting, left to right: Ian Poole, Will Street, David McCarthy. Don Taylor, Brian Chester, Col Lutz and Grahame Jurott

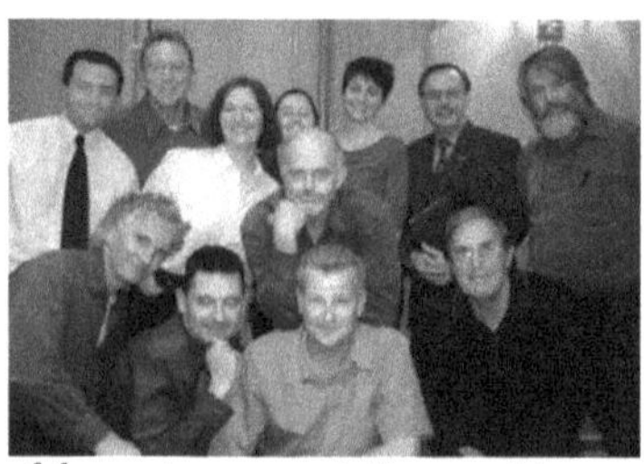

In 2003 representatives of the various associations met to organise an International Festival of Photography for Sydney in 2004. The five day event included a major exhibition of photography called the Festival Global Gallery and set a new record as the southern hemisphere's largest exhibition of photographic and imaging equipment and materials. In this photo by North Sullivan are, standing, left to right: Paul Stewart, Canon; Bruce Pottinger, PICA; Jackie Dean, AIPP; Rosslyn Richardson, Canon; Catherine Gasmier, ACMP; Terry Rimmer, PMA; Richard Bennett, Awards Chairman; Front: North Sullivan, ACMP; Jacques Guerinet, Fujifilm; David Simmonds, ACMP; Ian van der Wolde, AIPP and Paul Curtis, PICA.

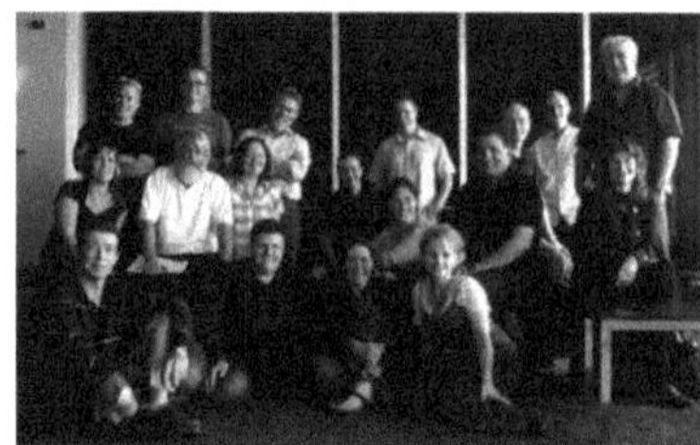

Every year, the AIPP Board invites delegates from the state divisions and subcommittees to a policy and planning meeting. In this 2006 photo are, back row left to right: Richard Muldoon, QLD President; Ian van der Wolde, Mediation; Geoff Comfort, ACT President; Ian Wallace, Vice President; Robert Edwards, Co-opted Board member; Peter Eastway, APPA; Ian Howell, VIC President; Middle Row left to right: Ann Vardanega, North Queensland Chapter Representative; Richard Bennett, Honours; Jacqui Dean, President; Russell Barton, WA President; Alice Bennett, Vice President; Phil Kuruvita, Chairman, Janie Boyd, TAS Representative; Front row left to right: John de Rooy, Treasurer; David Sievers SA President, Jessica Dean, National Office Co-ordinator; Kylie Lyons, NSW President

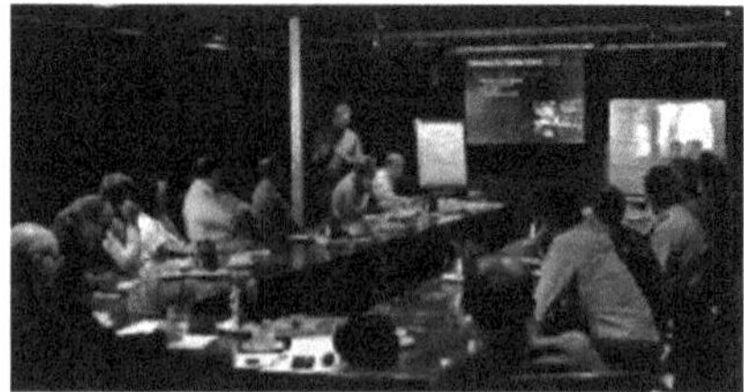

The inaugural meeting of the PMC (Professional Marketing Committee) was held in 2008. In a six-hour session drawing pro market leaders from around the country, the meeting reviewed where the opportunities for greater effectiveness may lie. Paul Curtis, PICA's consulting executive director, acted as facilitator for the day. In this photo by John Swainston, the delegates were, PICA: Bruce Pottinger, Rob Gatto, John Swainston, Kevin Cooper, Michelle Tuddenham, Alan Brightman; AIPP: Alice Bennett, John de Rooy, Robert Edwards; Peter Eastway ,(APPA); Greg Hocking , (AIPP Commercial Div); ACMP: David Simmonds; Mark Monro; Fiona Wolf, (Trampoline) Joseph Feil (Trampoline) Brent Williams; Arts Freedom Australia: Ken Duncan; and Paul Burrows.

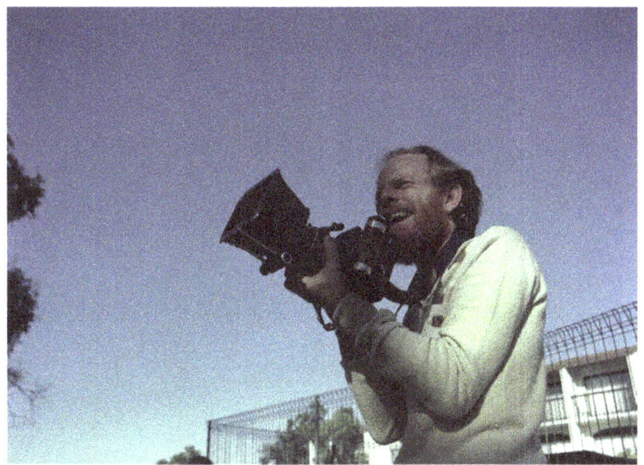

John Whitfield King in action. Photo by Robert Gray

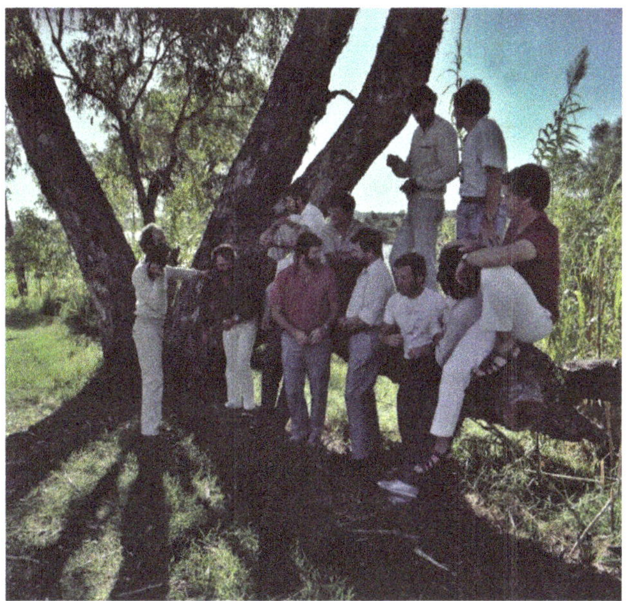

At a workshop, John Whitfield King jollies a group of reluctant photographers into position. Photo Robert Gray.

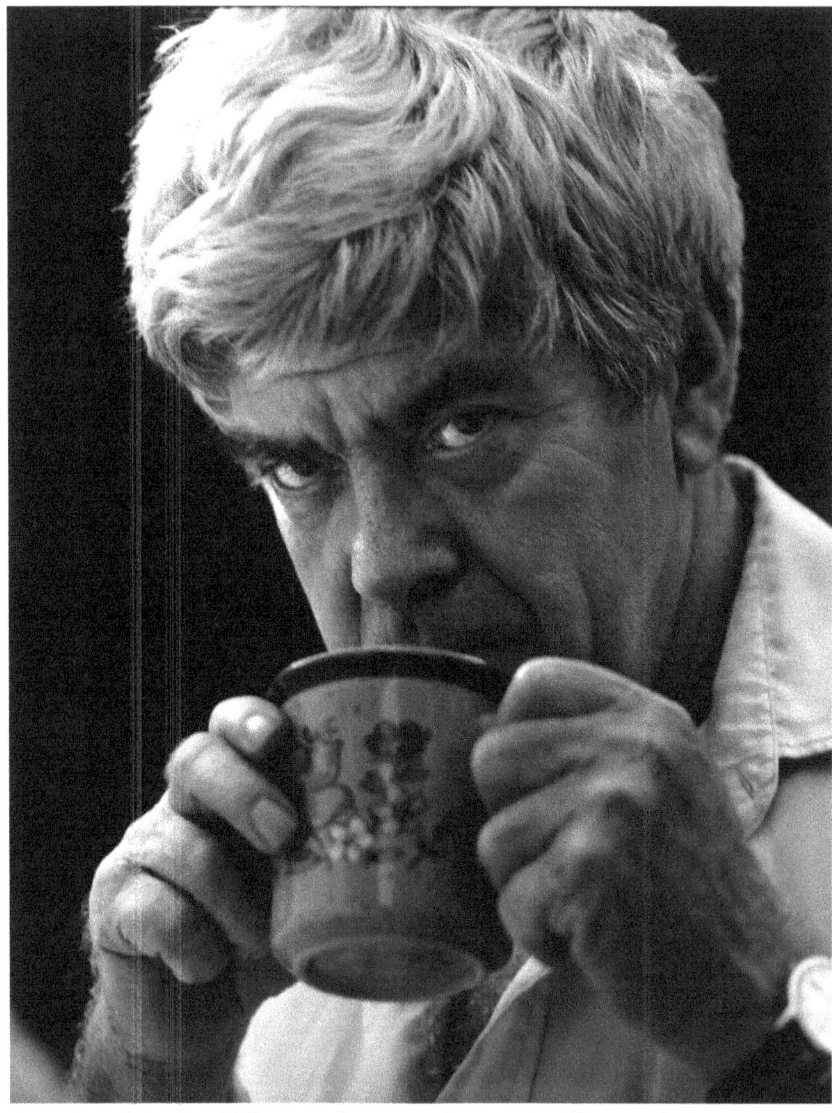

Brian Brandt, leading Melbourne advertising photographer Photography by Heide Smith

Chapter Five

The Nifty Nineties: The Approaching Digital Tsunami

The Nineties were a decade of accelerating technological change. Everyone started talking digital and a few professionals were even daring to wonder about the future of film. Behind closed doors at its 1990 Photokina booth in Germany, Kodak showed a privileged few a glimpse of its first digital camera. It stored its images on a floppy disk and boasted a record breaking 1.3 million pixel image sensor. Real professional stuff! In another move that really had Kodak jumping out of the frying pan into the fire, it began promoting the concept of storing images on compact discs. Polaroid too, which was much used by professionals to check lighting and arrangement before risking a costly exposure on film, was beginning to feel the winds of changes. Polaroid Inventor, Dr Edwin Land died in March 1991 and although he was a great futurist, it was mercifully doubtful that at that time Edwin could see all the ramifications the digital age would bring to his company.

The December 1996 issue of Professional Photography magazine dared to use a digital picture on its front cover. A large slash across the picture claimed it was an 11.4 mb file. Wow! The magazine also began devoting a third of a page each issue to list all the photography websites. A great idea and by the end of the decade the listing was occupying an entire page. I doubt that there would be enough pages in the entire magazine to print them all now! Few in the profession were overly aware of the digital tsunami building on our shores and which near the end of the decade was about to sweep away all before it.

Seeing a great divide between the business needs of wedding and portrait photographers, in 1990, commercial AIPP photographers and others created a special division of the institute known as FACE. This stood for Fashion, Advertising, Commercial and Editorial and when it was launched as part of the Institute it had more than 150 members in Melbourne and more than 300 in Sydney. In the following year, while still an affiliate division, the group renamed itself as the Advertising Commercial and Magazine Photographers (ACMP). In a bid to lower costs the ACMP decided to go it alone in 1993. Although the two groups continue to work together on mutual issues and in spite of discussions of the two organisations coming together again, at the time of writing this has yet to happen and in the end the Institute formed a new commercial division.

Taking over from Kevin O'Daly, who now became the first chairman of the board of the newly incorporated AIPP with for the first time an actual board of directors notifiable to the Australian Securities and Investments Commission, Malcolm Mathieson became president in 1991. Malcolm started in photography when he was 18, working as a cine cameraman for Channel Ten in Victoria. When television went to electronic news gathering, Malcolm turned to stills and bought a photography studio in Orange, New South Wales. He ran this for over a decade before moving his practice back to Bairnsdale in Victoria.

Although most of his work is wedding and portraiture, Malcolm has a wider interest in photography and has produced both an exhibition and a book on the people of Bairnsdale. Large framed and bearded, Malcolm likes to go on energetic landscape photo safari expeditions on his bicycle.

This unusual choice of transport for photographers might give a closer connection to the countryside around you, but certainly could leave you a little tired. However, Malcolm points out that he found a shot that had to be taken while lying on his back and waiting for the light to be right often could take at least an hour!

During Malcolm's term the Institute introduced accreditation for staff photographers and, with Malcolm representing the Institute on Viscopy, published a manual on copyright and worked with the awards committee to help promote the fact that with the Professional Photographer of the Year Award, they were now open to all professional photographers in Australia, whether or not they were a member. Under Doug Spowart's chairmanship of the awards committee, other changes introduced included the accreditation of judges and panel chairs, the acceptance of images made by this strange new digital imaging and the expansion of the event into a self-supporting financial activity. Evolving computer technology also enabled advances in awards processes from tracking, scoring, and collation of results, documenting and preparing category winners. Judging 450 prints was a mammoth task to complete in a two day program. But Doug developed the 'event team' concept that turned the volunteer helpers into a highly organised and professional events team.

Malcolm also began tackling the problems of government restrictions on taking photos in public places and imposing such fees as $250 for taking photographs on the streets of Melbourne.

In a campaign supported by Max Dupain and David Moore, Malcolm lobbied National Parks and Wildlife and the Minister for Tourism Roz Kelly. However, the issue did not make it onto her famous whiteboard and in a kind and diplomatic moment, Malcolm described the minister's response as 'unsympathetic'! Some years later, famous Australian landscape photographer Ken Duncan took up the cudgels and the campaign continues to this present day.

In 2002, Malcolm also became the first Australian to become president of the World Council for Professional Photographers. Malcolm was always quick to point out the power and responsibility of being a photographer and used to stress, 'We have the power to change the way the world views things'.

In June 1993, following the Institute's usual practice, Malcolm moved to the chairman's position and Richard Bennett was elected president. Richard was born in Hobart in 1945 and his first job was

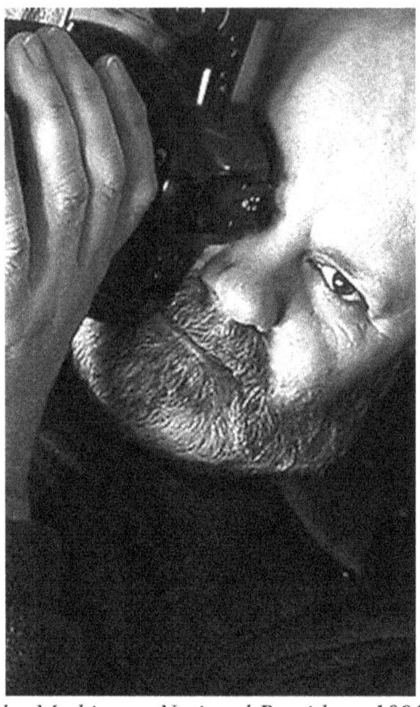

Malcolm Mathieson, National President, 1991-1993

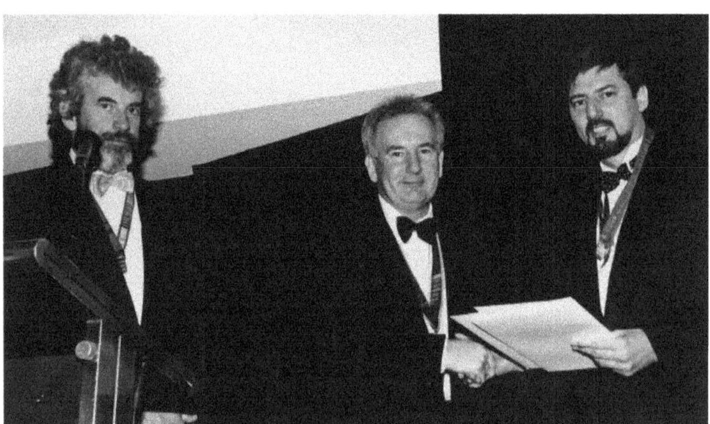

*Ian McKenzie Mark Fitz-Gerald and Doug Spowart at the
Award Night in 1995*

in his father's apple orchard in the Huon Valley. As a teenager he developed a love of bushwalking – a path which lead to an interest in
photography. Possibly in the quest for an always higher view point,
Richard then literally took to the hills. After attending a moun-

tain climbing training school in New Zealand, Richard became a mountaineer with the 1969 Australian Andean Expedition. When he wasn't climbing mountains or bushwalking, he was out sailing. With this great love of the outdoors and photography it was almost axiomatic that Richard would become one of Australia's greatest land and seascape photographers. His specialist area is aerial photography of yacht racing. He has now covered every Sydney to Hobart yacht race for the last 40 years. To get his prize winning pictures he became known for the daredevil stunt of perilously hanging out of the door of a fixed wing light aircraft, beard and 120 roll film camera flying in the wind,. The wilder the weather, the happier Richard is!

So being president for Richard should have been all smooth sailing, but he says he found the job very challenging. Photographers are highly individualistic by nature, and welding them into a common direction is not without its challenges. But this was a man who thrives on obstacles and to say to him that something is not possible only feeds his determination to quietly and without fanfare win through.

Said Richard, 'I believe I owe my success to the help and encouragement I received from my fellow members. They moulded me: people such as Max Townsend, who from 1974 introduced me to high quality lab services and the inspiration that can be obtained from international speakers. On the local speaking front, along with Garry Glenn, Peter Foeden was a great presenter for Townsend's lab and he greatly affected my life when he introduced the Awards in 1977. Val Foreman shared his commercial skills and business ideas while David McCarthy, Peter Eastway, John Whitfield King, Greg Hocking, Ian van der Wolde and Phil Kuruvita have not only greatly influenced me, but have become great friends. None of this personal development could have been brought about without the Institute.'

Richard worked both sides of the Tasman and introduced the Trans Tasman Photo Competition with the New Zealand professional photographer association and worked closely with Bruce Pottinger, professional vice president of the PICA importers and distributors group. This eventually lead to the bringing together of the Institute, the awards and the industry at the one cohesive annual show. This proved to be of enormous benefit to all parties. After he finished his term as president Richard Bennett became chair of the awards in 1999 and in this role spearheaded, with the national board, the gaining of a long-term major sponsor to ensure the growth and development of the event. This was a difficult quest as while the board was keen to raise funds from a major sponsor, Richard as chair of the awards was fighting a hard battle to not just take the money but form a steady relationship with a sponsor that could take naming rights while still preserving full recognition of the AIPP and its creative control over the judging process.

Eventually, after many discussions a deal with Canon was struck. Thus the awards for the last 13 years have been known as the Canon Australian Professional Photography Awards. Said Richard Bennett," Canon has been an ideal sponsor and very generous in its willingness to allow us a high degree of flexibility in managing the event and we take pride in the fact that our relationship with Canon is now in its fourteenth year. Over this time, all the people from Canon we have worked with have always been encouraging and helpful.'

During his presidential term, Richard also enjoyed the success of the Institute's lobbying of the Australian Parliament on copyright. He was sailing on his boat when he got the call from Senator Brian Harradine's office to tell him the bill on copyright law would be changed in favour of photographers and passed the following morning.

Toward the end of his term in 1995, the first steps towards the certification of practising photographers were initiated. Before Richard moved onto the position of chairman and his eight year association as chairman of the Awards, he also oversaw the moving of the national office from Bryan Pascall in South Australia to Christine Chester in Queensland who was to have an enormous influence on the development of the Institute over many years.

She began her career in Sydney studying at the Ultimo TAFE in the early seventies, becoming a student member of the Institute in 1973. As a wedding/portrait photographer in Sydney and then

Taree, she moved to Brisbane in 1983 and in 1988 was elected AIPP Queensland president. From here she moved to the national board and played an active role in administration with a very much hands on approach and became national vice president. After she resigned in 1993, the board realised that her experience and sense of history of the Institute were invaluable. So she agreed to take on an expanded role of national office coordinator in which she played an active role in administration with a very much hands on approach which continued with subsequent boards.

Chris says she luckily married an understanding and Institute-sympathetic husband, Bryan, a very fine commercial photographer, shares her passion for the industry and was invaluable in supporting her role in the national office. After eight years, Christine handed the role over to the board-appointed Brian O'Shea and moved to the Gold Coast and to Tasmania, where she remains a member and Honorary Fellow of the Institute.

In July 1995, Mark Fitz-Gerald was elected president. Starting as a photographer in the eighties, Mark is a South Australian medical photographer who works mostly in pathology but also handles some corporate work. Coming from a large organisation rather than a small studio, Mark brought a good working knowledge of business systems to the Institute to enable it to improve its back of office management functions.

A quiet and unassuming man, he played a key role in the campaign for copyright reforms for photographers. He also became chair of the visual arts copyright agency Viscopy. The successful changes that came about as a result of the lobbying included resale rights for visual artists, the extension of copyright from 50 to 75 years after the death of the artist and equitable secondary rights returns from all forms of published content.

During Mark's presidency, he and the board gained as part of the Institute's membership package, the publication on the business of photography, written by Peter Eastway, called at that time Profitable Photography.

Mark worked to bring the professionals and the industry closer together and, with particularly helpful input from Des Birt, introduced a special policy and planning committee to the Institute's organizational structure. Said Mark, 'The idea came from our need to engage with our industry partners on a long term basis. To do this we needed the policy and forward organisational stability to do it. PICA and others needed to know they could rely on us to commit to partnerships over time. The implementation was probably a bit unwieldy, and many, coming from small business where you 'just do it' struggled with the idea, but it set the tone.'

Mark's long contribution on this issue led to him becoming an inaugural recipient of the Photo Industry of Australia's (PICA) Golden Tripod Hall of Fame award for industry contribution.

Succeeding Mark Fitz-Gerald as president came West Australian Greg Hocking in 1997. Greg had first joined the institute as a student member in 1979 and had been on the West Australia divisional council and then the national board for many years. By the time of his tenure as president, he had become one of Australia's leading landscape photographers. Greg has had a long and continuing involvement in the Institute's affairs and his contribution has covered many issues. But the British Royal Family was about to bring him another.

For most of the twentieth century, the status of photographers in Australian society had been on a roller coaster ride. In the early part it was a very scientific profession and was much respected by the population at large. In those days it took great skill to take a photograph that actually came out. As cameras advanced and consumers began taking their own photographs, the mystery was disappearing and the profession was becoming viewed less highly. The Institute had worked hard to improve the photographer's standing and have it recognised as a profession and not as a trade or an industry. These efforts were given a significant boost, however when photography gained a new cache with members of the British Royal Family. The Queen herself was known to be a keen movie maker, and for a while, Bell & Howell ran full page advertisements in magazines showing a close up of the Queen using her camera. However, it is believed that pressure from the palace was brought to bear and the advertisements ceased to appear. But when Lord Snowdon married the Queen's sister, professional photographers were in! Then came the Queen's cousin, Lord Lichfield and any talk of the photographer being a tradesman all but disappeared! Photographers had evolved from the world of scientists and trades people to becoming recognised as true artists. The old chestnut question of was photography an art seemed forever to have been dumped in the dustbin of history.

But Princess Diana's death in a car crash while being hounded by persistent paparazzi led to a public outcry against photographers of all stripes and colours. In interviews, the Institute was keen to distinguish between the work and approaches of its members from the snappers that were being paid huge sums as a direct result of the public wanting to see the pictures they grabbed.

Said Greg, 'First the Royals gave us a leg up socially and now they have taken us down.' The public apparently revelled in the more mundane and intimate moments of the royals as portrayed by the spying lenses' Through some peculiar process, these pictures seem to have morphed Diana into being a favourite and valued part of everyone's family. This eerie transition was evidenced by the massive hysterical outpouring of grief at Princess Diana's death. They blamed the photographers for the accident. They did not blame themselves or see themselves as being the ones that all the paparazzi were working for. Is it just me, or isn't this all rather odd? No? Ah well, never mind.

In 1998 it was decided to move the awards judging out of the annual imaging show being held that year in Sydney in May to Adelaide a month later. While both events were successful, it was felt both were the poorer for being separated and it was decided to bring the awards and the show together again.

At the conclusion of his term, Greg observed that email and mobile telecommunication were causing many to become more isolated in the way they do business. Emails and messaging had replaced getting together for a cup of coffee. Greg pointed out that while it was arguably good for some, it was bad for others as for the past thirty or so years the AIPP has not only been a forum for the craft of photography but also a meeting and discussion point for photographers to share their knowledge and experiences.

Assuming the role of Institute Chair, Greg also became chair of the newly formed commercial photographer division. With more than 700 members working in commercial photography, there was a need to set up a register of commercial photographers for state divisions organising workshops or seeking judges and to produce business material to assist photographers and clients better understand what is involved in working with a commercial photographer. Ross Eason and Eric Victor-Perdraut had urged the board to adopt a mentoring program to help emerging photographers.

After a year's pilot program at Eric's Momentum Studio, a special committee was appointed to see it through to fruition. On the new division's committee were Ian McKenzie, long term future chair and Ian van der Wolde from Victoria; Chris Shain and Robert Edwards from New South Wales; Ross Eason and Eric Victor-Perdraut from Queensland, South Australian Milton Wordley and Greg Hocking from West Australia.

In July 1999 Marc Fenning, a salaried photographer at the Australian National University in Canberra and the former treasurer of the Institute, succeeded Greg Hocking and became president. Marc served until May 2000 when the presidency passed to Queensland photographer Eric Victor.

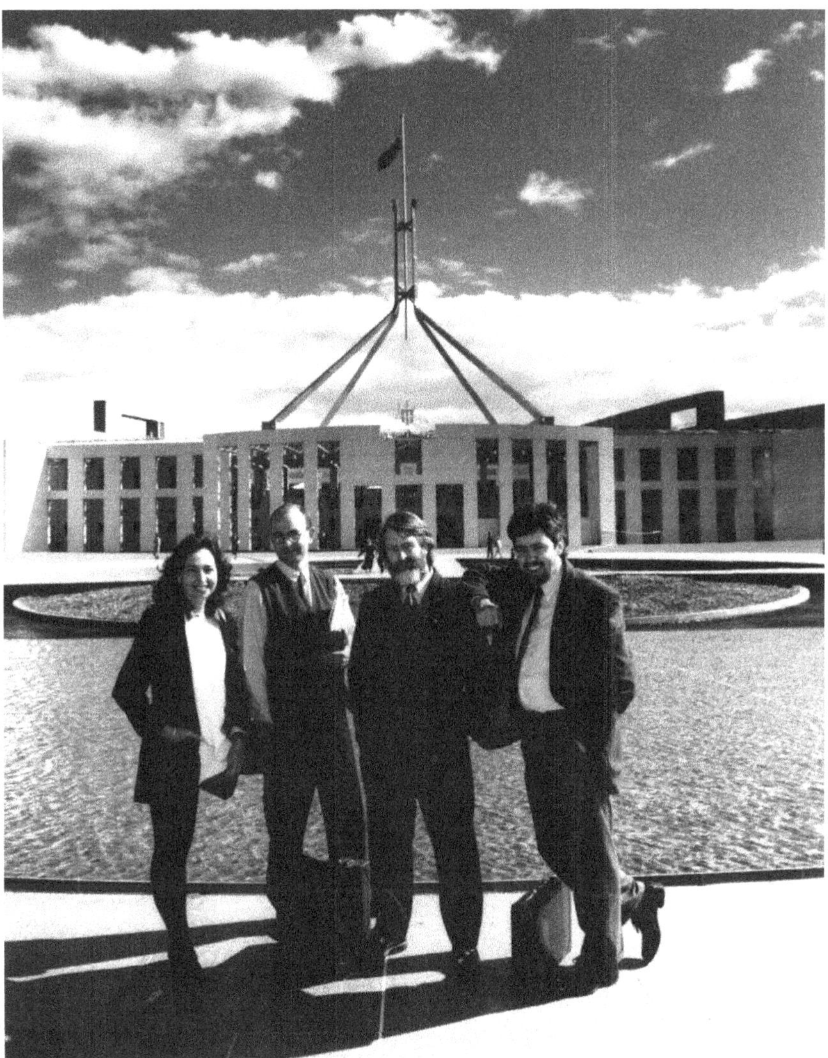

Copyright delegation to Canberra in 1992.
Left to right, Nancy Cohen, Chris Jones, Richard Bennett, Greg Hocking

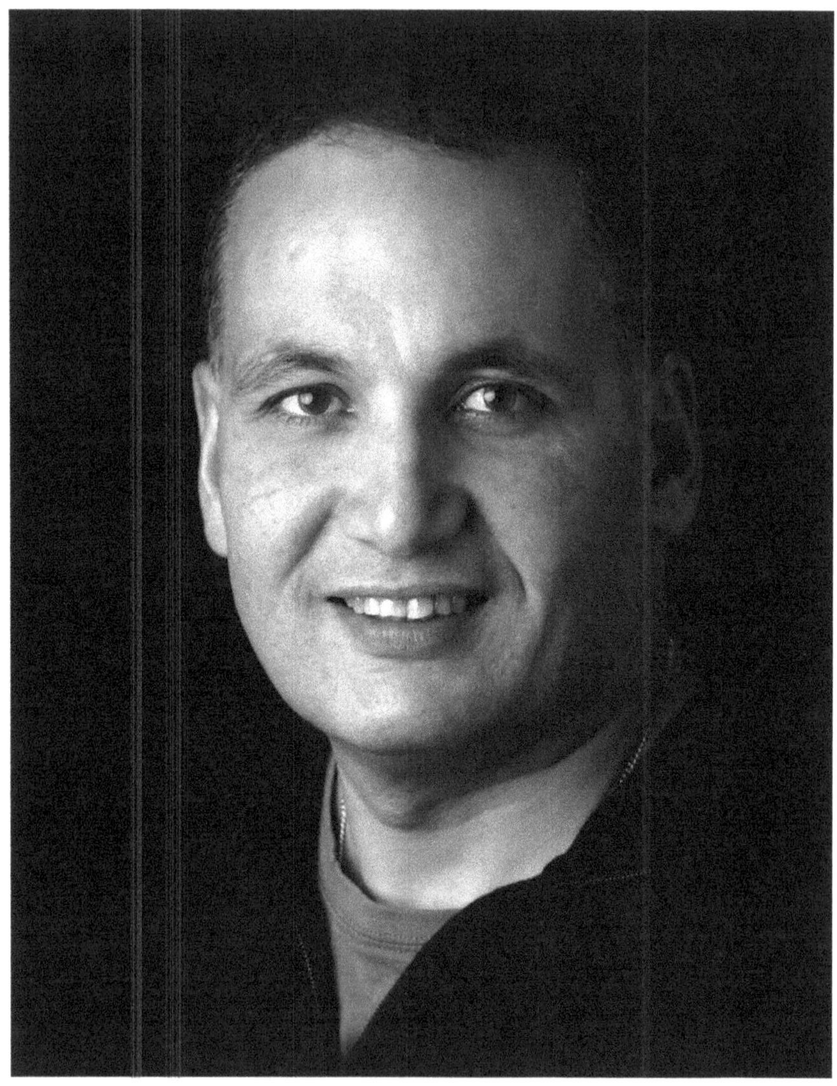

Philip Kuruvita National President 2004-2006

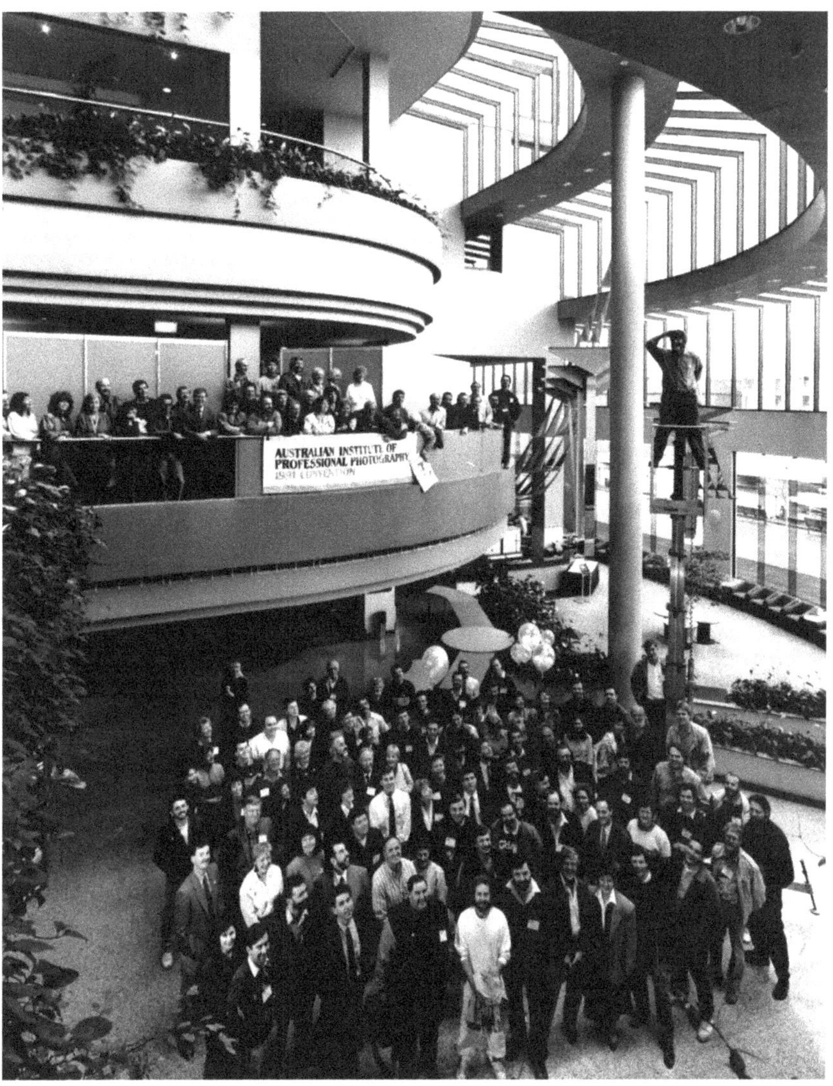

At the 1991convention in Hobart, convenor Richard Bennett stands high on the hoist above some of the more than 100 delegates. Photo by Ian McKenzie risking life and limb while perilously perched on a balcony flowerbed.

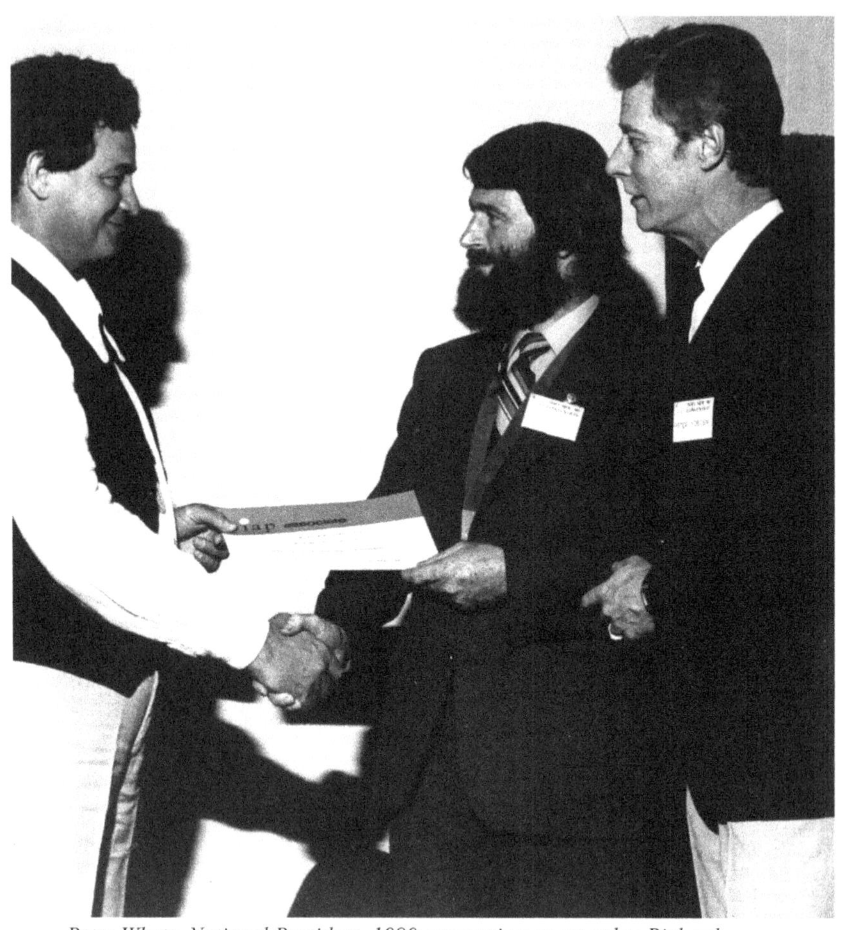

Peter Whyte, National President, 1980, presenting an award to Richard Bennett under the watchful eye of Peter Foeden.

Chapter Six

The Noughties: A Millennium of Pixels

In the run up to the year 2000, doomsayers were predicting the first day of the new millennium would be the end of the world. Planes would fall out of the sky, nuclear missiles would launch mysteriously, nuclear reactors explode and banks, along with the entire world financial system, would collapse. A scare campaign like no other gathered faster and faster momentum as the years and months to the first day of January 2000 remorselessly counted down. On talk-back radio, families were urged to fill the bath with water, grab some candles and matches and stock up on food and toilet paper. With such dire predictions, it is easy to understand the generous requirement for the last item!

The cause of all the media hysteria was an article published in a computer magazine in 1993 which pointed out computers only recognising two digit years for the 20th Century would mean that software would not identify the year 2000. The Y2K or millennium bug had been discovered. Once first mentioned, you might have thought that would be the end of the panic. There was plenty of time to fix it and besides, what business, in those heady days of fast computer technological development, was running either computers or software more than five years old? However, the hysteria mounted as the computer industry delivered the biggest sucker punch of all time and politicians and the media jumped on the bandwagon. Come the day, the bug had no bite and there were embarrassingly few prob-

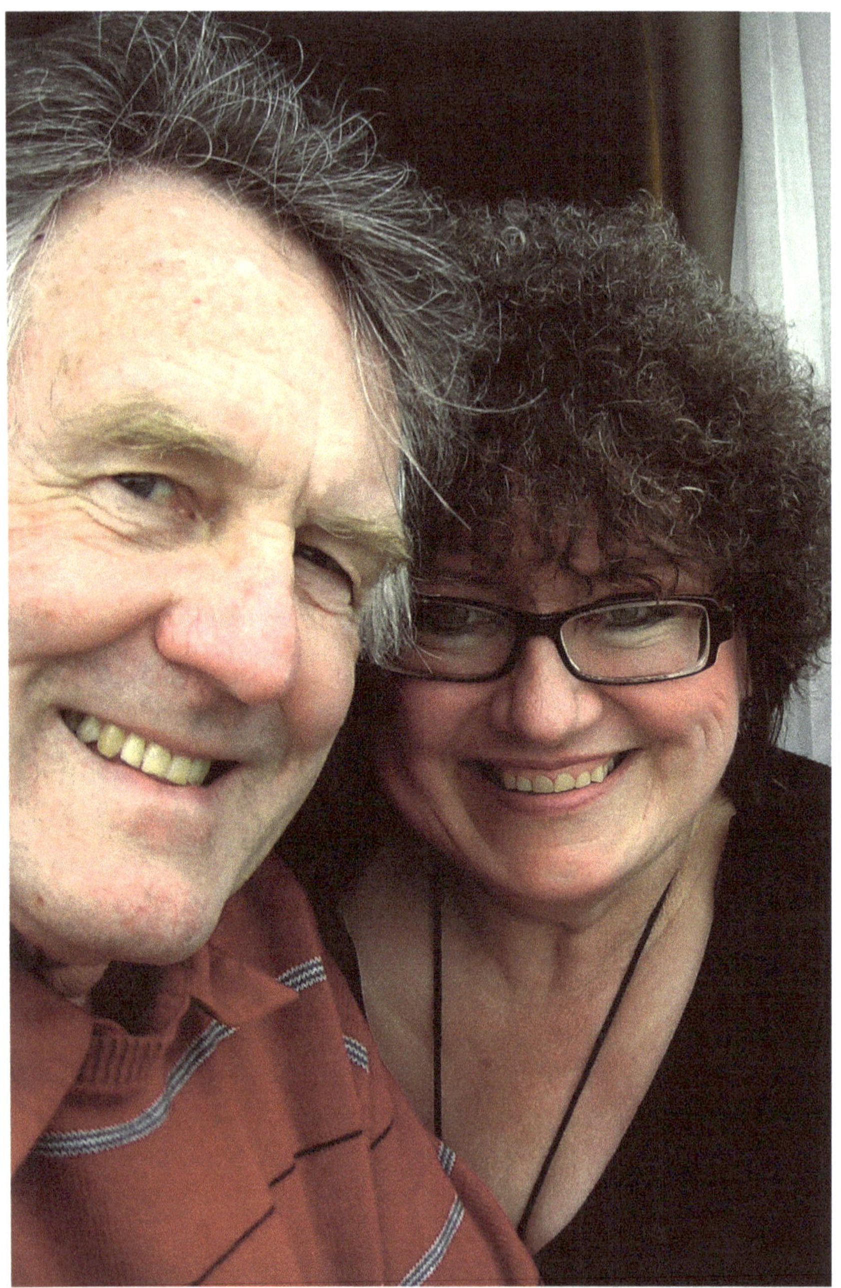

Queensland's Brian and Christine Chester played an active part in the Institute

lems. Even cameras still worked!

Even so, Australia did make world news: bus-ticket-validation machines in two states failed to operate. But to the average Aussie suffering public transport, that just felt like any other day!

However, the Institute's finances were not getting off so lightly. Newly arrived president Eric Victor, had his hands full. A number of problems had begun to surface and there was concern over the rising costs of communication. These included the annual awards book costs, the Working Pro Newsletter and Pro Photo, the official magazine of the Institute. In a bid to lower costs, some changes and rationalisation were being called for. Eric felt he was parachuted into a difficult position, but he had the steely strength and strong determination to undertake a number of sweeping changes.

Born in London as Eric Victor-Perdraut, Eric lived in France until he was nineteen. Then, in 1970, he came to Australia as a £10 immigrant. While studying at university in Brisbane he joined the varsity camera club and got hooked on photography. A chance meeting with a Vogue Living editor led to freelance work for the magazine and eventually to his own advertising and commercial studio.

Eric's problem was there was a shortage of funds and the Institute was supporting two separate publications to keep in touch with its membership. With articles especially slanted to professional photographers, the role of the publications had always been one of the key benefits to members. But it came at a cost. But there had been a long historic association with Professional Photography in Australia magazine. Launched in 1932 this publication had become the official journal under the editorship of Clive Stuart Tompkins in 1948. In the mid sixties the publisher role came to Gordon Hill. Gordon started in photography in 1951 at the Melbourne Technical College and after three years as a photography assistant to Arthur Dickinson of Dickinson Monteath in Melbourne, he travelled to Toronto Canada where he spent two years in advertising photography.

On his return to Dandenong he formed a partnership with Herb Secomb as Beaver Photographic. In 1963 the pair entered the pre-press area and formed Beaver Lithographic Pty. Ltd.

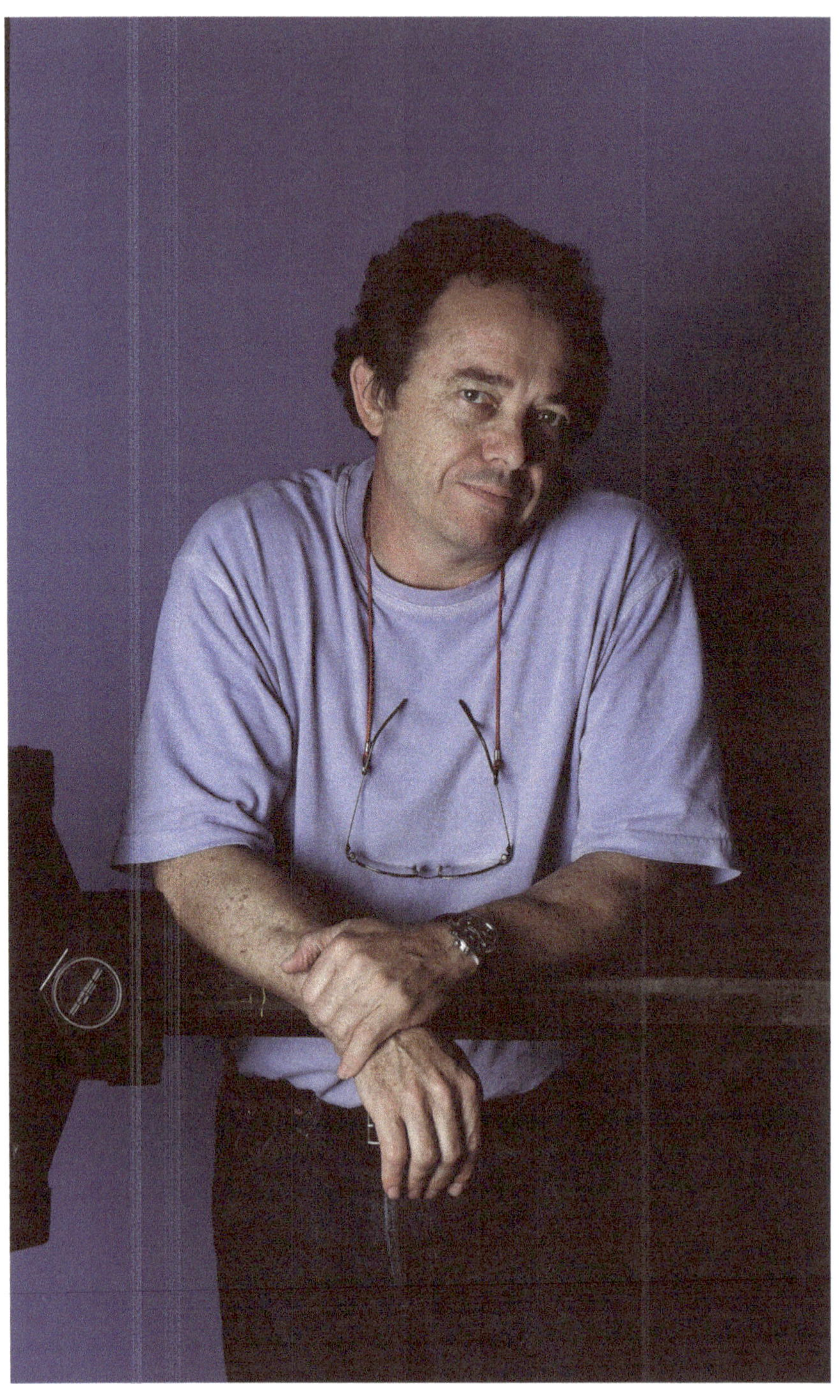

Eric Victor-Perdraut National President 2000-2002

To handle the publication of the magazine they formed an editorial committee with Stuart Tompkins, Val Foreman Alan Friedman, Max Williams and Gordon Hill. Ian McKenzie and Neil Murray joined the committee in the following year. Gordon was an active member of the Victorian branch of the Institute and played a key part in the organisation of the first convention of the Institute held at Newport in Sydney.

The magazine was given a new look and in 1968, long time magazine contributor Neil Murray took over as editor from an ageing Tompkins with Max Williams remaining his main contributor. After Gordon Hill retired in 1975, Neil also took on the role of publisher. Neil was an old school gentleman, always immaculately dressed and fired with a passion for the institute and the profession of photography equalled only by a select few. Most of his photography work was in the advertising, industrial and commercial area and he had a long involvement with the Preston College of TAFE in Melbourne as a lecturer in photography. This was a role he relinquished in 1985 to act as projects officer for the Institute after Ian Howell left his post as executive officer for a life in New Zealand.

In 1982, Neil tired of the dual role and the difficulties of being a single editor publisher, sold the magazine to Iris Publishing Company, which already had four other magazine titles. Under the new arrangement, that meant this writer was the publisher and Neil Murray remained as editor.

Two years previously, our small editorial team at Iris had been swelled by two new recruits. One was a very youthful Peter Eastway and the second was an even younger Paul Burrows. I like to tell the story that when I discovered Peter he was stacking shelves in Woolworths and Paul was fixing castors onto office chairs. So by joining our fledgling company, neither had much to lose! So I can claim to be their saviour! Reluctantly, I will also concede that Peter had a degree in accountancy and Paul was a qualified school teacher. But both wanted to get into something different, had a great passion for photography, a tremendous attitude and the potential to be great writers.

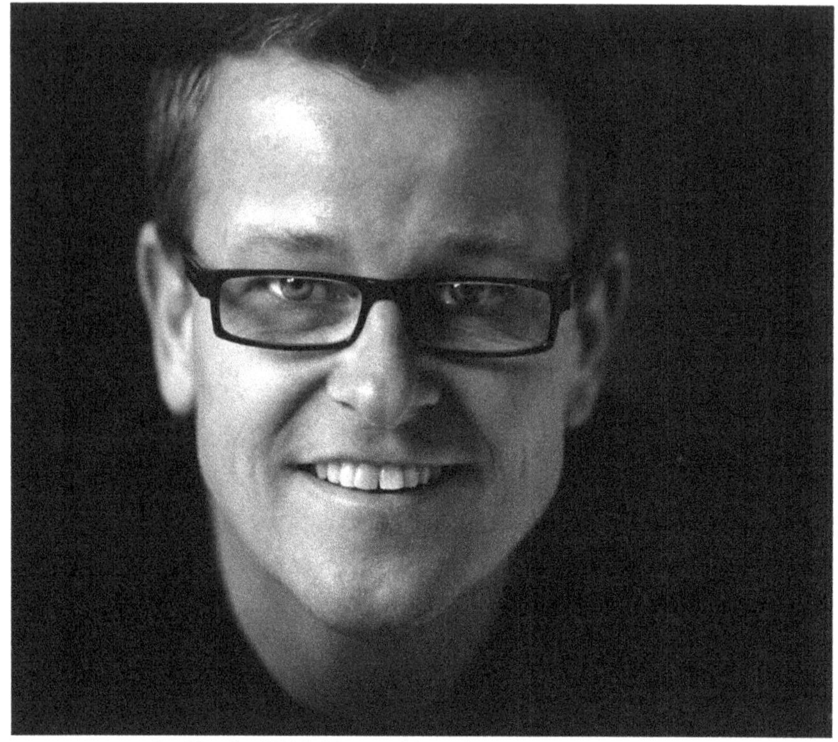

Ian Van der Wolde National President 2002-2004

Over the last 33 years this has been more than proven. So to that description you can add great commitment. For the high pressure environment of a busy publishing house, we all got on very well and Peter and Paul were firm friends.

In 1985, Neil asked to step down as editor and suggested I give the editorship to Paul Burrows. Peter was already in the group managing editor position. Under this new arrangement, Neil continued contributing articles until 1995. Neil died in 2007 aged 80.

Due to a health problem I encountered, I sold Iris to a large publishing company in 1989 and I took up a career as an industry consultant. Paul Burrows continued in the editorship of Professional Photography through another three owners and to this day is still the editor of the same magazine, which is now called Pro Photo. Paul, with his reporting on cameras and accessories, has both informed and entertained tens of thousands of his readers for more than thirty years. With his deep in-depth technical knowledge, his analytical reviews have led to him becoming an acknowledged expert on the subject of camera design. His comments are noted by camera manufacturers and are often included in overseas publications.

Peter, however, was not quite so enamoured with arrangements at the new publishers and left to form his own publishing company. Along with Better Photography magazine, in 1990 he produced a monthly newsletter for professional photographers called Profitable Photography, a title that some jokingly claimed was an oxymoron! This put Peter into the same marketplace as Professional Photography in Australia and although now rivals, Peter and Paul remained friends.

Peter had become a very active member of the Institute and was having great success in the Awards.

In 1989 Peter joined the council as federal treasurer. With his experience as a practicing accountant, Peter was a real godsend to the Institute at a difficult time. He was also much in demand as a lecturer on business management for photographers and was to become chair of the Awards for many years. Paul, on the other hand, is first and foremost a greatly admired writer. He is always at his happiest when reviewing the latest camera or other piece of photographic equipment and he is mainly content to leave the publishing business side to someone else.

So when Eric-Victor Perdraut and his board had to choose between Peter's professional newsletter and the sixty year association with the glossy Professional Photography Magazine it was a decision that in the end had to be made on costs. In a cross membership deal with the ACMP in 2000, Peter's newsletter, now renamed The Working Pro, got the nod. I am pleased to be able to report that Peter and Paul are still friends...again!

With regard to the title Working Pro, Eric commented, 'I like it very much, but I gave second thoughts to the possibility that it carries other meanings. It needs to be viewed in good humour.'

In 2013, even the printed newsletter fell victim to the digital age.

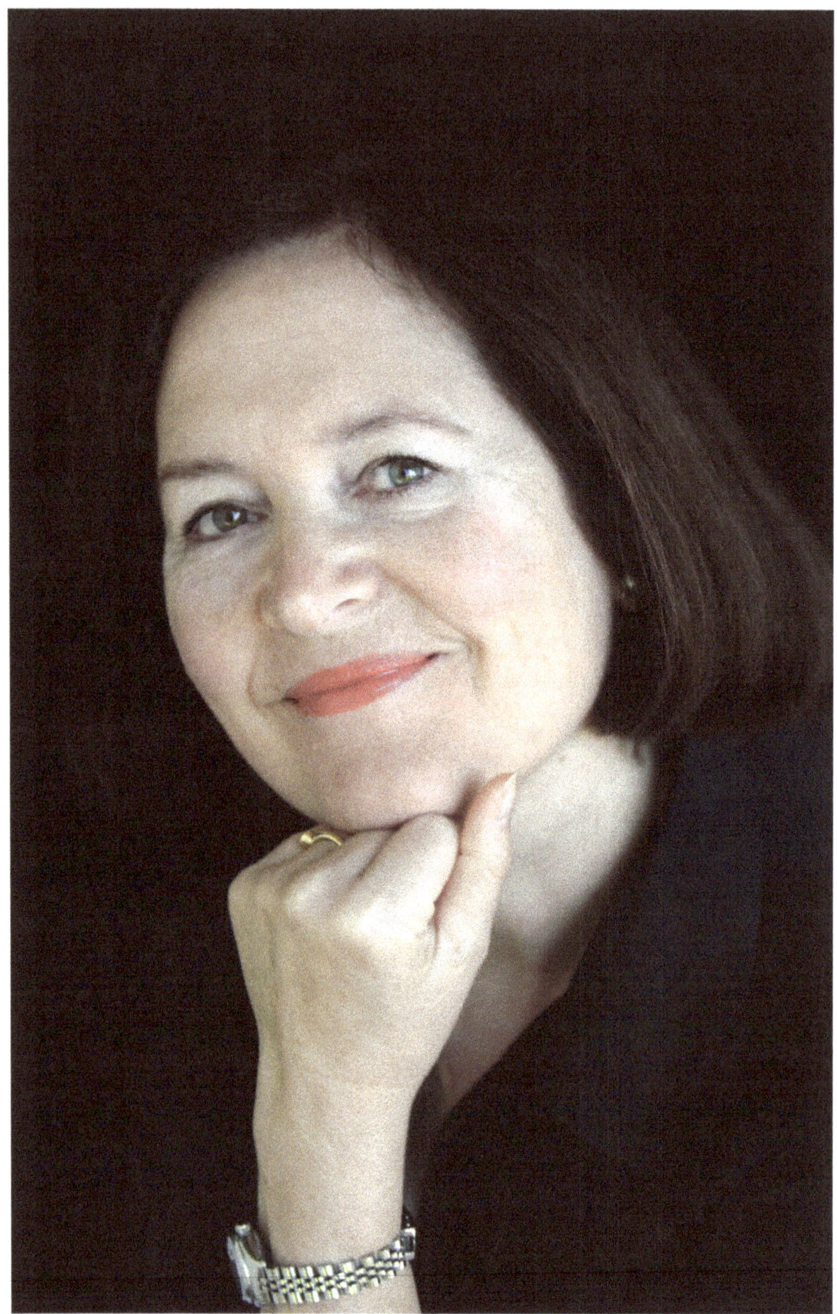

Jacqui Dean, National President, 2006-2008 Photo by Tim Dean

Due to high cost of postage and printing, the Working Pro went digital only. It is up to the subscriber to print it out. This is a very risky process from a history point of view.

I feel beholden to point out that I could not have compiled this book without having access to all the printed copies of the publications. By law, a copy of every printed periodical has to be lodged with both the National Library in Canberra and the main state libraries in which it is distributed. It was only with thanks to this requirement, and a heap of additional support from editors Burrows and Eastway, that I was able to compile this history.

Now that publishing is increasingly becoming less printed and only viewed on e-readers, it is a very real threat that future histories could be lost forever. It's the same with photographs. At the beginning of the decade I launched an industry campaign under what I thought was the catchy slogan of 'Print It or Lose It'. I was quite proud of it but it was much criticised by one of the major brands for being 'overly negative.' However, it had good cut through with the popular media and had an impact on the broader consumer market. Years later, every so often, some bright spark comes up with the idea of reviving it, but mainly it's a case of all talk and no action. In the meantime, I am pleased to report, Pro Photo magazine is still being printed.

The next big issue Eric and the board began to tackle in a turbulent period was the issue of sponsorship. The relationship between the Institute and the photo industry had always been a bit tricky. Some professional photographers felt sponsorships should be freely given and any quid pro quo in return tended to taint the artistic side of photography. At the same time, some sponsors were feeling that they were getting poor value for the amount of money invested.

The Awards were growing in strength every year and were now the key part of the Institute's calendar of events. But as the number of entries grew, so did the costs.

A considerable increase in sponsorship fees was needed if the success of the Awards was not going to drive the Institute broke. So the controversial idea of selling the naming rights was raised.

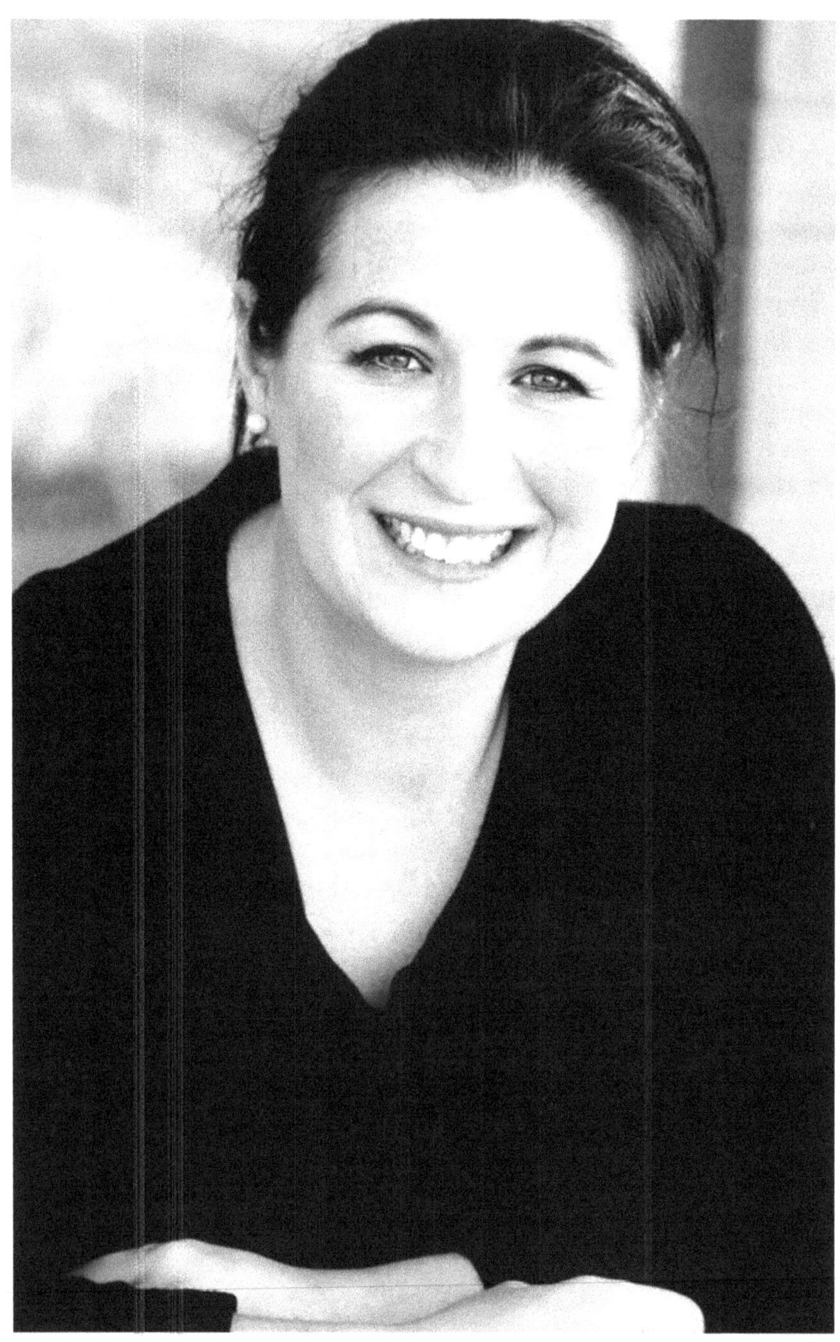

Alice Bennett, National President, 2008-2010

APPA chairman Richard Bennett was particularly concerned that the judging process remain completely free of any commercial influences. Fortunately for the Institute, Canon stepped up to the table and with compromises from the Institute, the Awards Committee and Canon itself, an equitable solution was reached. This resulted in renaming the Awards to be the Canon Australian Professional Photography Awards, a strong relationship that continues to this present day.

Explained Eric Victor, 'We agreed that APPA as a judging process was not for sale, but the by-products of APPA (namely the Professional Photographer of the Year, the Awards Book and the Travelling Collection) were available for sponsorship. To make the process even cleaner, it was felt that the judging itself would be clean skin, carrying no endorsement at all.'

By July 2001, the Institute's membership was again more than 1000 members and financially had edged back into the black. A survey, sponsored by PICA was taken to determine public attitudes to professional photographer services. One of the interesting facts that emerged was that while fifty three percent of people chose a photographer on a referral basis, twenty three percent came from Yellow Pages. There was no mention of the web in those days!

Before moving on to the role of chairman, as in accordance with the Institute's tradition, Eric said, 'The Board over the last two years has also worked hard at stabilising the finances and getting major sponsorship. There have been a few hiccups along the way, but these are now forgotten as part of our colourful history. The situation today is a solid base on which to build a great association. We have nurtured a very positive and competent Policy and Planning team and the good performance of the Board and the P&P committee is crucial to the health of the AIPP.'

Former Victorian state president and Institute national vice president, Melbourne photographer, Ian Van der Wolde became president in 2002 and Antonia Cornwell, based in Melbourne took over as national secretary from Brian O'Shea.

The following year, Jessica Dean, daughter of national treasurer,

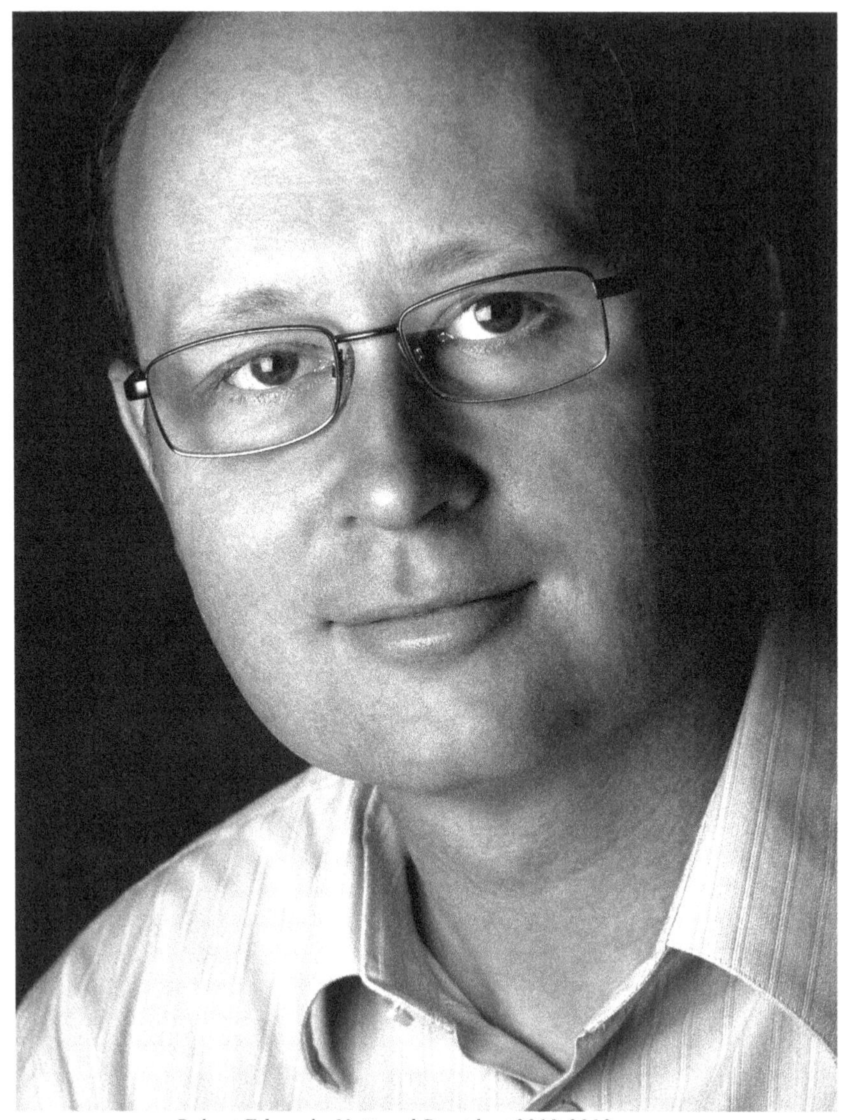

Robert Edwards, National President 2010-2012

Jacqui Dean, was appointed as the new national coordinator.

Ian Van der Wolde was aged 38 years of age and at that time, the second youngest president ever appointed. Ian was only two years older than when David McCarthy was elected in 1976. Ian was a graduate of Melbourne's Photography Studies College and he opened his own studio, Altered Images, in 1986 and became a successful commercial photographer.

Ian has been described as energetic, accomplished, good humoured, unassuming and with the memory of an elephant. Along with board members, Eric Victor, Phillip Kuruvita, Jackie Dean, Alice Bennett and Melissa Anderson, Ian introduced new member folio assessments and an accreditation system.

The role Ian played at the Institute was key to its growing success. After the tumult of the major restructuring and the return to profitability of the Institute's operations, Ian embarked on a healing mission to get rid of all the angst amongst the various divisions and cliques and to raise the morale of being an AIPP member. He took the first steps as a president to meet with the Awards committee and to sit down with them to better understand what their problems were. He succeeded in creating an environment in which everyone could work more happily and productively together. He even moved to re-establish relations with the ACMP

As well as visiting all the other states, Ian regularly flew to Tasmania to meet with Philip Kuruvita and thus formed a solid working relationship with the person nominated to be his successor. On the industry front, Ian was equally diligent. During some periods of its history, the professional organisation allowed itself to drift from it industry colleagues working in the distribution and marketing of equipment and materials. Ian became a moderating and cohesive force that heralded in a new era of cooperation.

In July 2004, Tasmanian photographer Philip Kuruvita took over the presidency. His board included Jacqui Dean, Melissa Anderson, Alice Bennett, Fran Howlett and immediate past president Ian van der Wolde as chairman.

Born in England in 1959, Philip came from a peripatetic fami-

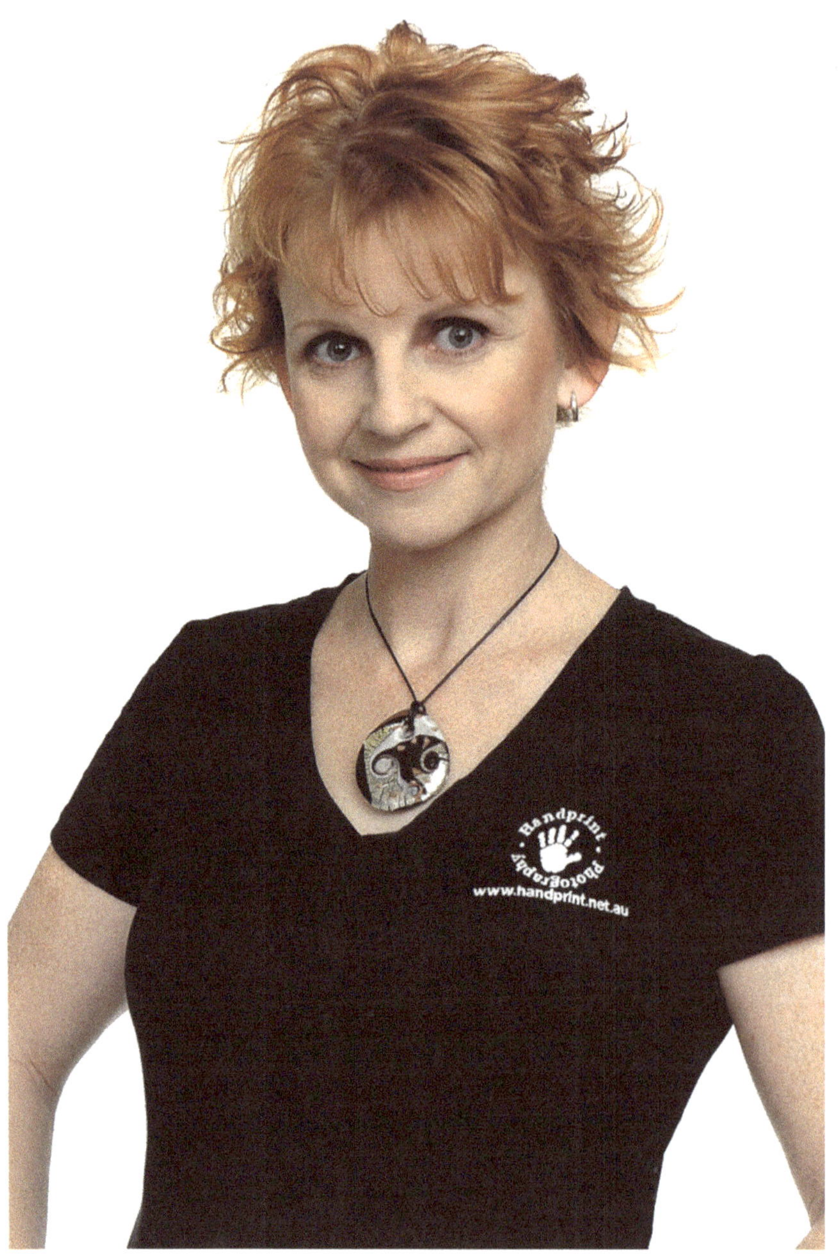

Kylie Lyons, National President 2012-

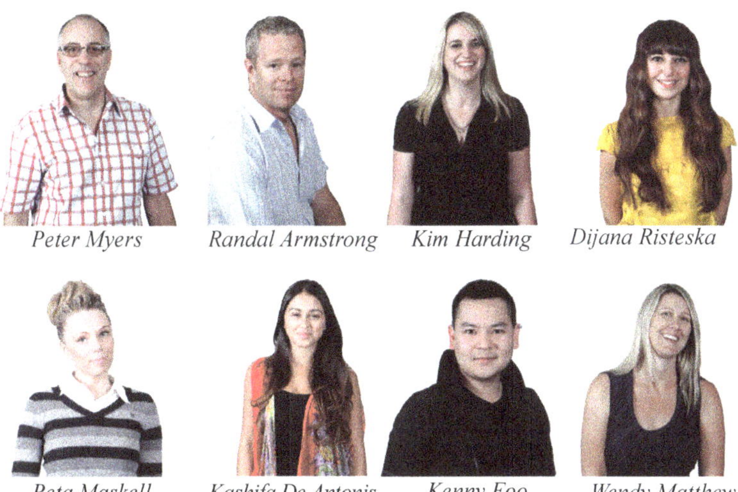

Peter Myers   Randal Armstrong   Kim Harding   Dijana Risteska

Peta Maskell   Kashifa De Antonis   Kenny Foo   Wendy Matthew

The 2013 Team at the Institute's Head Office in Melbourne.

ly. In 1968 they migrated by car to Sri Lanka for five years before travelling onto Australia. After studying biochemistry and serving in the Royal Australian Navy, in 1985 Philip enrolled in the Sydney Institute of TAFE where he studied photography. While studying at TAFE, Philip answered an advertisement on the college noticeboard for a medical photographer at Concord hospital. He worked here for two years while completing his studies. In 1989 Philip married Vicki, a qualified architect and they had two daughters. The family moved to Launceston, Tasmania and opened business as Still Light Photography. Vicki abandoned her profession to manage the busy studio, thus allowing Philip the opportunity to join the Institute's national board.

Philip is a quiet achiever with an infectiously dry sense of humour and during his term he developed the Institute's relationship with the New Zealand Institute of Professional Photographers. He also played a key role in the organisation of the Tasmanian Bicheno Weekend: an informal get together which various people giving talks and slideshows.

Said Philip, 'We discovered that as much could be learnt from sitting around a log fire with a glass of wine as from a formal classroom situation. Milton Wordley was one of our speakers, and he was so impressed with the concept that he went back to South Australia and started the Barossa Weekends. For the next Tasmanian event we moved from Bicheno to Freycinet and this was so successful it is still held every year.

'The Fujifilm Weekend Aways were based on the Freycinet weekend, and these eventually morphed into the national Nikon Event. At each stage, there were numerous people who grew and improved the concept and took it to the next level.'

Other issues Philip and the board were involved in was the increasing restrictive impositions on photographers by National Parks and other government agencies .The Institute became involved with the formation of the Ken Duncan initiated Arts Freedom Australia. Also, the Institute was active with the photographers' forum on the web with Better Photography, a national tour by photographer Michael Coyne in association with Sandisk and a visit by Steve McCurry in association with Kodak.

In 2005, the board also worked with the Awards committee to establish a new ranking that had been discussed for more than ten years: the title of Grand Master of Photography. In 2005, Lyn Whitfield-King became the first recipient. In the following year Peter Eastway was also awarded the title.

In 2006 the Institute elected its first woman president: Jacqui Dean. Jacqui was a Sydney Corporate and Architectural photographer who coincidentally was a fellow student at Sydney TAFE with previous President Philip Kuruvita.

Born in England, Jacqui, husband Tim and their three children, emigrated to Australia in 1982 to start a chain of minilabs in Australia. After graduating with honours from TAFE with an Associate Diploma of Arts Photography, in 1990 Jackie joined Tim in starting a commercial lab and studio. Jacqui was particularly interested in editorial photography, travelled widely and regularly published in travel and sporting magazines around the world.

Jacqui Dean's passion for the AIPP was immense. As a previous treasurer of the Institute, Dean was acutely aware of the need to strengthen the membership and with the board set about particularly growing the student and emerging photographer category. This together with special membership promotions at the annual photo show and at the Vivid Festival of Photography in Canberra organised by David Paterson, led to a 25 per cent increase in membership.

At the 2008 annual general meeting, following its normal custom, the Institute elected Jacqui as Chairman, thus becoming the first woman to ever be elected to the position as national chair. Tasmanian photographer Alice Bennett was elected as the new National President along with a board comprising John de Rooy as National Treasurer, Ian Wallace and David Sievers as National Vice Presidents and Robert Edwards.

Alice had an unusually early start in the Institute's activities. She started by first helping out at the Awards when she was six! In 1976 the offspring of a previous president was elected when Institute icon Claude McCarthy's son David took the reins. Now, 33 years later, history was repeated. Alice is the daughter of previous president Richard Bennett and was literally brought up in the photography business. Alice had an unusual opportunity to meet and learn from many of Australia's best photographers and gain a strong insight into the profession.

Setting up in Tasmania in a separate business from her father, Alice used wedding photography as her financial stable while pursuing photography for book publishers.

Explained Alice, 'I've tried to make my business diverse because I don't want to get bored doing the same thing. During her term as president, Alice found she was spending about 60 percent of her time on weddings, 20 percent on books and the other 20 percent on the Institute.

Alice and the board introduced an AIPP Scholarship aimed at encouraging photographers in the beginning of their careers and to fuel their passion for the profession. The scholarship consisted of an overseas photo safari with leading Australian photography mentors

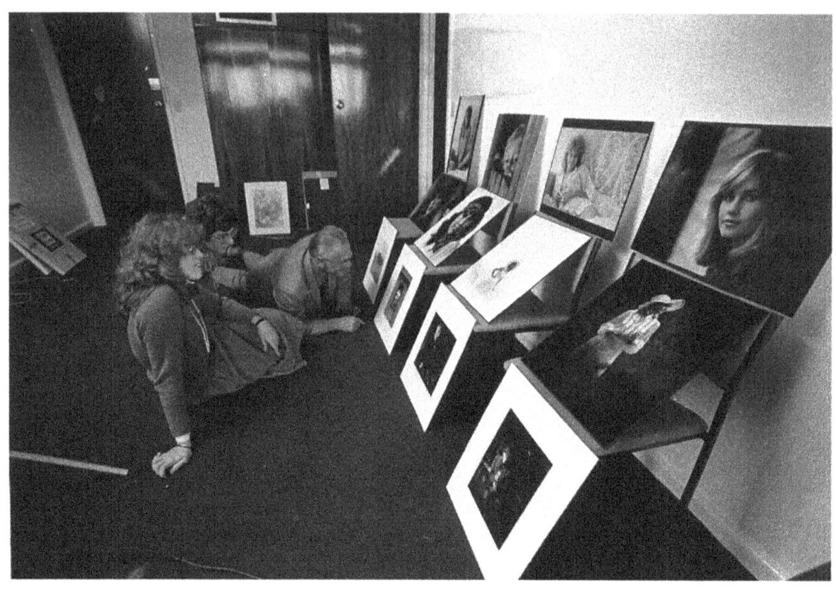

*In the early days of the Awards. Judging conditions were very primitive!
Sue Lewis shows how it should be done in 2012!*

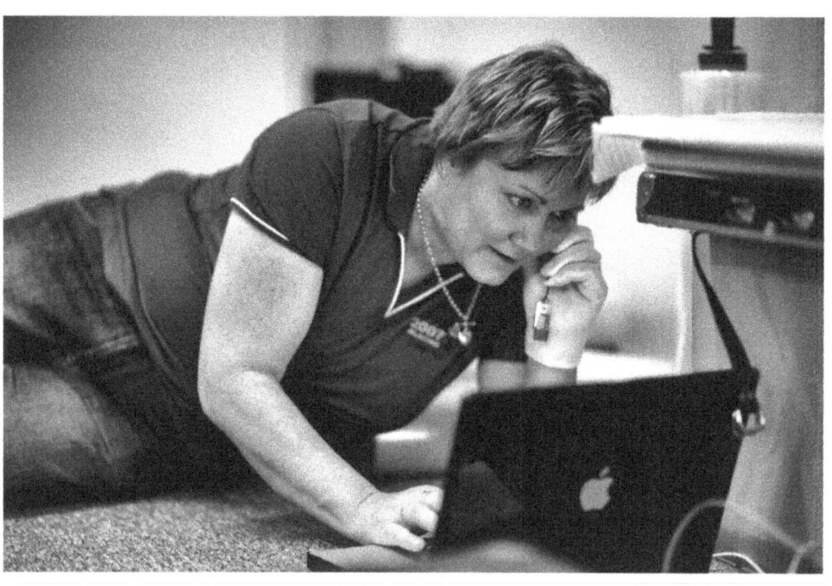

followed by an Australian tour with an exhibition of photos taken on the safari. Alice also organised a special event for women in photography.

With the membership now exceeding 2200, Jessica Dean, the national office manager for six years moved on and Peter Myers became the Institute's executive officer in December 2009. Peter brought a wide range of managerial skills to the organisation.

Born in England in 1957, Peter qualified in accountancy and became a Fellow of the Chartered Institute of Accountants. In 1986 he undertook a change of direction and started up a video production company first covering weddings before extending the company's activities to include providing live television coverage of premier league football matches. Peter also studied psychiatry and became a behavioural analyst and established the Peak Performance Institute for management training. In 2003, Peter visited Australia to set up a branch of business here and fell for the idea of life in this country.

As a qualified Microsoft technical engineer, Peter was also ideally placed to begin the redesigning of the Institute's website and to introduce a new range of business activities for the profession.

Work was proceeding at a busy pace at the Institute and in 2009 a team led by Ross Eason, a team of members began the task of organising a range of workshops, activities, tutorials, demonstrations and lectures for the national conference in 2010. This became known as The Event.

Alice's board also requested a review of the membership structure. The most contentious point that arose was the discussion on whether or not to allow enthusiast photographers, who only accepted occasional assignments, to join the Institute. The board was of the opinion that it was best to embrace those enthusiasts and help educate them on best business practice as a professional photographer.

Urging support of the idea, Alice said, 'If we are to create a unified, recognised professional body, we have to make these changes. We all need to look at this from a broad, unified community perspective.'

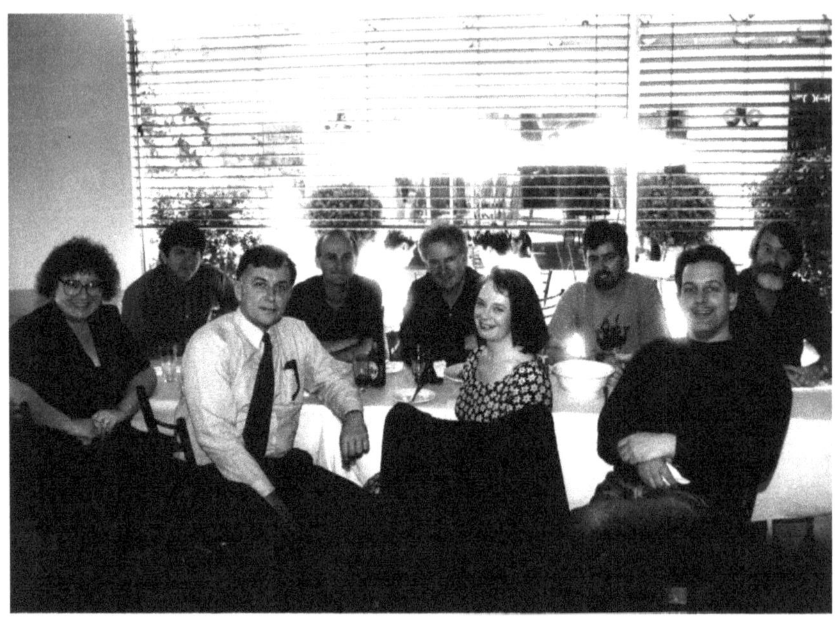

Left to right, Christine Chester, Des Birt, Kodak's Dr Andy Sierakowski with Rosemary Sharman, Mark Fitz-Gerald, Kodak Pro Division, Chris Shane and Richard Bennett

Chapter Seven

The Tensies: An Era of Change

The Tensies began as the age of gadgets. Smart Phones and social media networks were raging faster than a wild bush fire and numerous sites began the bid to control our picture files. And what an odd piece of marketing hype they used! Photographers were looking for servers that were safe, vault like and deep, deep underground. So what did the marketing gurus at the IT companies offer us? The Cloud! A light, fluffy, blow-away cloud! A case of too much marijuana smoke in the advertising agency art room I suspect.

However, there was nothing ethereal about the impact smartphones were having on the camera business. Major camera and consumer electronics manufacturers not named Apple or Samsung began experiencing deep financial doo-doo.

While the consumer side of the photographic industry was under great distress, in the professional field the digital tsunami has already passed and the survivors were building a new future.

The new board elected in 2010 had Robert Edwards as president, Alice Bennett as chair, Janie Boyd and Kylie Lyons as vice presidents, John de Rooy as treasurer and Ross Eason. In spite of all the digital change over trials that beset the professional photographer, membership now stood at more than 2700.

Robert, a Sydney based commercial photographer was passionate about education and raising standards. He was involved in the Universal Photographic Digital Imaging Guidelines and while studying in Adelaide saw Murdoch introduce colour to newspapers in the 1990s.

Said Robert, 'When I talk to new photographers about the good old days, they have no relationship to it. Right now, today, this is their good old days! In the very near future, the job of a professional photographer will be vastly different. Either we embrace this change, ignore it, or turn and run. Of course we have to embrace it. But we must do more than that. AIPP members must be amongst the leaders. Enter the Enthusiast photographer. Years ago we'd derogatorily call them "backyarders". Today they can easily access our market with camera in hand and compete for some of our work. This won't change. Rather than shun them, we can embrace them, welcome them into the fold. And then we educate them in how we do business and how to respect their intellectual property. '

After an extensive review conducted by Peter Myers for the board and much discussion with the membership, on 24 May 2011, members voted to amend the Institute's constitution to have three categories of membership: Member, Associate and Affiliate. A Member was defined as a practising professional. Affiliate membership was made available to those intending to become a professional photographer; Associate membership was made available to those with an interest in the profession of photography, but who are not a practising professional photographer.

At the conclusion of his term as national president, Robert Edwards reflected on some of the unsung heroes he had worked with during his term. Said Robert, 'The majority of AIPP volunteers who give their time and energy at events, on councils, subcommittees, and the board are not seen by the membership. They work bloody hard, away from family and their businesses, to help improve professional photography.

'One such quiet achiever is our National Treasurer, John de Rooy. Before joining the Board, John and his wife Pam started the North Queensland chapter of the AIPP. Maybe it's the climate up north, but John and the chapter members are a warm bunch who support one another closely. John has a passion for the AIPP and helping fellow members succeed.'

Robert Edwards clearly recalls soon after he joined the national board how John shared his vision for the Institute. John foresaw enormous changes to the profession and set out how the Institute should prepare its members and itself for that change. That same year the AIPP Policy & Planning meeting voted to grow the Institute to afford members a way to differentiate themselves from non-members. To make a clear and marketable definition of 'AIPP Member', John undertook the mammoth task of amending the AIPP constitution.

Robert also made special mention of Ross Eason, an AIPP Master of Photography, a former New South Wales state president and at the time of writing the national vice president. Said Robert, 'With his level headed approach, Ross played a pivotal role during the AIPP restructure. Ross also serves on the commercial sub-committee. In this role he has fully documented and passionately pursued the AIPP mentoring programme over three years, as well as being a major contributor to its success.

'He has coordinated from the ground up our national conference: The Nikon AIPP Event. This is the largest professional photography event in Australia and organising it has had a large impact on Ross' own business.

'Ross is also the most prolific contributor to the AIPP Forum giving advice to young and established members. He has selflessly mentored many Queensland photographers openly sharing his knowledge to improve their businesses all the while promoting the benefits of the AIPP. Ross is a humble man not wanting the limelight. Everything Ross does for the AIPP he does with his heart, and mind, in the right place.

In his end of term report on behalf of the board, Robert said, 'We embarked on the AIPP Accredited Professional Photographer campaign. To prove that there is a difference to the public, Continuing Professional Development was introduced along with more rigorous folio and business assessments.'

'The AIPP is the de facto industry regulator that the photo buying public will look to qualify a professional photographer. More photographers and other associations are joining the AIPP since membership was tightened up.

'Emerging members, and applicants who don't meet the membership requirements, have access to the AIPP Mentoring program. That program features internationally recognised professional photographers tutoring new members in best business practices.'

At the conclusion of Robert Edwards' term, membership for the first time topped 3,000 members. Interestingly, in spite of the new category for associates, the major increase in membership came in fully accredited members. The Institute's budget now exceeded two million dollars. This enabled the Institute to launch its first national TV advertising, print and social media campaign and to introduce on line streaming of training events for members unable to attend.

With a strong office team in place under the direction of Peter Myers, the board of directors was evolving to one of governance and undertook regular training on planning and corporate compliance.

The Canon sponsored Australian Professional Photographers Awards continued to grow. In 2012, now in its thirty-sixth year, the Awards attracted more than 850 photographers. With David Paterson as the new Awards Chair, Sue Lewis led an enthusiastic team of volunteers to assist in the judging of 3,100 images. An extra judging room had to be built at that year's photo show, bringing the total number of concurrent judging rooms in operation to four.

Explained Institute Executive Officer, Peter Myers, 'The Awards are open to all professional photographers around the world, including students of professional photography courses.

Each of the thousands of images entered is individually critiqued in detail by experienced judging panels before a live audience and on line video streaming.'

Taz Nakamasu, the managing director of sponsor, Canon Australia, described the Canon AIPP APPAs as the most sought after accolade in Australian professional photography and was proud of his company's support for the development of professional photographers.

In 2012, Kylie Lyons was elected president with fellow board members John de Rooy as chair, Ross Eason and Mel Neumann as vice presidents, Andrew Harrison as treasurer and Felicity Biasi and David Watson as board members.

Kylie, a Sydney based wedding and portrait photographer took her first photograph with the family Kodak Instamatic when she was aged six years old. This picture is framed and hangs on her wall. After attending the schools darkroom lessons in years eleven and twelve, Kyle knew she wanted to be a professional photographer. She would spend her lunchtimes in the school's darkroom and became a key photographer for all the school sporting events and functions.

Kylie began as a commercial photographer in a North Sydney studio, but after friends began asking her to take their wedding photos she decided to strike out on her own as a wedding photographer. Becoming interested in portraiture, Kylie bought a block of land which had two deconsecrated churches and adapted one for use as a studio and the other as a hired out special occasions venue.

Smart as a whip and a barrel load of fun, Kylie helped burst the Institute into a new age of communications. Gone is the hard copy of the president's report to members and in its stead is a treasure trove of fireside video chats delivered in a friendly and entertaining way. A new age of communication has arrived. This can be seen at vimeo . com / 57814382 and vimeo . com / album / 2180384 / video / 47233406.

The printed edition of the Institute's newsletter, The Working Pro was also abandoned in favour of an e-magazine. This allowed the introduction of colour and video, but it can only be hoped that some future researcher wanting to write the next hundred year history of the Institute can find access to the files!

But publishers have to adapt and change just as the photographer has had to do. This was a fact very ably demonstrated by photographer Geoff Harrison at an Awards dinner in 2005, Geoff said, 'In the last 50 years I think the main difference between now and when

I started in photography is that, back then, I was smarter than the equipment!

'Well, I had to be. In 1958 I had cameras that were sold as "fine precision instruments", but they: would let you make an exposure without removing the darkslide; let you remove the darkslide with the shutter open; let you make an exposure with the lens cap on; let you make more than one exposure on a sheet of film; let you take a shot with the aperture wide open (as you left it after focusing); let you make an exposure with the front shutter while the back shutter was closed; let you insert a flashbulb with the shutter open, which made it fire immediately, temporarily blind you, and cause painful blisters on your burnt fingers; let you fire an electronic flash on the M setting, resulting in no sync; let you open the back before the film had been rewound; tear sprocket holes in 35mm film so that you could make 36 exposures all on the one frame; let you make flash pictures on speeds that were not synchronised resulting in partial or no exposures and allow an exposure even if the subject was completely out-of-focus. Also, when using flash you were constantly doing mental arithmetic and aperture adjustments as you moved closer or further away And just at the exact moment for that perfect picture you could press the shutter release only to find you hadn't cocked the shutter!'

Moving into the essential darkroom, Geoff encountered other problems: 'You had the opportunity to load your darkslide with a sheet of film and the black paper interleaf on top; load your darkslide with the film back to front; expose your print with the enlarger lens still wide open (as you left it after focusing); turn on the white light before replacing the lid on the box of paper or film; make glossy finish prints only by drying them on a glazer; keep in stock bromide paper in four different contrast grades.

'But fifty years later in 2008, all of these fun camera options are no longer available. Instead your only amusement today is: "Delete all files?" and then accidentally select "Yes". Oops!'

The ability to take good pictures easily has undoubtedly had an effect on the professional photographer. A 2012 IBISWorld Industry

Report claimed that the business of professional photography had shrunk by 5.6% each year from 2004 to 2009, and that it would continue to shrink by 0.3% per year until 2014. The report's author, Edward Butler stated that ordinary citizens with digital cameras, colour printers or just the ability to view them digitally, were creating a new society that felt no need to hire a professional.

But the report does not allow for the fact that advances in technology equally open up new opportunities for professional photographers. While new cameras might be able to shoot motion with the same quality of stills and make that decisive moment technically easier to capture, you still have to be able to recognise that moment, frame it, light it and compose it. And that is the true mark of a professional image maker. A new type of professional image maker will emerge. It might well involve the ability to shoot motion, record appropriate voiceovers, make television commercials and even Hollywood movies. The essential skill is the ability to communicate a vision to the world.

Peter Eastway said 'There will always be a need for professional photography and while the nature of a professional photographer might change, if you have the passion for the business, you can make it work. Note I mentioned 'business', not photography. Professional photography involves two words and many people forget the first one. Many people in photography look for quick, get-rich solutions. A lucky few find them, but for most successful photographers, it's a matter of doing lots of small things properly for a long period of time.'

Robert Edwards said, 'There is one thing that never changes. That is the image. It's all about the image. That is what got me into the profession. It is a passion for expressing how we view the world, a passion for the photographic image and a passion to champion professional photography'

Peter Myers said, 'The challenge for us in the future is to distinguish between photography and professional photography. We have to be clear who we are and who we are trying to help. We have to meet the changes and adapt to meet the demands of the photographers of the future.'

As president of the Institute, Kylie Lyons said her vision for the future was to see all members become more engaged with ongoing improvements to the educational programs, to get involved with the high quality workshops organised and for the Institute to improve its advocacy and better value propositions for all members.

In the face of all the current challenges, the Institute has never

been stronger and it is full of confidence for a successful future. In a message to members, Kylie urged, 'I want you to come with me. I want you to strap yourself into the front seat of this roller coaster with me. Keep your eyes wide open, throw your arms in the air and scream at the top of your lungs as we navigate the twists, turns and loop the loops of our profession.'

Chapter Eight

The Teensies Revolution

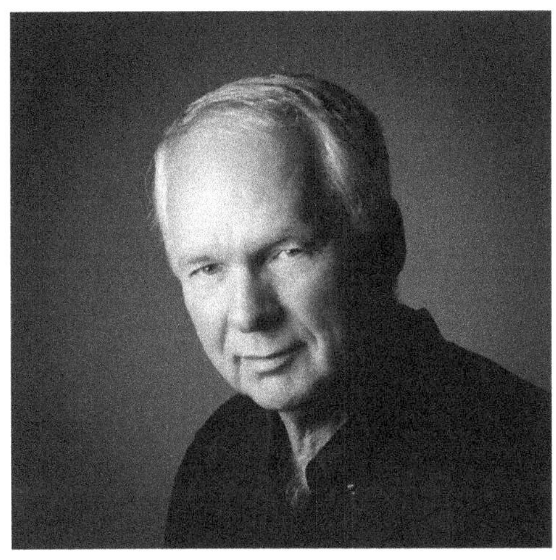

Ross Eason

How right Kylie proved to be. The AIPP was nearing one of its more dramatic rides. At the end of her term, Kylie passed the presidential baton in 2014 to Ross Eason. Ross began his career in Sydney in the field of public relations, photojournalism, commercial and advertising photography but in 1991 moved to operate from Queensland. He served as an AIPP board member and convened four national conferences for the AIPP. A trained photographic judge he helped establish the AIPP's national mentoring program and conducted many educational workshops and tutorials. He also served as an association advocate supporting Chris Shain for the AIPP's submissions to the Australian Law Reform Commission. In 2003 Ross was awarded the distinction of Master Photographer and in 2013 was made an honorary life member. In 2018 he was made an Honorary Fellow.

In September 2014, the ACMP and AIPP boards met to explore

consolidating resources while still maintaining the integrity of both brands. It had been a long-running battle to merge the two associations but many on both sides were reluctant to take the step. However, with the incentive of a declining number of people being able to make a sustainable career as professional photographers, and with six months of discussions, an agreement to merge was finally reached.

'Together we are stronger' said Ross. 'With greater representation for commercial photographers, we can more effectively influence the industry with advocacy, standards and education.'

ACMP President Richard Weinstein said 'This union is in the best interests of the industry and all our members. The ACMP logo and brand now represent a newly created Accredited Commercial and Media Photographers division of the AIPP.'

As a further sign of the changing times, Canon brought its thirteen-year sponsorship of the APPAs to an end. But the Awards events remained one of the most important events in the AIPP calendar. With its 36-year history, the Awards structured peer review program continued to form the cornerstone of the Association's philosophy to raise the standard of professional image making in Australia.

In another move in 2016, the AIPP decided to change it main news communication vehicle from the Working Pro to the AIPP Journal. Ross Eason said the AIPP Journal would be a system rather than a publication as research showed that different members wanted their news in different formats. Some simply wanted the basic facts; others wanted details; some wanted a short email, while others sought an online option to read at their convenience. The new format was designed to include content tagged news, features, education, awards and events and a detailed contents page with hot links to allow quick and easy searches.

Following the passing of institute legend Ian McKenzie, the board introduced the Luminous initiative, a system that each year recognises members who make a significant contribution to their community by giving an educational "Luminous" grant in their name to a worthy student. To fund the project the Luminous fund was established based on philanthropic donations with a mandate to raise funds as required.

During Ross's term, the Institute also initiated The Reflections Project to honour Australian World War II Veterans. This was an inspired undertaking comprising 6500 portraits photographed over two years by 450 photographers and gift the images to the nation as a demonstration of the importance of the professional portrait. Director of the Australian War Memorial Dr Brendan Nelson was Patron of the project and the digital archive now resides in the War Memorial where it is on permanent display, a two-volume set of books, created by book printing company Momento, was also presented to the National Library in 2018.

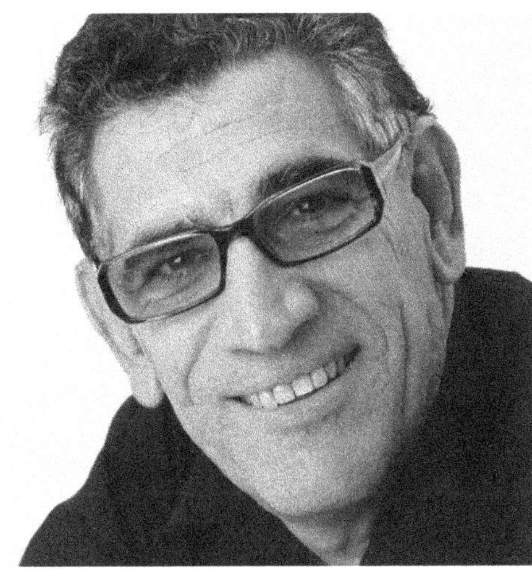

Vittorio Natoli

In 2016, the AIPP elected Vittorio Natoli as its new president. First co-opted in Ross Eason's terms to add commercial business expertise to the board for a potential re-structure, Vittorio was a Grand Master photographer notable for both his winning of multiple state and national awards and his entrepreneurial business skills. He opened his first wedding and portrait studio in Sydney in 1983 and in 1991 he founded Viva Photography, a premium wedding and portrait photography franchise which had ten studios operating in both Western Australia and Victoria. Viva photographers had collectively won more than 150 AIPP awards. To further strengthen the board's business management skill, Vittorio also co-opted former industry wholesaler, John Swainston.

With new Platinum sponsors, Olympus, Aon and Panasonic, the 2017 APPAs and the gala dinner were highly successful. Displayed

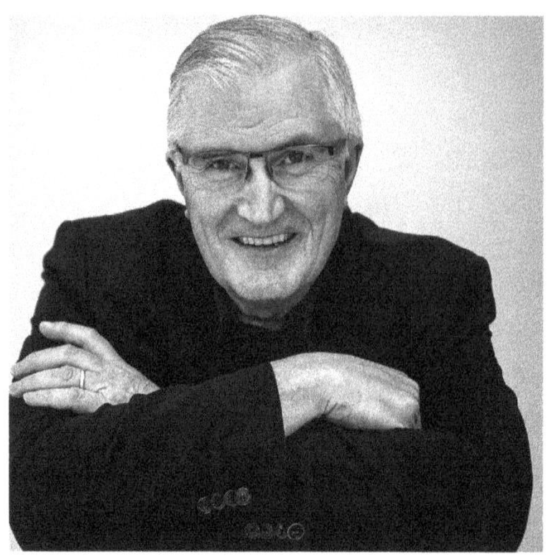

John Swainston

on the walls outside the Melbourne judging rooms, was an amazing variety of work across all genres, both in digital illustration and traditional image making. They served as a great pictorial insight into where the profession was heading, while also allowing visitors to view 200 of the Reflections WWII veterans, produced by Chromaluxe.

While the Association's membership had been growing, under the challenge of the digital age, the number of practising professional photographers was decreasing. With less demand for their services, many professionals were looking to supplement their incomes by lecturing and schooling hobby photographers. In a way teaching, such skills could be considered as hastening the demise of the professional photographer. But facing the avalanche of digital technology changes brought a need for a major rethink of how the AIPP could remain both relevant and financial. Managing this was a balancing act akin to weaving a unicycle on a wire over a shark pond.

A few of the more established members were beginning to question some of the board's moves into new areas and felt that too much of the association's funds were being spent on maintaining a well-staffed office and the associated administrative costs of trying to attract a wider group to membership. They thought there was not enough time and money going back into advancing the needs of the people who were practising professional photographers. The suggestion to include under the APPA's a new level for enthusiast photographers also drew concern as it might lessen the established prestige of the existing awards.

This growing groundswell of unrest was thrown into the cesspit of social media. Some criticisms of the association were made on the AIPP Facebook page. A few of these were moderated as they showed either the association or individuals in a poor light. But this only caused the complainants to seek other avenues to vent their ire and thus caused the broader social media spectrum to light up with a mix of bad-tempered and carelessly written comments.

This kerfuffle lead to an increasing number of people not renewing their membership and alarm bells began to ring. When the situation developed to personal attacks, the hard-working volunteer National Board began to wonder if the only recognition of their unpaid efforts was to be in terms of abuse.

Social media was still a relatively untamed beast without normal boundaries, and many were unschooled in the disciplines to use it. Anyone could fire off comments in an easy and careless way at any time of the day or night and thus sometimes cause utter chaos. U.S.A President Donald Trump perfected this practice to a fine art.

Probably It could have all been solved more easily if more complainants had simply decided to do the old-fashioned thing of simply picking up the phone and directly calling each other. In the early days of email, I remember well some brave soul had a jibe at Tasmanian wilderness photographer Richard Bennett for sometimes making him wait for answers. When you spend half your life hanging out of helicopters or trekking in remote wilderness, dealing with emails was not always easy. Richard simply shrugged his shoulders, sniffed and said, 'Well, you could always try calling.'

If more people have spoken directly to the Board, the whole kerfuffle might have been avoided. Although, throughout its long years, the AIPP had encountered it share of ups and downs, never before had its internal decision-making been so publicly aired.

The culmination came at the end of February 2018 when National President Vittorio Natoli dropped a bombshell e-mail on every member advising the board had resolved to make all staff redundant, close the national office, and resign en masse to allow for a new way of thinking.

To ensure a pathway to the future, four of the eight-member board, Louise Bagger, Melinda Comerford, and John Swainston, decided to remain in a caretaker mode to help a new board be elected. It was a strategic move that brought home to the membership the fact that if it didn't work together there would be no AIPP. It proved the successful catalyst to reinvigorate the entire association

The Institute was solvent, just, but it was relying heavily on the work done by volunteer members. But of its 2800 members, it was estimated that only around 600 photographers were running a full-time active studio and of those, many were not members. And of the members who were Accredited Professional Photographers, not all were interested in running a professional photography business.

To steer the association onto its new path, in 2018 the members elected a new president: industry veteran John Swainston. John did not have a professional photographer background, but as the former managing director of Nikon distributor, Maxwell Optical Industries, he was extremely familiar with both the art and business side of professional photography. Under his auspices, Nikon had long been a major sponsor and supporter of the AIPP. Also, a Fellow of the Australian Institute of Management, John, an Hon.FAIPP was a regular speaker at photographic conventions in Australia and overseas and had the benefit of a long involvement with photographic industry associations. He was thus and well equipped to tackle the work ahead.

The other new board members elected were: Chair, Melinda Comerford APP M.Photog; Treasurer, Melissa Neumann APP.L M. Photog; Education, Craig Wetjen APP M.Photog I; Awards, Steve Wise APP M.Photog II; Sponsorship, David Simmonds APP.L M. Photog II and Bruce Pottinger APP.L M.Photog I Hon.FAIPP

The first task was to revisit the constitution and bring it into the modern era by allowing video and other forms of electronic communication to be given the same status as physical meetings. Recognising the importance of the individual States and to ease the load of individual volunteer work, the number of permitted board members was increased. A new position of National Vice President was created with Louise Bagger as the first person to hold this position.

Commented John Swainston, 'Compared to five decades ago, time and financial pressures are generally much greater. Photography is almost unrecognisable compared to the profession or enthusiast practice of that era and has a strong state and territory council is once again the lifeblood of the organisation, just as it should be.

'2018 was a year was one of consolidation and restructuring, but the Board is determined that the AIPP looks forward, informed by its heritage, but not stifled by it. New technologies, new demand patterns for photography, and changing income possibilities, all require the Institute to be nimbler, more outward-looking and of more appeal to a very large number of working photographers. As we move towards 2020 our vision is to move forward to a brave new world that is rather different from the norms of the last 55 years of the Institute's life.'

Chapter Nine

The Institute's Honours: A Who's Who of the Profession's Achievers

The Photo industry and the professional photographers associations are awash with acronyms. We have everything from the AIPP, PICA, PMA, and APPA to McDonald's EIEIO. But an important part of the Institute's activities has been to honour those who have played a key role in helping to capture the Australian way of life in pictures. The various types of honours are:

Fellowship (FAIPP)

A Fellowship is the highest achievement that the AIPP can bestow and is a rare honour with only a few having attained this level of recognition in the Australian photographic industry. Because of the high level of entry, there will only ever be a small number of people with this title.

Honorary Fellowship (Hon. FAIPP)

This title is awarded for recognition of outstanding and long service to the Industry. This is usually given at the successful completion of a large project or a long period of service time. It is given for consistent and exemplary service within our profession, a reward for hard work and unselfish commitment to the industry.

Honorary Life Member

An Honorary Life Membership is granted for consistent and extended service over a long period and can include work on the national board, state divisions and other sub-committees. It is a reward for hard work and unselfish commitment to the Institute.

Claude McCarthy Award

This award recognises a long period of effort and dedication to the Institute and is named after the founding father of the Institute, Claude McCarthy.

The following awards are earned through the Canon Australian Professional Photography Awards system, but are not honours per se.

Associate - A member of the AIPP can earn their Associateship by accumulating five Award points in a four year period.

Master of Photography, the next step, requires a further 10 Award points in a five year period. Photographers who continue to enter the Awards can gain bars for their Master of Photography, each bar requiring an extra 10 Award points.

Grand Master, the highest APPA award, requires at least 65 full Award points to be earned - (at least five Gold Bars), including at least five Gold Awards and ten Silvers with Distinction (85 or higher). Given very few photographers earn more than four Award points each year, it takes not only a considerable time to earn the Grand Master, but also consistently high standard of excellence.

Grand Master (G. M. Photog.)

The Grand Master of Photography is also awarded by the AIPP, but is not an honour per se. It is earned through the Canon Australian Professional Photography Awards system. A member of the AIPP can earn their Associateship by accumulating five Award points in a four year period. The next step is Master of Photography, requiring a further 10 Award points in a five year period. Photographers who continue to enter the Awards can gain bars for their Master of Photography, each bar requiring an extra 10 Award points. However to achieve the status of Grand

Master, at least 65 full Award points are needed (at least five

Gold Bars), including at least five Gold Awards and ten Silvers with Distinction (85 or higher). Given very few photographers earn more than four Award points each year, it takes not only a considerable time to earn the Grand Master, but also consistently high standard of excellence.

Those honoured, in alphabetical, order include:

Peter Adams, M.Photog. FAIPP

Peter Adams grew up in the UK. After high school, Peter took a position as an apprentice toolmaker. Two and a half years later he became a London advertising photographer, taught photography at a regional art school and painted and sold 'ghastly abstract paintings under the name of Retep Smada'. That is Peter Adams spelt backwards.

In 1966 Peter emigrated from Britain to Australia as a ten pound Pom and was hired by Bryce Courtenay as an advertising agency art director. Adams worked in the advertising industry for 14 years - including a six-year stint in New York where he started and ran the Graphic Design and Packaging Division of Ogilvy & Mather. He also started a jewelry business called 'Hi-ho Silver': the logo was a silver bullet.

Back in Australia he returned to his first love of photography, opening a studio in Sydney. Devonshire Street. He combined photography and film direction for a while, before turning to directing commercials full time, working with several blue-chip film companies including, Challenges Accepted, Eureka Films, Ross Wood Productions. Later, Peter launched his own film company.

After fourteen years as a film director, Peter returned once more to photography co-founding the Blue Mountains Photography Workshops in Katoomba, where he now lives. Adams has published 8 photography books, has won many awards including twice winning the Hasselblad Masters and twice winning the AIPP Professional Photographer of the Year. He lectures extensively, has been exhibited in 'Head On' and twice in 'The Moran' and has had his sculptures exhibited in Sculpture by the Sea three times. His work is included in many collections. He now spends his time making furniture, writing and he is still taking photographs.

Rick Altman, AAIPP, Hon. LM

Rick Altman joined the Institute in the 1960's while working as an assistant to well known Victorian photographer Val Foreman. Rick worked as an assistant on industrial locations as well as in the darkroom. These were the early days of colour processing and Rick went on to help Val set-up the colour lab, ' Foreman Colour', teaching himself to process colour film, make colour prints and print film transparencies.

At 22, Rick decided to start his own business, setting up a darkroom at home and making portfolio presentations to PR companies. A year later Rick moved to business premises in St. Kilda Road where his business grew and developed. Rick was quick to embrace the digital revolution and was always upgrading to the latest digital camera. Rick is a pioneer of creative industrial photography and was highly sought after by corporations to illustrate their glossy brochures and covered every aspect of industry from off-shore oil and gas to open-cut and underground gold mining and the construction industry.

In the late 1980's Rick served on State Council and was the Victorian Delegate to the Federal Council. For over 40 years Rick showed great passion for photography, the AIPP and the photographic industry. Rick is now deceased.

George Apostolidis, M.Photog. FAIPP

George was given a camera by his aunt at the age of 11 and became infatuated with photography. After completing the illustrative photography course at Royal Melbourne Institute of Technology, he secured himself a job as an assistant at the studio of Brian Brandt. In 1981 George began working in his own right as an advertising photographer. Through hard work and determination George excelled and in 1983 won the Australian Professional Photographer of the

Year Award with an industrial portfolio.

He has won the Ilford Trophy twice, the Australian Commercial/ Industrial Photographer of the Year three times and the Australian Advertising Photographer of the Year. A Hasselblad Masters winner, George has won an impressive collection of international awards from New York and Chicago to London. A master of photography with four gold bars George has photographed some of the biggest high profile jobs in Australia and around the world. He was included in Luzens Archive in 2004 as one of the best 20 advertising photographers in the world.

George's outstanding photography is driven by his enthusiasm, honesty and integrity which he instills in young photographers . Carrying on Brian Brandt's legacy of the big studio, George's studio "Heaven Pictures" encourages the next generation of young photographers to share and learn together.

Andris Apse, Hon. FAIPP

Born in Latvia in 1943 Andris Apse arrived in New Zealand when he was just six years old after having spent five years in a refugee camp. While working for New Zealand forestry as an eighteen year old he found himself in the country's fiord land. This was a turning point in his career because Andris fell in love with the scenery and wanted to record it, to be able to show people how beautiful it was.

Since those early days Andris has gone on to win many awards including the Olympus 17th anniversary photographic competition and the gold award in the Pacific Asia Travel Association travel photograph category. He has been a guest exhibitor at the International Photography Hall of Fame in Oklahoma. USA. He won third prize in the Linhof International Photographic competition in Germany and in a competition run by the National History museum of Great Britain he won the Animal Behaviour section of the International Wildlife Photographer of the Year. During his career he has published 23 major books. In 2007 Andris was awarded life membership of the New Zealand Institute of Professional Photograph and was recently made a member of the New Zealand order of merit for services to photography.

Paul Arthur, Hon. FAIPP

Paul Arthur was a Kodak professional division sales representative who in the 1990's gave unstintingly of his time in order to assist the promotion and organisation of events for the South Australian division of the Institute.

John Atkins, Hon. FAIPP

Born in 1944 into an Adelaide horse racing photography family, John couldn't wait to work on a racecourse taking photos. He started at 13 then left school at 14 to chase his dream. Although he left school early, he says he never stopped learning about photography and business.

During the 60's John experimented with colour photography, and was the first to take and print racing photos in full colour in Australia. He changed to all colour work in 1970 and other photographers' began bringing their work to him for processing. Thus Atkins Colour Lab was born.

John joined in the sixties and served on the council for many years, including five as state president. During those years there were conferences in Adelaide with international speakers which brought attendees from across Australia.

The SA Division also promoted professional photography to the public, via stands at the Royal Show, Rundle Mall and other venues. On receiving his honourary fellowship from the Institute, John said, 'I can't understand the fuss, I only did what I loved doing'.

Sandy Barrie, Hon.LM

Sandy Barrie has collected a wealth of history, hardware and ephemera about photography and photographers in Australia. Few organisations have amassed the tons of memorabilia in this collection, including an original Daguerreotype camera, a mammoth graphic arts camera, and perhaps two thousand other cameras of a widely diverse nature. Hundreds of thousands of negatives present another aspect of the Sandy Barrie Collection, ranging from early glass plates by early documentary photographers, to near complete studio outputs of later photographers.

This collection, acquired by diligent hunting through flea markets, garage sales, studio basements and antique shops, has saved much history from scattered anonymity, the dump, incineration, or destruction for silver recovery. Unfortunately, a large part of the collection was damaged in the Brisbane floods.

Sandy has also conducted considerable research into photographers of the past. To date these studies have resulted in the publications; "Professional Photographers in Australia 1900 - 1920", "Queenslanders behind the Camera" - Professional Photographers in Queensland 1849 - 1920, a contribution to the "Mechanical Eye in Australia", and numerous articles in professional and amateur publications.

Brian Barrow, Hon.LM, FAIPP

Brian Barrow started in photography in 1961, and like many who started at that time had no formal training. After eight years working as a photographer, he became a photography teacher. He spent twenty two years building the Mt. Lawley course into one of the best and most innovative in Australia. His contribution to the Institute has been substantial. In the West Australia he attended more than 200 council meetings as variously president, vice-president and treasurer; organised many seminars and workshops and became a champion for change for both the Institute and photographic educators. For several years, Brian was the Institute's national education convenor. Brian is now deceased.

Craig Bassett, Hon.LM

A Melbourne based photographer, Craig managed the backroom running of the Australian Professional Photography Awards for more than 15 years. Craig started his association with the Awards by being one of the people placing the photos on the swing board for the judging panel, but moved on to manage a team of more than

40 volunteers required to process all the entries. This could require twenty hours a day of work for a straight eight days while the judging process was completed. His unselfish commitment to the business of professional photography resulted in him being awarded the Photo Imaging Council's Gold Tripod for an outstanding contribution to the industry and being made an honorary life member of the Institute.

Richard Bennett, M.Photog.IV, Hon.FAIPP, FAIPP

Richard has brought the beauty of the wilds of Tasmania to the world and has published 12 books on subjects including Tasmania's Huon Valley, Tasmania's Wilderness, Islands, yachting, forest regeneration, colonial architecture, Lord Howe Island, and most recently Bruny Island food. Born 1945 in Tasmania, Richard joined the Institute in 1974. He was elected national president in 1993 and national chairman in 1995. In 1998 Richard was elected chair of the Australian Professional Photography Awards, a position he held until 2004. During his time as chairman of APPA he oversaw the introduction of the Australian Professional Photographer of the Year Award. He has also served as a judge of the awards for twenty years. Since 1998, Richard has served as chair of the Honours Committee. He also convened the 1990 National Convention in Hobart and started the Trans Tasman Challenge, a competition between New Zealand and Australia.

Richard's awards include the Ilford Trophy, a Professional Photographers of America Gold Merit, a Master of Photography with four gold bars, and becoming a New York Alfred Eisenstaedt Awards finalist for excellence in magazine photography. Richard is also the holder of the Australian photo industry's highest award for outstanding service, The Gold Tripod and the Centenary Medal for his contribution to the promotion of Tasmania through photography. In 1999, he was the winner of the Australian Press Photographer of the Year Award for the Best Sport's Photograph of the Year and in 1996 one of his pictures became the world's biggest photo diorama when displayed at the International Photography Hall of Fame in

Oklahoma City.

Robert Billington, M.Photog. FAIPP

Born in England in 1954, Robert moved to Australia at the age of 18 where he began working for Elton Ward studios in Parramatta. After studying portraiture and the art of photography in 1994 he won the Institute's Professional Photographer of the Year Award. He continued on to win more than 100 medals in both Australia and England and has twice won the prestigious Hasselblad Masters Award. Robert has also served as a long term judge for the Awards and has delivered numerous seminars.

He has published nine books and his images have been collected by national and state galleries. The Museum of Sydney has held two special exhibitions of his work and his photographs have been exhibited in galleries in New York, London and throughout Europe.

Des Birt M.Photog, Hon.LM

On leaving school in 1978, West Australian Des Birt worked on a mushroom farm before joining Murray Moore's studio in Busselton. This involved photographing everything, from weddings, portraits, commercial and advertising, to debutant balls and cattle sales.

After working as a government photographer for the West Australian Water Authority, in 1987 Des opened his own business which mainly focused on wedding photography. In the same year he became the West Australian Divisional Secretary for the AIPP. In 1989 he graduated from Mt, Lawley College of TAFE with a Diploma in Photography.

Between 1987 and 1998 Des served the AIPP on both state and national committees holding the positions of chair of the WA Canon PPY, national director, national vice president and national treasurer.

Ray Blackbourn, Hon.FAIPP

Ray Blackbourn first started as a newspaper messenger boy but retired in 1988 from the position of Pictorial Editor at The Age in Melbourne. Ray had been at the newspaper for 46 years and 11 months. During that time he photographed a Royal Tour, the Commonwealth and Olympic Games, football finals and test cricket. His overseas assignments took him to the US, UK, Greece, Yugoslavia, Italy, Asia and Papua New Guinea.

In 1942 Ray was reluctantly granted leave by his employer to join the forces. His active service came to an abrupt end the day after the war ended when he was injured while working with a bomb disposal unit in the Solomon Islands. Returning to The Age He served with seven editors and for 19 years was its Pictorial Editor where he had considerable influence on the development of press photography.

Said John Lamb, one of Australia's best press photographers, 'Ray encouraged me, and so many other young press photographers around Australia that you can't count them'. Under Ray's leadership The Age was one of the first to employ women photographers. He was a judge of the Nikon Press photography competition and Rothmans awards and instigated a schools photography competition. His photographers, here and overseas, have for many years been winners of the highest awards for press photographers.

Gavin Blue, Claude McCarthy Award

For more than 25 years, Gavin's personal and creative approach has earned him a reputation of producing truly outstanding images for the advertising, editorial and corporate markets. Based in Melbourne, Gavin's clients include Volvo, Australia Post, Fonterra, Tourism Victoria, Suzuki, Singapore Power, Sunday Life Magazine, Financial Review Magazine, KPMG, National Australia Bank, Mercedes Trucks and Boeing to name a few. He is especially sought after for his people photography. Subjects include CEO's of multinational companies, politicians, Olympic athletes, actors, and other celebrities.

Gavin is highly active in the professional photography industry. He was president of the Australian, Commercial and Media Photographers (the ACMP) for 5 years, was Chairman of the Fuji ACMP Australian Photographers Collection for 7 years when it was at its most prestigious level.

John Bodin, M.Photog, Hon. LM

John Bodin graduated with a Bachelor of Arts degree from the Royal Melbourne Institute of Technology in the 1980s. First freelancing for Peter Walton and Brian Brandt, John joined the AIPP and served on the Victorian Divisional Council. Since then, John has judged at numerous Victorian Professional Photographer of the Year Awards and at the APPAs.

Specialising in the urban environmental photography, John's portfolio led to more than eleven shows in six years and to his work being collected privately throughout Australia and New Zealand. John has also served as chair of the RMIT BA Photography Program Advisory Committee.

For his outstanding service to the AIPP and to the Australian Professional Photography Awards the Institute awarded John honorary life membership.

Janie Boyd, Hon.LM , AIPP, BA (Photography & Art History)

Janie Boyd works as a portrait and wedding photographer and joined the AIPP in 2004. She became an active member of the Tasmanian Divisional Council and in 2007 she was co-opted to the national board as national sponsorship coordinator.

In 2010 Janie was elected National Vice President and has been involved in a wide number of projects for the Institute and also for the Bridport Surf Life Saving Club.

Brian Brandt, Claude McCarthy Award, Hon. LM., FAIPP

Victorian photographer Brian Brandt was one of the most talented, generous, and gregarious people in Australian photography. His first Melbourne job was with Latrobe Studios. He joined the IVP, the precursor to today's Institute, as a foundation member.

He was on the Institute's Victorian Council for 4 years from 1972 and served as a national awards judge for seventeen years.

In 1989, the Melbourne Art Directors Club awarded him the All Graphic Industries Award, for the most outstanding achievement by a creative person from any branch of the advertising industry.

The Brian Brandt Studios were the most prolific training ground for many of the great talents in Australian advertising photography. As role model and mentor, he was directly responsible for the nurturing and development of a number of today's top advertising photographers, including Rob Imhoff, Angie Heinl, Peter Bailey, Richard Millott, Doug Coates, Rob Slatyer, Peter Johnson, George Apostolides, Peter Thomson, Gary Smith and many others.

Don Burrows, Hon.LM

In 1941, Don Burrows, at age 13, was playing music professionally with four piece bands in suburban dance halls. Since this time Don has played with the many other great jazz artists of the world. In Australia, he became a household name, particularly through his television series on the ABC, and he is on the official list of Australia's Living Legends. His involvement in photography began at an equally early age and wherever he toured the world, his camera went with him.

For more than forty years, in a bid to foster music and photography, Don visited every corner of outback Australia to help aboriginal and white children alike onto a path of creative expression. Don reasons that the ear is to music what the eye is to photography. Both pursuits are outlets for self-expression, imagination, discovery, individuality and form.

Always working in black and white, Don was a keen and able darkroom worker. Some of his favourite pictures were those of Aboriginals but he never included these in his pictures for sale until the Department of Aboriginal Affairs set up a special fund in which all the proceeds of these photographs goes to aid young aboriginals seeking a career in music.

The Institute recognised Don's outstanding contribution to the photographic community by awarding him Honorary Life Membership.

Paul Burrows, Hon.FAIPP

A prolific journalist and long term editor of Australian Camera and Pro Photo magazines, Paul Burrows, with his reporting on cameras and accessories has both informed and entertained tens of thousands of his readers for more than thirty years. With his extraordinary in-depth technical knowledge, Paul has analytically reviewed every significant camera in that period and has become an acknowledged expert on the subject of camera design. His comments are noted by camera manufacturers and are often included in overseas publications.

Paul was an active participant in the Ken Duncan inspired Arts Freedom Australia campaign and used his publications to focus attention on the inequities of the people at National Parks and other bureaucrats imposing unnecessary restrictions on photographers.

His writing topics extend beyond photography and have included, travel, classical music, motoring and documentary TV travel script writing and a book on cats. With his wife Victoria Jefferys, he formed WriteLight Press, a boutique publishing house which with Ian McKenzie published the Contemporary Photographers Australia series. This included the works of which included the works of Ian Dodd, Lewis Morley, David Moore, Wolfgang Sievers Graham McCarter and Michael Coyne.

Jeff Carter, Hon.FAIPP

Jeff Carter was born 1928 in Melbourne, Victoria. Finishing his education in 1946, Jeff knew what he wanted to do: take pictures, write and travel. So he immediately set off into the Outback to photograph the people he admired most and described as 'the poor and unknown.' He sold his photographs to magazines such as Paris Match, People, Pix, Walkabout and Australian Women's Weekly. Later Jeff was also commissioned by National

Geographic and his black and white images, such as Tobacco Road and The Drover's Wife, became accepted as iconic moments in Australian photography.

Jeff wrote and illustrated seventeen books and from 1972 to 1974, Jeff Carter directed and filmed the award winning television series Wild Country for the Seven Network. From 1981to 85, he was head teacher of photography at the Wollongong campus of the National Art School.

His photographs are in the collections of the Art Gallery of NSW, the National Gallery of Victoria, the National Gallery of Australia, the National Library of Australia, the Art Gallery of South Australia, the National Museum of Australia, and the Powerhouse Museum. Overseas, his photographs have been exhibited in galleries in Osaka, Japan, Lisbon, Portugal, New York and Paris. Jeff died in 2010.

John Cato, Hon.FAIPP

John Cyril (Jack) Cato was born in 1889 at Launceston, Tasmania. His uncle was landscape photographer J. W. Beattie, who encouraged Jack into photography. In his early teens he also received training from the two local studios and Jack applied to be the official photographer to Mawson's 1911 Australasian Antarctic Expedition. Disappointed that he was passed over in favour of Frank Hurley, Jack travelled to London where he worked for society portraitists. Here he unfortunately contracted tuberculosis and left for South Africa's warmer climate where he continued to work as a photographer. By 1917, his standards of portraiture earned him of a fellowship of the Royal Photographic Society.

Returning to Tasmania, between 1920-27 Cato operated his own portrait-studio in Hobart before moving to Melbourne. His friendship with Dame Nellie Melba, whom he had met in London, stood him in good stead as Dame Nellie helped him to become quickly established on the Melbourne social and theatrical scenes. His studio flourished and became active in the Institute's forerunner, the Professional Photographers Association where he was made a life member.

In 1946, Jack retired from his studio to concentrate on his career as an author. In addition to a large number of articles in photographic, philatelic and other magazines, he published an autobiography, I Can Take It (1947), a pictorial documentary, Melbourne (1949), and The Story of the Camera in Australia (1955). In the first three years of the sixties, he was also the photography columnist for The Age.

He died on 14 August 1971 and a collection of his photographs is held by the National Gallery of Australia.

Fred Cherry, Hon.LM

A Brisbane photographer and long time employee of Kodak in Queensland, for his long period of outstanding service to the Institute, Fred was awarded an Honorary Life Membership.

Peter Cocklin, Hon LM

At the age of 18, Peter Cockin began his career apprenticed to a photographer in New Zealand. This led to him working as a ship's photographer on P&O. Back ashore he worked for Kodak in Sydney before moving to Brisbane to manage a commercial lab. Returning to Kodak, he built a long and distinguished career with that company and at the end of the Nineties he became manager of the professional division.

In this role he was a strong supporter of the AIPP education program and together they initiated a strong speaker program bringing in top overseas photographers. In 2016, thc Institute recognised Peter's long contribution by presenting him with Honourary Life Membership.

Nancy Cohen, Claude McCarthy Award

Nancy Cohen was born in New York but came to Australia to set up in business in Sydney as an editorial, corporate, travel, commercial, and industrial photographer.

During the 1990's Nancy worked closely with the Australian Copyright Council and represented the interests of photographers for both the Institute and the ACMP.

In recognition of her outstanding work on copyright issues that benefited all photographers, the Institute awarded Nancy with the Claude McCarthy Award.

Mike Connell Hon.LM

While still at school Mike Connell worked part time for a major Adelaide photographic store. On leaving school he continued with the same store for ten years before turning professional. With Drew Lenman they developed their business to the stage where they opened Orange Lane Studio in Adelaide's advertising agency heartland.

Mike joined the AIPP in 1988 and was awarded the title of Associate in 1991 and Master of Photography in 1994. In 1996 he was the South Australian AIPP Commercial/Industrial Photographer of the Year. Since then he has been the South Australian Advertising Photographer of the Year and twice the South Australian Illustrative Photographer of the Year.

In 2000, Mike was recognized by the Adelaide Art Directors Club and awarded the President's Award for services to the advertising industry. Mike has served on state council and is a past president and vice president of the South Australia Division. He also served as the national chair of the Honours and Ethics Committee.

Geoff Comfort, G.M.Photog, FAIPP

Based in the ACT, Geoff Comfort is a specialist aerial photographer and has presented at numerous AIPP events, business boot camps, print critique nights and judge training sessions.

He was ACT president from 2007 until 2010 and he has won the title of ACT Professional Commercial Photographer of the Year Award ten times as well ACT Landscape Photographer of the Year seven times and twice ACT Professional Photographer of the Year.

Keith Cook, Hon.LM

For many years black and white film, paper and chemical manufacturer Ilford dominated the professional photographic market. In Melbourne, Ilford had a large chemical and paper slitting plant and was represented to professional photographers by Keith Davis from the mid 1960's to the 1990's. Keith Davis was extremely supportive of the Institute, and to show its appreciation of his many years of help made him an Honorary Life Member.

Dr Michael, Coyne Hon. FAIPP, FAIPP

A gentle and spiritual man, Michael has covered the harsh reality of war for several decades. His assignments have taken him from trouble spot to trouble spot, In the 1980s Michael was one of the few western photo-journalists allowed into Iran and he spent eight years travelling back and forth, photographing the war between Iran and Iraq and life under the reign of Ayatollah Khomeini. His inside access to the regime even lead to him being questioned by the American CIA.

Michael Coyne's photographs have appeared in such great magazines of their day as Newsweek, Life, Time National Geographic, New York Times, Sports Illustrated, Paris Match, Vogue and the London Observer. His published books include Numurkah Lakes & Roses, The Oz Factor, A world of Australians, The Jew Called Jesus, Tour of Duty- East Timor, Lonely Planet's People Photography and Contemporary Photographers Australia, Michael Coyne and a major volume on the Regeneration of the Jesuits, Second Spring, which involved living in communities around the world.

Michael did a thesis on the ethics of photography in contemporary society and was made a Doctor of Photography by Griffith University. He was also granted the title Adjunct Professor of Photography by RMIT. In April 2003 Michael Coyne was awarded a Centenary Medal by the Australian Government for Service to Photography.

 Michael is also a powerful and motivational speaker and has he always been willing to share his knowledge with fellow photographers.

Bryan Chester, M.Photog, Claude McCarthy Award

For more than 30 years, Bryan Chester was a stalwart and active member of the Institute. One of the first members to achieve qualification by folio submission in four separate categories, Bryan quickly established himself as one of Australia's top image makers. His career encompassed work in the armed services, both here and overseas, before running one of Brisbane's leading commercial studios and in-house labs.

A past Queensland state president, Bryan served on its state council over three separate terms. His willingness to help others included mentoring both students and fellow professionals. Bryan wrote numerous articles for state and national newsletters and magazines and organised an annual seminar program. In 1989, Bryan began serving a long time period as an Awards judge.

In addition to his Institute support, Bryan was the strength behind his wife Christine's seven year role in the national office and always helped out with the annual show's Awards gallery and national office information stand.

Christine Chester, Hon.LM, Hon.FAIPP

Christine Chester played a long and vital role in the Institute's development and had a long lasting effect on the way the Institute was managed. In the early seventies she began her career studying at Sydney's Ultimo TAFE and became an IAP student member in 1973. Working first in Sydney then Taree as a wedding/portrait photographer Chris became a NSW state councilor.

She continued her career in Brisbane from 1983 and was elected AIPP Queensland president 1988. She moved to the Federal Council and participated in the change to the national board during her time as AIPP vice president. After she resigned in 1993, the board realised her experience and sense of history of the Institute were invaluable and so she agreed to take on an expanded role of National Office Coordinator. She played an active role in administration working closely with subsequent boards.

After eight years, Chris handed over to the board-appointed Brian O'Shea and moved to the Gold Coast and then to Tasmania.

Neville Coleman, OAM Hon.FAIPP

Born in 1938, Neville Coleman was a marine photographer that built a greater awareness of the need for the preservation of fragile and irreplaceable marine ecologies. Coleman started scuba diving in 1963 and six years later commenced a project aiming to document the entire marine life of Australia with meticulous and technically ground-breaking underwater photography. He has discovered and documented over 400 new marine species and logged over ten thousand dives. With his camera he compiled the world's largest library of underwater images with more than 100,000 images. This lead to 39 books, a number of TV documentaries and countless lectures tours. Neville died in 2012.

Melinda Comerford, Claude McCarthy Award

In 2017 the Institute's Honours Committee took the unusual step of presenting the Claude McCarthy Award for an outstanding contribution to the Institute to not one, but two people at the same time. They were Melinda Comerford and Mark Zed.

Melinda and Mark were co-chairs of the newly formed Awards Committee at a time of a controversial change in direction by the board. The duo worked tirelessly to build bridges and keep the AP-PAs strong through a difficult period. Their commitment ensured the APPAs continued to be a strong force.

Victoria Cooper, M.Photog.Hon.FAIPP

Victoria Cooper came to photography as a second career in 1990 and became involved in the Institute's Awards. Victoria completed a Graduate Diploma in Visual Arts at Monash University in 2002 and has become recognised as one of the world's twelve foremost pinhole image-makers. The unusual nature of her work is due to its origins in the history of the process. Her images of Van Dyke brown, cyanotype, and pinhole photography challenged the Awards judges and created for many a new relevance for heritage imaging. Victoria has also served in valuable roles on AIPP subcommittees, such as education and accreditation.

Olive Cotton, Hon. FAIPP

Olive Cotton started photography in 1922, at the age of 11. She was educated in Sydney, achieving a Bachelor of Arts, studying subjects such as Mathematics, Biology, Botany, Geology, and Music. These were unusual subjects for a woman in the 1930's.

In 1929 she joined the New South Wales Photographic Society and the Sydney Camera Club. Her first print was exhibited in 1932. Olive Cotton commenced work in 1934 in the studio of Max Dupain, whom she married. Her famous Teacup Ballet photograph was shown in London in 1935. For the next thirty years Olive continued to create images that have become photographic icons.

In 1964, Olive opened her studio in Cowra, in Central Western New South Wales, and photographed the events of her community. In the 1980's and 90's Olive's work became recognised and her images have featured on Australian stamps, been purchased by the National Gallery, and her life has been the subject of a documentary.

David Cumming, FAIPP

David Cumming is a Balmain photographer specialising in aerial mapping and survey work. For many years he played a very active role in the Institute. He played a major role in the development of the NSW division in the 1980's and served a term as its president. In addition to the time he gave to the Institute, he also gave studio space and other resources for AIPP meetings.

Geoff Cummings, Hon.FAIPP

Geoff Cummings started his career in photography when he was seventeen. In 1961 Geoff was elected president of the New South Wales branch of the Professional Photographers Association and in 1963 became a founding member of the new institute. He was its inaugural New Wales Division president, a role he filled for many years. David also played a key role in beginning the national conventions and was the organiser of the first national convention.

Geoff abandoned his career as a professional photographer to concentrate on a new job as the managing director of Group Colour which supplied high end processing services to professional photographers. However, he continued his long term role of supporting the institute.

Paul Curtis, Hon.FAIPP, Hon.LM, Claude Mcarthy Award

Born in 1943, Paul Curtis began contributing photographs and articles to newspapers and magazines while still at school in England. Before he turned twenty he became a cruise ship photographer.

He became manager of the ship's photography and retail shop units and served on ten different cruise ships, traveling and covering most of the world's cruising grounds. Towards the end of his six years sea time, he traded his camera for a microphone and became an entertainments officer aboard the original Queen Mary.

In 1978 Paul formed the Photographic Dealers Association which later became the Australian Division of the Photo Marketing Association. In the same year, he returned to writing and established a magazine publishing company which become Australia's largest photographic publishing company.

For many years Paul was the executive director of the Photo Imaging Council of Australia and the organiser of the industry's annual shows which grew to attract more than 20,000 attendees. Paul also served as a director of the Australian Centre for Photography.

Des Crawley (Professor), Hon.FAIPP

Des Crawley's commitment to photoimaging education and training extended over a thirty year period. As an academic, he led the establishment of significant photographic and digital imaging facilities within the University of Western Sydney.

In 1997, he became the foundation president of the Australian Photoimaging Educators Association, a branch of PMA International. He also served a term as vice president of the United States division where he had the responsibility for international program development.

Des has travelled and lectured extensively on the art and craft of photoimaging. As much as Des is known for his activities within academia, he is equally known as for his personal imagery and activities within the camera club movement. His passion for photography has extended into and influenced the camera club movement where he has held the position of lecturer and judge, exhibitor and motivator.

Keith Davis, Hon.LM

For many years black and white film, paper and chemical manufacturer Ilford dominated the professional photographic market. In Melbourne, Ilford had a large chemical and paper slitting plant and was represented to professional photographers from the mid 1960s to the 1990s.

Keith Davis was extremely supportive of the Institute and to show its appreciation of his many years of help, Keith was awarded an Honorary Life Membership.

Jacqui Dean, M. Photog. FAIPP, Hon. FAIPP

A commercial and editorial photographer, Jacqui has travelled widely and has been published in numerous travel and sporting magazines around the world. After graduating from Sydney TAFE with an Associate Diploma of Arts/Photography with Honours, she joined the AIPP in 1990.

She first entered the Awards in 1994 and achieved one Silver Award. In 1996 she gained her Associateship, won the Val Foreman Award and the AIPP Commercial/Industrial Photographer of the Year. By 2000 she was a Master and the NSW AIPP Professional Photographer of the Year.

Jacqui was the 2002 AIPP Editorial Photographer of the Year and the following year achieved her first Gold Bar. Her work is also represented in two Fuji ACMP Collections. A dedicated board member of the Institute, Jacqui Dean has played a vital management role as national treasurer and became the first woman to serve as national president and chair.

Tim Dean Claude, McCarthy Award

Tim began his photographic career at the age of 17 with Studios 51 in Greek Street London. He also worked for Copeland, Douglas and Dyer as a representative and for Hatton, a photographic agency that syndicated images to papers around the world. It was here that he worked closely with the UK photographer Terry O'Neil and in 1971 they started Microtrans, a business supplying advertising agencies with the services of dye retouching, duplicate transparencies and black and white printing. The business was very successful and Mictrotrans moved from Covent Garden to Brewer Street in Soho.

In 1982 Tim Dean with his wife Jacqui and their three children emigrated to Sydney Australia to start a chain of mini-labs. In 1990 Tim and Jacqui started a commercial lab and studio. Following his terminal illness, in 2010 the AIPP posthumously awarded Tim Dean the Claude McCarthy Award.

John de Rooy, Hon.FAIPP

The son of a Dutch migrant family, John de Rooy, became a cadet at age 15 with the Queensland Police Force. In 1980 he became a Scenes of Crime Officer, where he trained in forensic investigation and photography. As a sergeant, John transferred to Townsville and married Pam. Pursuing John's long interest in photography, the couple set up a wedding and portrait photography business. In 1993 John gained an Associate Diploma of Arts in Applied Photography from James Cook University. He also completed Business and Taxation Law subjects with honours in 1984.

In 2000 the couple was instrumental in setting up what was to become the North Queensland Chapter of the Institute, which successfully convened many great events, such as the Fuji Getaways.

John and Pam also cemented a strong working relationship with highly regarded educator, Les Walkling, and for the past nine years they have been running the Orpheus Island Fine Art Workshops.

In 2006, John joined the AIPP Board as national treasurer and in 2012 became chair of the national board.

Pam de Rooy, Claude McCarthy Award

Pamela de Rooy worked in the health, education and police departments in far North Queensland where she met and married police photographer, John de Rooy. In 1998 Pam and John left the police service to work in their burgeoning private photography business.

Pam's considerable organizational skills were not only of great benefit to the business but to the Institute as well: first at regional level and then when John moved onto the federal board at national level. For her long and outstanding service to the Institute, Pam was awarded the Claude McCarthy Award.

Keren Dobia, APP M. Photog, Claude Mccarthy Award

Keren Dobia gained her Master of Photography in 2015 and has added a further two Gold Bars and, was the 2017 AIPP Australian Professional Photographer of the Year. Keren was invited to be an official member of the APPA Event Team in 2014. After showing her commitment over the past few years, volunteering at APPA and VPPY, she became an integral member. Keren proved a strong leader and quick to step in when tasks needed to be done.

Ken Duncan, Hon. FAIPP

Ken Duncan and his partner Pam have built an extremely successful, international photography and publishing business based on his own images. Through his extraordinary business acumen and talent, Ken Duncan has created the largest group of privately owned galleries in Australia and raised the profile of professional landscape photography. Ken has also campaigned for photographers' rights in regard to copyright and photography in national parks.

In the United States Ken published his first international publication In God We Trust in 2001. This was followed by Spirit of America in 2003. Ken's association with long time friend Mel Gibson led to his book The Passion – Lessons from the Life of Christ in 2004. Another book about Jesus, Where Jesus Walked, took Ken on a journey through Israel, Palestine, Jordan, Lebanon and Egypt.

Ken's many awards include numerous gold and silver awards with APPA, an Award of Distinction at the NSW Tourism Awards, and in 2002 he was honoured with the Rotary International Award for Excellence in his field. But Ken doesn't take all the credit and has been known to admit that on occasion he is assisted by God himself.

Max Dupain, Hon.FAIPP, FAIPP

The name Max Dupain is synonymous with Australian photography and he is renowned as a modernist photographer that made one of the most outstanding contributions to the medium as an art form in the twentieth century.

Born in 1911, Max took an early interest in photography and after completing his tertiary studies he worked for Cecil Bostock in Sydney. In 1934, Max opened his own studio in Sydney's Bond Street. During World War II Max served with the Royal Australian Air Force in Darwin and Papua New Guinea where his artistic skills were brought into play to create camouflage.

His 1937 photograph of the Sunbaker is internationally recognised as one Australia's greatest iconic images. His 16 books and numerous one man exhibitions in Paris London and New York have made an important social and historical contribution to Australia. In 1982, he received an OBE for his services to photography. He was also at one time married to photographer Olive Cotton.

Max Dupain died in 1992.

Peter Dombrovskis, Hon.FAIPP

In 1945, Peter Dombrovskis was born in a refugee camp in Wiesbaden, Germany of Latvian parents. The protégé of noted wildlife photographer and activist Olegas Truchanas, his photographs of the Tasmanian Wilderness brought images of once remote and inaccessible areas of the state into the public realm. Dombrovskis founded West Wind Press in 1977 and later went on to print calendars entirely of his own work featuring incisive commentary from pre-eminent environmental professionals.

Peter's most famous photograph was Morning Mist, Rock Island Bend which was taken on the Franklin River. Due to the Franklin River dam controversy, some commentators believe the use of this photograph played a part in the victory for Bob Hawke in the 1983 federal election.

Peter's works are represented at the National Gallery of Victoria, the Tasmanian Museum and Art Gallery, the Australian Heritage Commission and in private collections. Peter was inducted into the International Photography Hall of Fame in 2003. He is the only Australian photographer to have achieved this honour.

In 1996, at the age of 51, Peter died of a heart attack while photographing near Mount Hayes in the Western Arthurs mountain range of South West Tasmania.

Judy Eason, Claude McCarthy Award

Although not a photographer herself, Judy is married to former AIPP president Ross Eason and thus threw herself wholeheartedly on a volunteer basis into the organisation of the first Nikon AIPP Event held. It was so successful that Judy was brought back for the next Events. Together they made a great contribution to the Institute throughout the Tensies of the twenty-first century.

Ross Eason, APP.L, M.Photog. HON.FAIPP, Hon. LM

Ross Eason joined the IAP in 1984 and was active on the NSW Council from 1985 until 1989, which included a year as state president. After fifteen years working in Sydney, Ross moved to Queensland in 1991 where he established his studio, Eason Creative, catering for resort tourism and property development. Ross was co-opted onto the National Board in 2009. He established a national conference, The Nikon Event. He was elected National President in 2014. During his term as President, the Board as a team introduced the merging of AIPP and ACMP; and The Reflections Project, honouring our World War II Veterans.

Robert Edwards, APP.L, Hon. FAIPP

Robert Edwards began his career at Australian Capital Television in Canberra and went on to attain a BA (Visual Arts) at the University of South Australia. He joined the AIPP in 1992 and was also active in the ACMP. A Sydney based commercial photographer and early proponent of digital, Robert is passionate about education and raising standards. He was a contributor to the Universal Photographic Digital Imaging Guidelines and chief author of the Australian Photographic Digital Imaging Guidelines. Robert presented several workshops on managing digital archives for the AIPP and ACMP as well as PICA, PMA and tertiary institutions.

Robert joined the National Board in 2007 and was elected National President in 2010. He managed the constitutional changes surrounding membership categories. He further developed the Accredited Professional Photographer and the Continuing Professional Development Program and the resulting benefit is the certification of AIPP Accredited Professional Photographer.

Robert also served on the constitutional committee, represents the AIPP at Standards Australia and the International Organization for Standardization on ISO, Technical Committee 42. In 2016 he was made and Honorary Fellow.

Peter Eastway, GM.Photog. Hon.FNZIPP Hon.FAIPP, FAIPP

After qualifying as an accountant, in 1984 Peter Eastway joined the photographic magazine company Iris Publishing as a writer before becoming an editor and shortly after, the group managing editor. The company's titles included Professional Photography magazine. Peter joined the Institute in 1985 and he won the Illustrative Photographer of the Year award in 1986. In the following year, he achieved his Associateship, was invited to join the APPA judging panel and was awarded the Kodak Professional Achievement Award.

He was elected to Federal Council in 1986. After Iris Publishing was taken over, Peter left to start publishing on his own and in 1992 began producing the Profitable Photography newsletter. This was later renamed the Working Pro. Through has publications and his numerous seminars around Australia and overseas, Peter has disseminated his deep knowledge of the craft and business management of photography to thousands.

Peter has become one of the top award winning photographers in Australia. He has twice won the Australian Professional Photographer of the Year Award and served as chair of the Canon APPA awards from 2006 to 2009.

Max Farrell, Hon. FAIPP

Max became a full time self-employed photographer after his discharge from the Royal Australian Navy. He initially photographed wedding and then later started freelancing for The Australian Women's Weekly. On the commercial front, his advertising clients included clients such as B.H.P, Tube makers, Chrysler (later

Mitsubishi) and the Adelaide Steamship Co.

In 1952 Max joined The Professional Photographers Association (PPA) in South Australia and served on the executive for many years. In 1963 he was elected president of the South Australian Division of P.P.A. and in 1964 represented South Australia in Melbourne at the formation of the Institute of Australian Photography. Max was thus a foundation and executive member of the Institute. In 1974 and 1975 Max became the forth elected national president and represented the Institute to the government on the issue of metrication.

He was also on the Education Panel at the South Australian Institute of Technology and played an important part in establishing a course for photographic technicians which became a diploma course in photography. Max died in 2012.

Katrina Ferguson, APP AAIPP Claude Mccarthy Award

Katrina achieved her Diploma of Applied Photography in 2008 from TAFE and joined the AIPP as a student. Katrina became an emerging member in 2009, a full member in 2012 and achieved the level of Associate. Kat served as an active member of the APPA Event Team, one of the leaders prominent in the training of volunteers and explaining the importance of getting the right print ready for judging. Even after marriage and three children, Katrina continued to participate as a valued team member on bump-in day and judging.

Denny Field, Hon.LM

Denny Field worked for the Government Weapons Research Establishment and later for the CSIRO as a scientific photographer. He attended the foundation Newport in 1965 and was a keen advocate of the Institute to his fellow government photographers.

Mark Fitz-Gerald, Hon. FAIPP

A South Australian medical photographer, Mark's contribution to the photographic industry and arts sector includes being South Australian state president in 1993 and 1994 and national president from 1995 to 1997.

Following two years as chairman of the AIPP Board and involvement with the campaign for copyright reform for photographers, Mark became a board member of the visual arts copyright agency

Viscopy. He became subsequently chair and in this capacity Mark was involved in the major campaigns on resale rights for visual artists, the extension of copyright from 50 to 75 years after the death of the artist and equitable secondary rights returns from all forms of published content. Also during his time as chair, Mark oversaw the transition of the Viscopy budget from substantially funded to break-even as the funding periods wound up.

Mark is the co-editor and producer of the IMVS Pathology Newsletter which has a target audience of clinicians. He is also the editor and producer of The Handbook which is an international publication in local language for training technicians in low income countries in the diagnosis of TB.

He has also been a speaker at numerous photographic and medical conferences and in 1996 Mark was awarded the PICA Inaugural Gold Tripod for a long and outstanding contribution to the industry.

Peter Foeden, M. Photog. Hon.FAIPP, FAIPP

During the 1970's and 1980's, whenever photographers came together to discuss portrait photography technique, the most frequently mentioned name was Peter Foeden. Peter was a Melbourne photographer born in Holland in 1930.

After arriving in Australia and first starting a career in physical education, Peter turned to photography in 1960. He rapidly built a reputation as an outstanding photographer. He was a Member of State and Federal Council for several years and served as both State and Federal president. His most lasting legacy was the introduction of the Awards. He was the chair of the committee to design the Awards system, worked as a judge for many years and spent five years as chair of the jurors.

He was the Wedding Photographer of the Year in 1982 and has presented dozens of one and two day seminars as well as filling many speaking engagements at professional photography conventions in Australia and New Zealand. His photographs have been accepted by the Professional Photographers of America Loan Collection and exhibited at the Kodak Pavilion at Photokina.

He sold his studio in 1985 and five years later sold his shares in

Nulab. Peter also started the key wedding album supply company Albums Australia which he sold in 2002.

Val Foreman, M. Photog. Hon.FAIPP, FAIPP

Val Foreman was a leading Melbourne commercial photographer who played a key role in the development of the Institute. He was the third person to be elected as national president and served the Institute for one of its longest terms: covering the years 1970 to 1973.

Val Foreman died in January 1989 and Neil Murray, editor of Professional Photography, described him as 'having most of the better qualities we look for in a human being. So many of us received far more than we gave in our dealings with him. He dealt only in the big picture, rarely thinking on a local scale. It mattered not that he lived in Melbourne, his work for the AIPP encompassed Australia, and his photography at times covered the world.

'The Institute was always close to him and he was always ready for a chat, to give advice, to expound a point of view, to push a colleague or the AIPP further. His financial counselling and often direct help made sure friends as well as the Institute came out on the right side of the ledger. His was a gregarious personality, quick-witted and had golf as a passion.'

Sudershan Gajree, OAM, FBIPP, Hon.FRPS, Hon.EFIAP, Hon.FAIPP

Sudershan 'Palli' Gajree first studied photography in England, where he was named best student and awarded the final prize of excellence. His lecturing began in Kenya in 1963 before joining Swinburne University in 1973 where he stayed until his retirement in 1995.

He is a much published author on topics as diverse as studio portraiture, wildlife photography and the history of photography in Kenya. In 1989 he was awarded the Order of Australia for services to photography. His contribution to photography was also made in India and Kenya.

His work has been exhibited around the world and is included in permanent collections in Queensland, America, and Great Britain.

John Gollings, AM, Hon. FAIPP

John Gollings holds a master's degree in architecture from RMIT University. However, in the 1960s he branched into fashion and advertising photography as well as covering tours of pop bands such as the Rolling Stones and Bob Dylan.

Returning to architecture, he developed a unique style of architectural photography and became recognised as an international leader in the field. John's work has been published in numerous books and his work is held in in significant national and international collections.

In 2016, John was made a Member of the Order of Australia (AM) for 'significant documentation of iconic architectural landmarks in Australia and the Asia Pacific region.'

Kate Gerahty, HON, FAIPP

Kate Gerahty is a five times Walkley winner and works for the Sydney Morning Herald andThe Age newspapers. Her first assignment for the Herald was to cover the 2002 Bali bombings. Since then, Kate has covered numerous stories of conflict and natural disaster around the world. In the course of getting the picture, Kate has been tasered and jailed by the Israelis. But in spite of this, as usual, Kate managed to get her pictures away.

Robert Gatto, Hon.FAIPP

A former ship's photographer, Robert Gatto is the managing director of Kayell Australia, a leading supplier of photographic equipment materials to the professional photography and graphic arts industries.

Robert has taken an active role in organising photographic workshops and seminars for professional photographers for both his own company and the industry. He was the organiser of the last ever Digital Show. In his role with the industry body IDEA he worked on the last combined trade show.

IBambi Gosbell, Claude McCarthy Award

Bambi was brought up a third-generation member of a photography enthusiast family and in 2005 she became a professional photographer specialising in portraits and business branding.

Based at her regional property just outside Gympie, all her shoots take place on location. Bambi was an active member of the Queensland Council and volunteered considerable time to assist with AIPP conferences and seminars and sponsor relations for project such as the Nikon AIPP Event.

Alice Gray, Hon. FAIPP

The daughter of iconic photographer, Richard Bennett, Alice is a Tasmanian photographer who quickly established herself with a formidable reputation in her own right. Apart from her prize-winning wedding and portrait photography, Alice has had many successful exhibitions and her photographs have been purchased as corporate and hotel décor.

Alice's publications include Country Houses of Tasmania and Living in History, coffee table books on beautiful historic Tasmanian properties, both published by Allen and Unwin. Bream Creek Farmers Market the Cookbook, and Africa. Alice served on the Tasmania council and became the youngest National President of the AIPP ever elected. Alice is now specialising in food photography, commercial portraiture and editorial work.

Robert Gray, Hon.FAIPP

Robert Gray played a key part in the Institute's affairs for decades. He began straight from school as a cadet photographer in 1969 at The Age and was with the newspaper group until 1976. He became picture editor of the Sunday Press and was the 1975 winner of the Best Action Picture (football) and winner of the Best Action Picture (cricket) in the following year.

Robert went onto to work in fashion in Hong Kong and then in advertising and corporate work around Asia until 1979. In 1978: he was one of a team of Official Photographers to produce the book for

The Edmonton Commonwealth Games.

Moving back to Melbourne Australia in 1980 he formed with Ian McKenzie, McKenzie Gray and Associates before moving to Cairns in 1987 at the start of the North Queensland tourism boom where his clients were mostly hotels, resorts and tourism companies. He also covered assignments in Papua New Guinea as well as returning to Melbourne to service his existing clients.

Robert also served as president of the Victorian Division, a national president, national chair and was one of the team that incorporated the Institute into a national body.

Tim Griffith, GM. Photog., FAIPP

Tim Griffith is a world leader in architectural photography. Born in Melbourne in 1961, Tim studied photography at the Royal Melbourne Institute of Technology. On graduating in 1983, he started working freelance from Richard Millott and Associates studio in St. Kilda. In 1985, Tim established his own company.

Tim has won the Australian Professional Photography Awards Commercial category thirteen times, as well as the Illustrative category once and in 1995 was the Australian Professional Photographer of the Year. Tim was the International Architectural Photographer of the year in 2005 and 2006, and became an AIPP Grand Master of Photography in 2007.

Tim has delivered talks and workshops at AIPP National and State events. He is a popular and insightful speaker and someone who will always take the time to listen and advise emerging photographers about the subtle art of light, form and function and how these relate to architectural photography.

Tim's architectural photography has taken him around the world and in 2002 Tim established an office in San Francisco where he continues to work worldwide on commissions for leading architectural and design firms.

Geoff Harrisson, Hon.LM

On leaving school Geoff went to work for Kodak as a film processor and t hen as a printer. After national service in the navy he went to work in 1957 f or J. Barry Laurance Studio as a social photographer. Geoff purchased the Hobart studio in 1959. In 1962 he joined the Institute of Victorian Photographers.

Geoff spent 15 years on state council as a newsletter editor, president, convention convenor and federal delegate. During the 1980s Geoff presented numerous workshops around Australia. In

1985, he made a presentation to the London Portrait Group.

Geoff was part of the TAFE Advisory Committee in 1989 and his articles have appeared in the Leica Historical Society of America's Viewfinder and in the Journal of the Australian Photographic Collectors Society.

Ian Hawthorne, M. Photog. Hon.FAIPP, FAIPP

Born in 1925, Ian Hawthorne was a Victorian photographer who left school the day he turned 14. Despite his lack of a formal education he went on to write 22 books, became a regular contributor to Professional Photography magazine and was an in-demand mentor to Australian photographers for more than 30 years

As a youth Ian became interested in photography and built his own enlarger. However, it was not until he turned 31 that he decided to become a professional photographer. In 1956 Ian attended a Kodak demonstration on colour photography and whilst many who attended dismissed the process as too complicated, Ian went ahead and consequently became one of the first colour studios in Australia.

This led to Kodak inviting him to give talks and share his knowledge and experience with other photographers... a mentoring activity which was to continue for the next 28 years

Ian Hawthorne joined the Institute in 1961. After he sold his business in 1986, he presented numerous talks around the country. A late night accident whilst he was driving home from an interstate talk almost took his life and this curtailed much of his further activities.

Ian first entered APPA in 1977, gaining three silvers at his first attempt. Within three years he became a Master of Photography. He then became a member of the APPA committee and in 1996 was elected as chair of APPA.

After losing a fight with cancer, Ian died in 2010, aged 84.

Peter Hay, Hon.LM

Born in 1934, Peter was a photographer with nearly fifty years of wedding and studio experience in both Canberra and Goulburn. While at his studio in Goulburn, Peter also shot everything from fashion to footage of news events for the local television stations. After returning to Canberra, he became a CSIRO photographer until his retirement.

Throughout his long career, Peter was strongly associated with the Institute, firstly with the Professional Photographers Association of Australia and then as a founding member of the Institute. He was a former president of the ACT Division, a regular judge on the Awards panel and worked for many years on the Federal Council. For his long contribution to the profession, Peter was made an Honorary Life Member.

Tony Hewitt, Hon FAIPP GM.Photog. Fellow, FNZIPP

Tony's career highlights feature over 150 state, national and international photography awards. He was Western Australian Professional Photographer of the Year 2004 and also in 1994. Tony Hewitt's photographic journey has seen him explore the genres of The Institute's Honours: A Who's Who of the Profession's Achievers Portrait, Landscape, Wedding and Fine Art Photography. He has exhibited both within Australia and Overseas, and has been invited to judge both nationally and internationally since 1995.

In 2010 he exhibited jointly in the exhibition "52 weeks on – the Pilbara Project", and featured in the publication of the same name. More recently he was an integral part of the South West Light Project and Exhibitions.

As a professional speaker and presenter Tony also has a broad skill set in the areas of personal and interpersonal communication and presents on subjects as diverse as rapport and personal awareness, often utilising his amazing images to illustrate various aspects of his message. A qualified Master Practitioner of Neuro Linguistic Programming, he has also co-authored a series of nine books, which stimulate and service the growing demand for information in the area of lifestyle and well-being.

Robyn Hills, M. Photog.IV, FAIPP

A highly innovative and motivated photographer, Robyn works in portraiture, landscapes and art photography. Passionate about photography and life, Robyn has a long list of solo exhibitions of her art and landscape photography and lectures to professional photographers as well as writing for several magazines.

Being one of the early pioneers of boudoir glamour photography in Australia, Robyn has developed a unique blend of all of her skills to achieve these looks that are contemporary and beautiful.

Success for Robyn is about how happy she is doing the things she wants to in life: going for a walk, playing the piano, flying a helicopter, adventure travel to Africa or Antarctica, being a property developer, enjoying her clients and business. All of this and constantly learning new techniques keeps Robyn at the forefront of the profession. Robyn has won the title of 'Australian Professional Photographer of the Year'

Greg Hocking, M. Photog. FAIPP, Hon FAIPP

In 1979 Greg Hocking was a student member of the Institute whilst studying for an Advanced Diploma of Photography at Mt Lawley TAFE. In the early 1980s he established Hocking Photography, serving design and architectural clients.

In the early 1990s Greg began exhibiting his fine art landscape work. His images have been and continue to be exhibited in many solo and group exhibitions, as well as published worldwide. Greg is highly sought after as a speaker for seminars and workshops on landscape and fine art photography.

In 2005 Greg was appointed a Hasselblad Master, the first photographer in Australia to receive this international award. He also won Australian Landscape Photographer of the Year.

For nearly three decades Greg served the Institute in important roles. In 1984 he held positions on the West Australian Division Council including president. Greg was elected to the National Board in 1993 and served for ten years.

He became AIPP National President in 1997. Greg was also the joint chair of the AIPP/ACMP copyright committee. In 2000 Greg was recalled to the board to serve another term as chair.

Ian Howell, Claude McCarthy Award

A onetime executive director of the Institute, Ian has had a long and passionate involvement with photography and photographers. A skilled businessman, Ian gave lectures both in Australia and New Zealand to help photographers improve their business practices.

Over many years he assisted many members to develop and enhance their businesses and in recognition of this Ian was presented with the Claude McCarthy Award.

Fran Howlett, M. Photog, Claude McCarthy Award

Fran's love of photography started when she was very young and shared a darkroom with her father in the family garage. She later studied and obtained a Diploma of Applied Science in Photography before embarking on a fulltime career as a photographer in Western Australia.

As a board member, in 2005 Fran took on the job of updating the Institute's website and in recognition of this was presented with the Claude McCarthy Award.

Owen Hughes, M. Photog. FAIPP

Born in 1940, Owen Hughes was raised on a small farm in Tasmania. Owen began photography as a hobby, but faced by the rural depression of the 1960s he gambled on a full-time career.

He established a business in Launceston in 1969 but was forced to photograph his subjects in natural surroundings because he could not afford a studio. Owen now believes this was a blessing in disguise because he developed an innovative style which has lead to his publishing several photographic books on Tasmania.

One of the Institute's first Masters of Photography, Owen went on to be Australian Wedding Photographer of the year in 1986 and 1987. He has also won Australian Landscape Photographer of the year. He has served for several years on the Council of the Tasmanian Division, and has enthusiastically taken part in the organisation of workshops in the State.

Robert Imhoff, M. Photog. Hon.FAIPP, FAIPP

Rob Imhoff is a Melbourne photographer who after studying photography at RMIT commenced a career with Brian Brandt and Associates in 1969. He soon created both a European and American client base as well as a network of clients throughout Australasia.

Rob made a dramatic input at the first judging of the Institute's awards in 1977 by scoring four Gold Award prints to handsomely win him the Ilford Trophy for the highest scoring entry. Rob went on to win t he Ilford Trophy again in the following year with four more Gold Awards and became the Institute's first Master of Photography. In 1987, he won the Institute's portrait category, and in 2003 he won the Australian Advertising Photographer of the Year. Rob opened his Lighthouse Gallery in 1982 with an exhibition of work by the renowned American portrait photographer, Arnold Newman.

Rob made an early transition to directing television commercials in which capacity he has won many awards, including the Australian Television Award for Professional Excellence in the category of Visual Effects in 1981, the Television Society of Australia Award in 1983 for Photography and Art Direction, and a CLIO Award for international television and cinema.

Marianne Irvine, Hon LM

In 1994 Marianne Irvine was one of APPA chair Doug Spowart's first student helpers. As part of the APPA event team, Marianne joined Ruby Spowart in coordinating the logistics and began a long term commitment to the Awards and played an integral part of behind the scenes management.

Marianne was a valued member of the Queensland council from 1996 until 2000, and again from 2004 until 2009. Her roles included Queensland Vice President, compiling the Queensland AIPP newsletter and helping with the Queensland Awards. In 2010, Marianne and her husband retired to a rural property near Toowoomba.

Dave Jarvis, Hon.LM

Dave Jarvis was a Kodak professional division sales representative who gave unstintingly of his time in order to assist the promotion and organisation of events for the Queensland division of the Institute.

Stephen Jones, GM. Photog. Hon.LM

Since the 1970s, Stephen Jones has worked as a portrait, commercial and event photographer based in Brisbane. In both 2006 and 2007 he won Australian Editorial Photographer of the Year for his portrait images. In 2008, Stephen won Australian Documentary Photographer of the Year and was the eleventh photographer to earn the title, Grand Master of Photography.

Stephen has applied his extensive knowledge of website construction to assist the Institute and he has been a judge at the Australian and Queensland Professional Photography Awards since 1996.

In 2011, Stephen was made an Honorary Life member of the Australian Institute of Professional Photography for his services to mentoring and teaching newer and younger photographers.

Attila Kiraly, Hon.LM, FAIPP

Attila Kiraly was a survivor of the 1956 Hungarian Revolution and throughout the sixties, seventies and eighties he ran Attila Studios in Canberra. In that time he photographed politicians, diplomats, businessmen and the citizens of Canberra. Utilising many of the thousands of photographs of his beloved Australian outback, he presented a staggering audio visual of these photographs at the Institute's National Convention in Canberra in 1975 involving 24 projectors and surround sound, on a 12x3 metre screen. He received a standing ovation. He published a book of his Red Centre photographs titled Australia, The Land of Lies in 1977.

He photographed the construction of the new Parliament House in Canberra from a fixed time lapse camera of his own design bolted onto the communications tower on Mt Ainslie. An engineering background enabled him to develop a laser triggering system which would only allow the camera to take shots when the tower, which swayed in the wind, was in the correct position. His photographs of the construction are now in Australian historical collections.

He served for many years on divisional and federal councils, and was federal vice president of the Institute in 1975 and 1976. Called Tilly by his friends, in 1975 he was made one of the two first Fellows of the Institute and was awarded Honorary Life Membership in 1980. On his retirement, for personal reasons, he returned to Hungary.

Leon Kozyrski, Hon. LM

Leon began his career in photography in London in 1967 before moving to Geraldton, Western Australia. There he worked as a photographer and manager of a family photographic studio and in 1972 began work as a photographer and cinematographer with the Audio-Visual Education Centre in Leederville.

In 1977, Leon was shooting weddings and portraits on the weekend and in the following year he became a lecturer at the Mt. Lawley Technical College. Leon worked closely with the AIPP on how courses were developed for the photographic profession.

Philip Kuruvita, G.M. Photog. FAIPP, FNZIPP

Born in England in 1959, Philip Kuruvita's family migrated first to Sri Lanka in 1968 and then seven years later on to Australia. In 1985 Phil studied at the Sydney Institute of TAFE's Certificate of Photography course before marrying Vicki and moving to Launceston, Tasmania. In 1989 the couple started Philip Kuruvita Photography.

He has served on the Institute's board as chair, 2006-2008; president, 2004-2006 and vice-president, 2001-2004. Philip has a regular schedule of exhibitions of his work with 15 solo exhibitions Including five 'Faces of Launceston' projects, inclusion in the M.I.L.K book and exhibition in New York, and has been involved in a number of books: the latest on Tamar Valley Pantry, will be published in 2013. He has been named Tasmanian Professional Photographer of the Year in 1999, 2004, 2006, 2007 and in 2010. Philip has been asked to speak at numerous events around Australia about his photography and at the Wedding and Portrait Photographers' International conference in Las Vegas.

Vicki Kuruvita, Claude McCarthy Award

Vicki Kuruvita was born in 1959, spending her childhood in Albury, NSW before moving to Sydney to study at the University of New South Wales. Graduating with a Bachelor of Architecture, in 1986 she married photographer Philip Kuruvita and moved to Tasmania where she worked on designing the new Launceston General Hospital.

After the birth of her children Vicki became an integral part of the family photography business. Vicki helped on Institute matters, supporting Phillip when he was on the federal board and giving her time to assist in the smooth running of conventions and award events. For her great contribution to the Institute, Vicki was awarded the Claude McCarthy Award.

John Lamb, HON FAIPP

John Lamb was a friend but a professional rival of fellow press photographer Bruce Postle when they were working together at The Age. Lamb had come to the newspaper via the office mail room in 1954, whereas Postle joined as a photographer.

Michael Smith, a former editor of The Age, said Lamb and Postle, along with some of their peers at The Herald and Weekly Times, "redefined press photography when the doomsayers were saying television would kill still pictures. They took pictorial creativity to new levels".

Both men won many awards: Lamb took 22, including two

Walkley's. Postle left The Age in 1996, Lamb a year later. Some of their photographs are imprinted on the national consciousness, such as Lamb's 1978 snap of a uniformed escort inadvertently saluting a woman as she walked past while the Governor left Parliament House.

Mike Langford, M. Photog. FAIPP, Hon FNZIPP

Mike Langford was born in Christchurch, New Zealand but since the nineties has been a true trans-Tasman photographer with representation in both countries. His strong, evocative pictorial imaging and his specialisation in both travel and location photography has achieved for him an enviable reputation for creativity.

Mike has been involved in many book projects on New Zealand, China, Korea and Japan. All of these have been hallmarked by his artistic vision and meticulous attention to detail.

He has been in much demand as a speaker and an Awards judge, both in Australia and in New Zealand. He is an astute and articulate observer who possesses the ability to freely share his knowledge with fellow photographers and is currently serving as national president of the NZIPP.

Susen Lewis, M. Photog. Hon. LM

Based in Queensland, Sue Lewis commenced her involvement with APPA as a student in 2001 and became leader of the Awards Event team. Like her predecessors, David Puddefoot and Craig Bassett, Sue has given up enormous amounts of time to ensure the smooth running of the Awards. In recognition of her dedication to this event, Sue was made an Honorary Life Member.

Sue has also served as the chair of the AIPP Education Sub-committee and runs her own wedding and portrait business in Toowoomba.

Lord Patrick, Lichfield Hon FAIPP

Lord Lichfield was educated at Harrow and Sandhurst, and joined the Grenadier Guards in 1959. On leaving the Army in 1962, he began to work as a photographer's assistant, and built up his own reputation, partly as a result of having access to the Royal Family. He was selected to take the official photographs of the wedding of the Prince and Princess of Wales in 1981, and subsequently became one of the UK's best-known photographers.

In 1999 he adopted digital photography and was chosen by the Queen and the Duke of Edinburgh to take official pictures of her Golden Jubilee in 2002. Lichfield made several trips to Australia to share his knowledge of photography and support for the Awards. In 2005, Lichfield suffered a major stroke, and died the following day, aged 66.

William Long, M.Photog. Hon LM

Speaker, mentor and educator; William Long is one of Australia's most successful and technically diverse professional photographers. He has been recognised for his excellence in photography with Fellowships from the British Institute of Professional Photography (BIPP) and the Royal Photographic Society (RPS). He has also served as Vice National President of both the AIPP and the ACMP.

Born in Rochford, Essex, from the age of six William trained as a classical ballet dancer. By his twenties he was touring the world's stages as a principal dancer with The Scottish Ballet, including performances with industry greats such as Rudolf Nureyev and Margot Fonteyn. After a crippling back injury, his professional ballet career came to an unexpected and premature end, William focussed his on his other passion: photography.

William's photography has been featured in publications, such the New York Times, South China News and Time magazine; and he has also photographed many international artists including The Rolling Stones, Neil Diamond and Willem Dafoe.

Kylie Lyons, M.Photog, Hon.LM

Graduating from the University of Western Sydney in 1994 with a Bachelor of Design / Photo Media Major, Kylie commenced work shortly after at Amazing Faces in North Sydney. As a pre-press and graphic design studio, it was her job to set up a photography department, focusing on commercial photography. In 2000 Kylie established her own studio handling fine art portraits, weddings, food and commercial photography.

For the Institute, Kylie spent ten years on the New South Wales council, the last five as president. Kylie joined the National Board as vice president in 2010 and at the time of writing is serving as the national president.

Dr. David, Malin Hon.FAIPP

Dr Malin is a world renowned leader in astronomical photography and has made a significant contribution to astronomy generally. As a chemist, he took responsibility for all the photographic work at joint Anglo-Australian facilities within Australia developing techniques for photography in low light levels when exposures in the order of one hour are very much the norm. To do this involves long and complex procedures of hypersensitisation in nitrogen and hydrogen gas to minimise low light level reciprocity failure. David has been extraordinarily successful at doing this and has single-handedly developed a whole series of techniques for enhancing and combining photographs to produce results much better than even the best single photographs can yield.

David has been recognised for his work with the award of Honorary Doctor of Science by Sydney University, being made chair of the International Astronomical Union's Working Group on wild field imaging, and as an Honorary Fellow of the Australian Institute of Professional Photography.

Malcolm Mathieson, M. Photog. Hon.FAIPP

Malcolm Mathieson was born in Bairnsdale where he started at an early age taking wedding photographs. When he was 18 he worked as a cine cameraman for Channel Ten but when television went to electronic news gathering, Malcolm turned to stills and bought a photography studio in Orange, New South Wales which he ran for over a decade.

Shortly after joining the Institute in 1986, he joined first the New South Wales and then the Federal Council and became president in 1991.

In the early nineties Malcolm was one of the first Australian photographers to adopt the style of wedding photography reportage. He then lectured and taught other professionals in New Zealand, The USA, Canada, UK, Spain, Italy, Belgium, Ireland and elsewhere in the art of reportage photography. At the time of writing, Malcolm is the only person in the Southern Hemisphere to be elected as president of the World Council of Professional Photography.

Although most of his work is in wedding and portraiture, he has a much wider interest in photography, from an exhibition and book on the people of Bairnsdale, to award-winning landscapes.

Grant Matthews, Claude McCarthy Award

In 2013, Grant Matthews is one of Australia's pre-eminent photographers and has photographed celebrities from the Prime Minister of Australia to Russell Crowe, Kylie Minogue and Nicole Kidman.

Grant's photographs have appeared in numerous publications, including Vogue (Australia, USA, UK & Italy), Harpers Bazaar (Australia & Italy), Elle (Australia, France & Japan), InStyle (Australia & UK), Grazia (Italy), and his advertising clients include Bloomingdales, J Crew, Karl Lagerfeld, Yohji Yamamoto, and Givenchy.

He has directed about 40 music videos for performers such as Tina Arena, INXS, Ice House, Kylie Minogue, Wendy Matthews, and directed around 100 commercials for clients as diverse as MasterCard, Ikea, Colgate Palmolive, Unilever, Arnott's, Goodman Fielder and Ray Ban.

He has won numerous awards in Australia and overseas, including a prestigious D & AD award in England. An IKEA commercial he directed was short listed with five other commercials as the best commercial produced in Australasia in 2002. At his company, Mondo Digital, Grant acts as mentor to young photographers within that business.

Graham McCarter, Hon.FAIPP

Born in England in 1940 and educated in Edinburgh, after leaving school Graham McCarter studied accountancy. However, the subject lost its appeal and in 1961, Graham studied photography at Guilford Art College in Surrey, turned freelance in 1964 and worked in London.

In 1966, Graham emigrated to Australia and became an ABC TV photographer and shortly after as a portrait and travel photographer for Gareth Powell Publications. In 1968 Graham returned to the UK, photographing for the charity Shelter and his photographs appeared in the Sunday Times and Observer colour magazines. Discovering the joy of teaching Graham became the senior lecturer at St Albans College, Hertfordshire and the Medway College of Design.

In 1973 Graham returned to Australia where he became actively involved with the Australian Centre for Photography as well as becoming the official photographer for the Rolling Stones tour of Australia and New Zealand. Graham also began working in advertising photography and his clients included Cathay Pacific, Thai, Malaysian and Qantas airlines, Coca Cola, IBM and Optus.

In 2002, Graham returned to photographic education with the commencement of the Blue Mountains Photography Workshops.

David McCarthy, OAM, Hon.FAIPP, Hon.L.M.

The son of Institute founder, Queenslander Claude McCarthy, David was born and raised in the profession. He also had the same energy and commitment to the concept of building a stronger Institute to develop the standards of professional photography in Australia.

Following in his father's footsteps, David became president of the Institute in 1976. He was re-elected the following year and during his presidency, David helped steer the Awards from being a concept advocated by Peter Foeden and Max Townsend into reality.

As the master of ceremonies at the Awards Dinners, he was renowned for his quick wit and astute observations.

A Hasselblad Masters Award winner, judge of the AIPP Awards for 17 years and a panel chair for 15 years, chair of Federal honours committee for 2 years and in his capacity as Federal President of the IAP, represented Australia in 1976 at the official opening ceremony of the Professional Photographers Association of America national convention in Washington DC on the occasion of the USA centenary celebrations.

Like his father, David was honoured with the Order of Australia for his services to professional photography in 1995 and was also made an Honorary Life Member of the Institute. David is now retired and living in Tasmania.

Claude McCarthy, OAM, Hon.FAIPP, FAIPP

Claude McCarthy became generally known as the Father of the Institute. In 1944 he was a representative of professional photography in Queensland when he gathered with his peers from other states together to establish the body that became known as The Professional Photographers Association of Australia.

In the immediate post-war years, activity was considerable, but enthusiasm was on the wane when in 1963, Claude took over the presidency. He reactivated interest throughout Australia in a national body and in Melbourne, May 1964, the PPA of A. formally changed its name to The Institute of Australian Photographers, with Claude McCarthy as its inaugural president.

He held the president's office for six years and in the process nurtured the fledgling body through its formative struggles. He made one other great contribution to the Institute, his son David, who continued his father's work by becoming Institute president in 1976.

Claude McCarthy was awarded an Honorary Fellowship in 1968 and the Order of Australia on the Queen's birthday in 1976. Claude died on the 14th of September, 1993.

Robert McFarlane, HON FAIPP

Born in Adelaide in 1942, Robert has been capturing defining moments of Australian life for more than half a century. From his early work in the 1960s capturing the now iconic images of a young Indigenous activist Charlie Perkins, to the Beatles arriving in Australia, Robert went on to photograph many historical Australian moments, both big and small, over the subsequent decades. Prime ministers, film directors, go-go dancers, photographers, artists, surgeons, activists and workers, all have found themselves in front of Robert McFarlane's lens as he uniquely chronicled the changing face of Australia.

John McKay, Hon.FAIPP

John McKay's passion for photography began in childhood when his grandmother, a keen amateur photographer, gave him her Thornton Pickard half plate camera.

From 1953 to 1959 John operated a Brisbane commercial and portrait photography business, Craftsman Studios, with the assistance of his wife, Rosemary.

John's teaching career started in 1960 when he was appointed photographic instructor at the Central Technical College in Queensland. A fortuitous combination of changing times, industry support and John's foresight brought about by study tours through Europe and America, saw the college change its name to the College of Art. In 1979 John was promoted to Senior Lecturer, a position he held until his retirement from the college in 1988. John's students will be found in all disciplines of photography from studio to government departments.

He was education officer for the Queensland Division of the Institute from 1962 to 1966, and contributed to the development of Australian Film Television and Radio School's Graduate Diploma in Media from 1983 to 1984.

After his retirement, John McKay continued to teach photography and digital imaging part-time at QCA until 1998. He is now deceased.

Ian McKenzie, M.Photog.ll, Hon.FAIPP, FAIPP

Ian McKenzie was born in Melbourne in 1939 and spent two years in chartered accountancy before becoming a professional photographer in 1958. Ian specialised in architectural and industrial photography and was also active in aerial and corporate work for company reports. He is a travel junkie, mostly around South East Asia working on oil and gas pipelines.

A passionate educator, in 1966 Ian designed and oversaw construction of the photographic educational facilities at Prahran College, Melbourne, served as department head for two years and laid the pathway to its degree course, before the politics drove him back into full-time practice.

In 1959, Ian joined the Institute of Victorian Photographers, thus becoming a founding member of the Institute when it became a national body. Few, if any, could compare with Ian's long-term support of the Institute and only a part of his involvement is included here. He gained his Associateship in 1969, became Victorian Vice President in 1971 and Victorian President and a Federal delegate from 1972-75, being elected Federal Vice-President in 1976 and 77. In 1978 and 1979 Ian was Federal President. In 1980 and 81 he was chair of the Federal Executive. He was the convenor of the national biennial Hypo conventions from 1973 until 1977, convened the National Convention Photina 79 held in Sydney, and was co-convener of Photographics 81. He attained his Master of Photography in 1982.

He joined the Awards committee in 1976, and still serves as a judge and chair of APPA judging panels. From 1991 to 1998, Ian chaired the Federal Honours and Ethics Committee.

In 2006 he established and became chair of the AIPP Commercial Group, of which he is the current chair. He developed the syllabus and course materials for the AIPP National Mentoring Scheme, which he currently administrates.

Ian has also been a speaker at conventions both in Australia and New Zealand, has contributed many articles to the Institute's magazines and has been active in publishing books on Australian photographers.

Ron McKenzie, Hon. FAIPP

Ray began his career in 1944 as a photography cadet with the Sydney Daily Telegraph. During the next twenty years he photographed royal tours, as well as having the plum job of following the Australian cricket team as News Limited's official cricket photographer. He rose to become picture editor of The Australian, The Daily Mirror, and in 1969, the founding and only picture editor of Newsday.

He developed an outstanding reputation in the news industry and mentored numerous photographers that went on to build successful careers. In 1991 he ended his own career while serving as picture editor of Sydney's Daily Mirror.

David Moore, Hon.FAIPP

Born in 1927, David Moore became Australia's most renowned and widely travelled photojournalist. His extraordinary archive covers both his homeland and the many countries and subjects he visited over a sixty-year career.

Moore commenced his professional photographic career in Sydney with Russell Roberts' studio in 1947. Later he worked with Max Dupain before travelling to London in 1951. He was the first Australian photojournalist to work consistently for the international picture magazines during their heyday in the 1950s. For seven years he photographed on assignment in the UK, Europe, Scandinavia, Africa and the USA, and his work was published in such journals as The Observer, Time-Life, Look, The New York Times and Sports Illustrated. He was one of only two Australian photographers included in the Family of Man exhibition in New York in 1955.

From 1958 Moore travelled the world for his New York agency, Black Star, working for Time-Life Books, National Geographic and corporate industrial clients.

From the 1970s onwards Moore was based in Sydney and here his work reflected his views of Australia. His photographs have been published in many books and are in many Australian collections including those of the Australian National Gallery. Collections are also held at the New York Museum of Modern Art, Le Bibliothéque Nationale in Paris, and the Smithsonian Institution in Washington DC.

David died in 2003.

Jeff Moorfoot, M. Photog. Hon.LM, FAIPP

At various times Jeff Moorfoot has worked as a gravedigger, an oil rig worker, a market gardener, a production welder, a university lecturer and an advertising photographer.

With a twenty year background as a freelance commercial photographer, educator, and photo artist, Jeff has been a vice president of the Victorian Division of the Institute, a member of the national education subcommittee and convener of the Victorian Photography Student of the Year Awards. Jeff also founded the photographic group Free Radicals in 2000 and became the editor of the Free Radical Notes

A respected seminar speaker and judge at various photographic awards, he has now semi-retired from commercial practice and concentrates on teaching and developing his own personal work. Now in his late sixties, Jeff is currently the long serving festival director of the Ballarat Foto Biennale.

Julie Moss, HON FAIPP

Julie Moss is the managing director Melbourne's famous Photography Studies College and has more than thirty years of experience in the education and training sector in Australia.

During that time, she has frequently represented the interests of private education and training providers at the state, national and international levels.

She was a founding member of the Australian Council for Private Education and Training and served as a Board member and Chair of the National Board for a number of years. Julie is Chair of the National Education Committee of the AIPP (Australian Institute of Professional Photography).

She is passionate about photographic education and brings this passion and experience to her leadership of PSC. She is determined to ensure that PSC provides a place where students can learn to see the world anew and be nurtured to develop and achieve their full potential.

Neil Murray, Hon.FAIPP

In 1964, Melbourne advertising, industrial and commercial photographer Neil Murray joined the editorial committee of the Institute's magazine and became a regular editorial contributor. The magazine was given a new look and within a few years, Neil took over as editor. After the publisher, Gordon Hill retired, Neil also took on the role of publisher.

During his time as editor and publisher, Neil continued with professional assignments and an involvement with Preston College of TAFE as a teacher. He left TAFE in 1985 and became projects officer with the institute filling the gap between Ian Howell and Tim O'Daly.

In 1982, Neil tired of the dual role and the difficulties of being a single editor publisher, sold the magazine to Iris Publishing Company, but continued in his role as editor. In 1985, Neil asked to step down as editor and suggested Paul Burrows as his successor. Under this new arrangement, Neil continued contributing articles until 1995. Neil died in 2007 aged 80.

Gael Newton, Hon. FAIPP

Gael Newton is the Senior Curator of Australian and International Photography at the National Gallery of Australia in Canberra. From 1974 to 1985 Newton was the foundation curator of photography at the Art Gallery of New South Wales. Gael then moved to Canberra and from 1985 to 1988, was the visiting curator for the Bicentennial Photography Project at the NGA. During this period she researched and mounted the 900 work exhibition Shades of Light: Photography and Australia 1839-1988 and published the major Australian reference book in association with the exhibition. She also became the curator of Australian Photography at the NGA.

Gale has curated many historical and contemporary exhibitions and oversaw the establishment of a new significant collection within the National Gallery.

Gael Newton is also the author of the standard reference work on the history of Australian photography, Shades of Light: Photography and Australia 1838-1988 and monographs on Australian photographers such as Harold Cazneux, Max Dupain, John Kauffmann and Tracy Moffat. Gael wrote Silver and Grey: Fifty Years Of Australian Photography 1900–1950 and is a regular contributor to magazines.

Adrian Nicholson, Hon.LM

Adrian Nicholson commenced his photography business in Longreach, Queensland, in 1973, and joined the Institute in 1979. He moved his business to Ipswich in 1983, and was co-opted onto the Queensland Divisional Council in 1984. In 1985 he was elected treasurer and introduced computerised record keeping to the division. In 1986 he was elected state secretary as well as treasurer. He held these positions through to 1989 at which time he was elected Queensland vice president.

In 1990 he was elected to the position of state president, an office which he held until 1992. In 1990 he was also selected as a National Print awards judge, was the convenor of the Divisional Convention, and was elected State Delegate to the Federal Council, a position he held for four years. Prior to Incorporation he spent considerable time on suggestions for revisions to the new draft Articles of Association - a majority of which finished up in our current Articles. For these outstanding contributions Adrian Nicholson was made an Honorary Life Member.

Kevin O'Daly, M. Photog. Hon.FAIPP

In 1968 Kevin began his photographic career as a public servant at the weapons research establishment in Adelaide, before in 1977 establishing his own large commercial studio complex in that city.

Kevin O'Daly has contributed greatly to the Institute. He was on the federal council for thirteen years, and helped forge the current strong links with other sectors of the photographic industry. In 1980 he became SA President before holding the following federal offices: South Australian Delegate 1982 - 1985; Federal Treasurer 1984 - 1987; Federal Vice President 1988 - 1990; Federal President 1991 and then in 1993, chairman of executive. Throughout this time he also served as a council member and divisional president in South

Australia.

One specific project instigated by Kevin was the introduction of the hardcover, yearly Awards Book. Kevin brought the proposal to Council and pushed it through. From modest beginnings in 1983, it has grown to the stage where it has a major sponsor and is an eagerly awaited publication on both sides of the Tasman.

On the Awards front, Kevin was the 2001 Advertising Photographer of the Year; the Commercial Industrial Photographer of the Year in 2002, 2003, 2004 and 2005. In 2005, Kevin was also the South Australian Professional Photographer of the Year.

David Oliver, GM. Photog. FAIPP

Emigrating from t he United Kingdom, David initially saw more of a financial future in being a courier rather than a photographer. He was eventually persuaded by his wife to give photography a try and he joined an established portrait studio shooting eighty sittings a week. While this taught David the essentials of both professional photography and people handling, it left David looking for more creative freedom in his approach to his subjects.

In 1986 David set-up his own wedding and portrait business in Sydney and thus gained full reign over his artistic process. His unique and distinctive style saw the business grow to quickly become of Australia's leading studios.

David has served the AIPP on various committees, including the APPA committee as well as being the NSW divisional president. David has won the Australian Wedding Photographer of the Year and is a three - time winner of the John Whitfield-King Award for reportage photography. Now, in addition to his running his practice, David lectures around the world and has acted as a source of inspiration for many.

Peter Owen, M.Photog. Claude McCarthy Award

Peter Owen is an award winning studio portrait photographer who with his wife established Lifeworks Photography in Melbourne. The studio has become well known for its natural and contemporary style and although Peter has had to retire due to ill health, the studio continues with an all female, award winning team led by his wife.

In recognition of his long term contribution to the Institute, Peter was presented with the Claude McCarthy Award.

Bryan Pascall, Hon.LM

Attending his first Federal Council Meeting as national secretary in March 1986, Bryan Pascall provided advice and support through the terms of four presidents, and four boards.

For his dedication and contribution to the Institute over ten years, the Institute awarded Bryan with an Honorary Life Membership.

David Paterson, M.Photog. Hon.FAIPP, Hon.LM, FAIPP

David is originally from Goulburn and moved to Canberra in the 1960s. He first started work at the Australian National University before transferring to the University of New South Wales. Now back at ANU as multimedia officer, David continues his long time involvement with the Institute's Awards.

David joined the Institute in 1985 and has been involved with the APPA awards for approaching twenty years. His roles have included deputy event team manager, deputy chair and since 2002, chair of jurors. He has coordinated the Award Book in 1996, 1999, and every year since 2002. Since 2010, David has been chair of the awards.

His participation in APPA has earned him a Master of Photography and three gold bars and in 2013 David won the Institute's ACT Professional Photographer of the Year Award.

Robert Piccoli, M.Photog. Hon FNZIPP, FAIPP,

Robert Piccoli has achieved a level of excellence and expertise that has won him awards from around the world. These include Fellow of the Institute of British Institute of Professional Photography, and Honorary Fellowship of the New Zealand Institute of Professional Photography and being a winner of D'Arcy Pforr Memorial Award.

For the last thirty years his portrait photography has become synonymous with sensitive inspirational images, impeccable craftsmanship and understated style. He brings empathy to every commission which allows the spirit and essence of each of his subjects to naturally emerge.

With his European sensibility he often lectures to fellow professionals and shares his passion and sincerity that only further enhance his already emotive works. The Piccoli Photographic studio is a converted warehouse space in inner city Melbourne Australia.

Ian Poole, Hon FAIPP

As a young man in 1972 Ian Poole partnered with another young photographer and began to make waves on the Brisbane weddings and portraits market. He joined the Institute in 1975 and was coo-opted onto the Queensland Council. He was a member of that Council for 22 years, holding the offices of Queensland President, vice president, secretary, treasurer, newsletter editor and education officer. He has been a judge or panel chair at the Queensland Awards since their inception in 1990.

In 1986 he was Australian Delegate to the World Photographic Conference in Cologne. In 1993 he was awarded the post-graduate degree of G.Dip Visual Arts from Griffith University . He was also awarded the title of Master Photographer of the New Zealand Institute of Professional Photography.

Bruce Postle, HON FAIPP

Born in 1940, Bruce Postle is one of Australia's greatest and most highly decorated photographers. For 50 years he has taken stunning pictures of Australian news, sport, entertainment, tragedy and the small moments in ordinary people's lives. He began his career when the new medium of television was threatening press photography's dominance of the visual news image. Postle helped lead the way for his generation of photographers to redefine the craft and prove that a picture could not only be worth a thousand words, but sometimes kilometres of videotape or gigabytes of digital data.

Bruce Pottinger, M.Photog, Hon.FAIPP, Claude McCarthy Award

Born in England and training as a camera repair technician, Bruce Pottinger emigrated from the UK to Australia to work in a specialist camera store.

In 1980, in partnership with Len Lindell, he formed L&P and opened a showroom in Sydney. The company became a leading importer and supplier of professional photographic products and following Len's retirement, Bruce became the sole managing director of L&P Digital Photographic,

Bruce worked closely with professional photographers and attended all photography events. For many years he was the vice president of the professional division of the Photo Imaging Council of Australia which represented photographic importers and mounted the annual industry photo show. Bruce served a long period as chair of the show and worked to improve relationships between photographers and their suppliers. In recognition of this, in 1995 the Institute presented Bruce with the Claude McCarthy Award.

This only fanned his passion for photography and after attending decades of professional photography lectures, he began to put this learning into practice. On entering the Awards, he became a prize winning photographer, gaining his masters and regularly gives talks and lectures to those wanting to learn more about photography.

Ian Poole, Hon FAIPP

As a young man in 1972 Ian Poole partnered with another young photographer and began to make waves on the Brisbane weddings and portraits market. He joined the Institute in 1975 and was coo-opted onto the Queensland Council. He was a member of that Council for 22 years, holding the offices of Queensland President, vice president, secretary, treasurer, newsletter editor and education officer. He has been a judge or panel chair at the Queensland Awards since their inception in 1990.

In 1986 he was Australian Delegate to the World Photographic Conference in Cologne. In 1993 he was awarded the post-graduate degree of G.Dip Visual Arts from Griffith University . He was also awarded the title of Master Photographer of the New Zealand Institute of Professional Photography.

David Puddefoot, Hon.FAIPP

The smooth running processes of the Awards event can be largely attributed to Melbourne photographer, David Puddefoot. Playing a key role in managing the Awards from 1979-2004, David was an extremely efficient organiser and handled the ever growing task of coordinating the judging process under the difficult conditions of temporary built judging rooms on the show floor.

His methods, calmness under pressure and good humoured demeanor set the standard for the teams that followed.

In addition to being awarded an Honorary Fellowship of the Institute, David received the Photo Imaging Council of Australia's highest award, the Gold Tripod, for his long and outstanding contribution to photography.

Laurie Rogers, Hon.LM

Laurie Rogers is a doyen of the camera service industry and has kept professional photographers' cameras going for generations. As a child Laurie had more cameras than conventional toys. He knew how and why they worked and could fix most things, well before reaching his teens.

Starting work in the repair section of RH Wagner and Sons in 1956, Laurie worked with European trained technicians and studied at RMIT. After thirteen years he left Wagner's and spent four years at Hanimex where he developed his managerial skills. He formed his own repair company, Camera Clinic, which is based in Melbourne and he has run with his family for the last 36 years.

Laurie has also designed and built cameras for specialist applications such as fingerprinting.

Chris Shain, HON. LM. AAIPP

Chris Shain began his career working as a photographer's assistant, including 10 years working alongside the Australian photographic icon David Moore. His photography has since been published widely in Australia and overseas. He has personal work in the Australian Photographers Collection and has been a finalist 3 times in the Head On portrait prize.

He has documented major infrastructure projects, produced high quality images for annual reports and capability brochures, as well as architectural photography of domestic housing, significant heritage structures and major public buildings. His heritage and architectural work have been used in a wide range of books and publications that are in major collecting institutions including the Historic Houses Trust, the National Trust and the NSW Supreme Court.

Chris was the first elected president of ACMP (Society of Advertising, Commercial and Media photographers), subsequent Chairman. He was a Director of the Australian Copyright Council for 8 years until 2014.

Rick Sherwin, M. Photog. Hon. FAIPP

Born in Canada in 1940, Rick worked at everything from a fur trapper to a bartender before moving to Australia. He graduated from Sydney TAFE in 1969 and joined the Institute in the following year. In 1970 he worked at Freeman Studios in 1971.

Rick started his own Sydney studio in 1982, photographing many of the city's business, political and society celebrities. Rick also was involved in organising many exhibitions of photography.

On the Institute front, he became the New South Wales president in 1974. Rick was Federal Delegate for two years and spoke at no less than 21 International, National and State Conventions and Open House Workshops over a sixteen year period. He has judged at the Australian Professional Photography Awards frequently and with distinction, as well as his own State Awards every year since their inception. He was the 1990 Wedding Photographer of the Year.

In 1995 Rick was honoured with an Honorary Fellowship. He moved to Noosa in 1997.

Ryan Schembri, GM.Photog, Hon. LM

Ryan Schembri photographed his first wedding at the age of 15 and has loved capturing people on their wedding day ever since. Throughout his more than sixteen-year career his passion has been to create images that don't just record the wedding day but capture and create images that become family heirlooms and works of art.

Throughout his career he has travelled the world to compete in photographic competitions, to judge photographic award prints and to speak and educate other photographers on the fundamentals of photography.

Wolfgang Sievers, AO Hon.FAIPP

Wolfgang Sievers was born in Berlin of Jewish parents in 1913 and studied at a progressive private art school. In 1938, he was retained as a teacher at the same school but heard of the school's imminent closure by the German authorities. He began preparations to escape, but was briefly questioned by the Gestapo, and then conscripted as an aerial photographer for the Luftwaffe. He fled the country immediately, going first to England before moving onto Australia.

On arrival he opened a studio in Melbourne, but after war was declared, he volunteered for the Australian Army and served from 1942 to 1946. Following demobilisation, he established a studio in Melbourne's fashionable Collins Street.

Wolfgang became a lifelong friend of fellow émigré photographer Helmut Newton and his Australian actress wife June Browne, who later made photographs herself under the pseudonym Alice Springs.

A valued member of the Institute, his significant corporate clients included Alcoa, Australian Paper Manufacturers, Comalco, Hamersley Iron, John Holland Group, John Lysaght, Shell and Vickers Ruwolt. He also received commissions from leading architectural firms.

In 1989, the Australian National Gallery staged a retrospective of his work, an exhibition which travelled around the country, often accompanied by Sievers' lectures. In 2000, he was the subject of a major retrospective exhibition held in Lisbon, Portugal at the

"Arquivo Fotografico Municipal de Lisboa". For his services to photography, he was appointed an Officer of the Order of Australia (AO) in 2002.

The National Library of Australia has an archive of more than 50,000 of Sievers' negatives and transparencies.

Wolfgang Sievers died died in Victoria in 2007 at the age of 93, a month short of his 94th birthday

Meaghan Simms, AAIPP. Hon.LM

Fascinated with photography from an early age, Meaghan completed a Diploma of Applied Photography at the North Melbourne Institute of TAFE in 2001. She then assisted several great photographers, including Bill Bachman, Ian Van der Wolde and David Williams, before making her mark in the advertising industry.

Meaghan was introduced to the APPA world by David Puddefoot in 2000 when she was a student. At her first APPA, she managed the judging rooms where a typical day started at six in the morning and often work ended with a pizza at midnight or later. Accommodation was at cheap backpackers, often a long way from the venue, and there was no budget for the comforts of life.

The APPA Event Team roughed it for very long hours at the back of the judging rooms where nobody is allowed to go, making sure that the prints kept coming in the right order, hour after hour and day after day. In 2004 Meaghan was invited to join the APPA committee where she has continued her work with David Paterson, Peter Eastway, Craig Bassett and Sue Lewis.

John Sinisgalli, Claude McCarthy Award

John Sinisgalli is a prominent lawyer based in Melbourne who has acted as the AIPP's lawyer since 2005. During that time, he has done a considerable amount of work on a pro bono basis for both the Institute and individual members.

In recognition of his long service and dedication to the AIPP, in 2106 the Institute honoured him with the Claude McCarthy Award.

Athol Shmith, OAM, FAIPP

Athol Shmith was born in Melbourne in 1914 and gained an early interest in photography. Supported by his family, Athol established a studio in St Kilda where he specialised in theatre work and society and wedding portraits. His approach won him a reputation and in the early 1930s gained the contract to take portraits of visiting celebrities for the newly formed Australian Broadcasting Commission.

Success followed and in 1939 he moved to a studio to Collins Street which he ran with the assistance of his brother and sister. Shmith's work expanded to include a range of commercial advertising and fashion clients and appeared in local society magazines. He exhibited his works in photographic salons at home and abroad, gaining a Fellowship of the Royal Photographic Society in 1933. At the age of just 19 he was appointed Vice-Regal Photographer in Melbourne. He long held the contract for stage and publicity photography for theatre producer J.C. Williamson.

Throughout the 1960s, Shmith remained energetic and dynamic in his development of fashion work, but by the close of the decade he took on roles in photographic heritage and education. In 1968 he helped to establish a photography department at the National Gallery of Victoria and in 1971 closed his business to take on a new role as head of the Photography Department at Prahran College of Advanced Education, on the same Prahran campus as is now occupied by Swinburne University of Technology. He taught there with his business partner John Cato and the film-maker Paul Cox. His support assisted the careers of students whom he closely mentored such as Sue Ford, Bill Henson, Carol Jerrems and Christopher Koller.

Ill health caused his retirement from the College in 1979. He was appointed a Member of the Order of Australia in the following year. The major holdings of his work can be found in the National Gallery of Victoria and the National Gallery of Australia. Athol died in 1990.

Anna Smith, O.B.E Hon.FAIPP

Anna Smith was one of the original members of the Institute who lived for 104 years before passing away in 2011.

She began photography at the age of 14 and her professional career spanned 63 years. During the Second World War, she managed her brother's photography studio in Young, NSW while her brother and husband went to war. Later, her husband's health suffered from war-inflicted problems and so it was up to Anna to support their only son. She opened a studio at Chermside Shopping Centre, and was president of the Queensland PPA, the first woman to hold a state presidency. It was during this time that she and presidents from other states agreed to form the Institute.

In 1978, Anna went to Buckingham Palace where Her Majesty, Queen Elizabeth II presented her with an OBE for service to the community and to photography. For many years she had also been a member of the United Nations and a supporter of UNICEF.

Heide Smith, Hon.FAIPP

Heide Soltsien was born in Germany, where her father was a graphic artist and designer. After an apprenticeship in photography which culminated in a diploma, Heide studied advertising, gaining a second diploma. After a spell as an industrial photographer, Heide worked as a photojournalist for four years until her marriage in 1963, travelling to England as Mrs Smith. In 1971 the Smith family emigrated to Australia, where Heide worked as a photojournalist and later in a professional colour laboratory. In 1978 the family moved to Canberra, where Heide established a studio, which she ran until 1997.

Since 1998, Heide and her husband Brian have lived in Narooma, a small fishing village in NSW. Heide continues to photograph families and celebrities, participate in exhibitions and competitions and has published thirteen books.

Heide has given workshops and seminars to professional photographers in most states in Australia and in China, Hong Kong, The Philippines, Holland, UK and Germany. In Australia the highlights have been two APSCON conventions, a Caxton Awards presentation to the Australian Advertising Industry in Cairns, and giving workshops at the Light of Australia convention in Sydney, alongside such icons as Helmut Newton, Art Kane and Jay Maisel. In recent years, Heide has held seminars for small groups and one-on-one workshops, at her home in Narooma.

Doug Spowart, M. Photog. Hon.FAIPP, FAIPP

Doug Spowart joined the Institute as a student in 1972 and became a full member in 1978. At that same, he became a member of the Queensland divisional council and was awarded the Queensland Pictorial Photographer of the Year. His awards from then on came thick and fast.

In 1983 he was awarded his Associateship, and won the Illustrative section of the national awards. In 1984 he was invited to be a judge for the national awards, a position he has held with distinction for many years. In 1990 he won the Ilford Trophy at the National Print Awards. In 1991 he again won this Trophy, adding to it the Athol Shmith Award for Black & White excellence. He was Queensland Professional Photographer of the Year in both 1991 and 1992 and was awarded his Master of Photography and was appointed National Chairman of the Awards between 1991 and 1998. In 1992, he was Queensland Illustrative, and Innovative Wedding, Photographer of the Year. With his mother Ruby, Doug opened the Imagery Gallery in Brisbane in 1980, a base from which they have launched many major talents, through participation in workshops and photographic tours.

Ruby Spowart, M. Photog. Hon.FAIPP, FAIPP

Ruby Spowart is a Master Photographer and the mother of Queensland photographer Doug Spowart.

With Doug, Ruby opened the Imagery Gallery in Brisbane in 1980, a base from which they have launched many major talents, through participation in workshops and photographic tours.

Ruby's work is in the National Library's Collection and has held numerous exhibitions of her work across Australia. Now in her mid 80s Ruby retains an active interest in photography.

Will Street, Hon. FAIPP

Will Street commenced professional photography on the Gold Coast, Queensland, in 1961, owning and operating various photographic studios there and in Brisbane until 1993 at which time he relinquished ownership of Selwyn Studios and became Queensland Director of Townsend Colour Laboratory.

He graduated with a Bachelor of Science degree from the University of Queensland in 1967 and in 1975 from six courses at Winona School of Professional Photography, U.S.A.

Will joined the Institute in 1971, serving as Queensland Divisional Secretary for seven years from 1977 - 1984.

He has also served as a judge at the Awards and served as national president in 1984 and 1985.

Dacre Stubbs, AAIPP Hon.FAIPP

Born in 1910 in Yorkshire England, Dacre first worked as a staff photographer for the British Broadcasting Corporation. On migrating to Australia in 1948, he began professionally photographing other migrants for the Department of Information. Following his success in this field he established a studio in Melbourne where he specialized in advertising and car photography.

Dacre also had a keen interest in anthropology and together with his wife Pauline, he contributed many articles to magazines such as Walkabout. He was also the author of the classic work Prehistoric Art of Australia which was first published in 1975. He died in 2001.

John Swainston, Hon.FAIPP

John Swainston has spent four decades in the photo imaging industry and has worked in Europe, the US, Australia and Asia. He is a past president of Photo Imaging Council of Australia and a recipient of the Photo Marketing Association International Distinguished Service Award. John has also served as vice chair of the Australian Centre for Photography.

For 25 years from 1979, he was responsible for Nikon distribution in Australia and hosted the annual Nikon Press Photographer of the Year Awards night for nearly twenty years. As Managing Director of Maxwell International Australia for the past six years, he has focused on lenses and accessory for digital products.

In 2009 he was appointed as Senior Vice President for Maxwell's parent company, DayMen Group Worldwide, in charge of DayMen's Asian sales. Today he spends as much time in Asia as Australia, servicing 22 national distributors and the top retailers in each country.

He has had a lifelong interest in strategic change, and the use of data to drive focused business decisions. Aside from being a keen photographer, John is also a Fellow of the Australian Institute of Management, New South Wales, and he is a regular speaker at photographic conventions in both Australia and overseas.

Bob van der Toorren, Hon. LM

In 1964, Bob van der Toorren was the first photography student to graduate with an associate diploma in photography illustrative from the Royal Melbourne Institute of Technology.

He launched his photography business in 1978 by setting up in Melbourne's Block Arcade and was one of the earliest photographers to take colour portraits and weddings. Nearly all the photographs were taken and printed in his own darkrooms.

With the advent of digital technology, his studio team, studied thoroughly, experimented, and is now one of Melbourne's finest photographic studio's for custom framing, passports, portraits, corporate and photographic restorations work.

Max Townsend, Hon. FAIPP

Max was the owner of Townsend Colortech, a wedding and portrait lab in Melbourne which had a major impact on professional photography from the 1960s.

Between 1973 and 1992, Max sponsored no fewer than 34 workshops and 47 seminars designed to help professional photographers improve the quality of their work and grow their business.

Aimed at wedding and portrait photographers, overseas names such as Monte Zucker, Leon Kennamer and Paul Yaffe were invited to show Australian photographers how to light and pose. While today we may look back on these techniques with a different view, at the time they were an essential part of Australia's maturation as a leading photographic force.

With Peter Foeden, Max Townsend was instrumental in starting the Canon Australian Professional Photographer of the Year Awards. Max had become a convert to the concept after seeing an Awards system in practice in the United States.

With his decades of emphasis on providing workshops and seminars, Max's favourite saying was, 'The cost of education will never be as expensive as the cost of ignorance.' Max Townsend died on 16 October 2007.

Michelle Tuddenham, Claude McCarthy Award

Born in Ballarat, Michelle majored in printmaking before taking up a position at the local Fletchers Fotographics. After a period as store manager, Michelle joined Canon Australia as an account manager and moved into professional imaging in 2004. In 2007, Michelle was promoted to Professional Imaging, National Account Manager. Her responsibilities included managing the wedding portrait segment, pro sales for Victoria, South Australia, and Western Australia, and specialist education. Michelle's role also includes managing Canon Professional Services at the Commonwealth Games and other high profile events.

For the Institute, Michelle's greatest achievement is maintaining a strong relationship between Canon and the Awards where she works behind the scenes to ensure its ongoing growth and success.

Ian van der Wolde, M. Photog. Fellow Hon.FAIPP

In 1984, Ian graduated from Melbourne's Photography Studies College with a Certificate of Illustrative Photography. Two years later he opened his own studio Altered Images and became a successful commercial photographer.

Ian joined the Institute in 1990 and became a member of the Victorian divisional council in 1995, before being elected Victorian president in 1998.

During very turbulent times Ian became National Treasurer in 1999, National Vice President in 2000 and national president in 2002. As president he implemented his vision to break down political barriers that existed at the time and he created an environment in which everyone could work more happily and productively together. After a two year term as national chair, Ian continued his involvement in the Institute at an executive level and is currently chair of Compliance and a member of the Honours and Commercial sub-committees.

Ian has assisted many photographers with colour management and has conducted numerous seminars Australia wide.

Eric Victor-Perdraut, M.Photog. Hon.FAIPP

Eric Victor - Perdraut was born in London but lived in France until he was 19. He came to Australia as a £10 immigrant in 1970. While at university he joined the uni camera club shooting some book covers for the University of Queensland Press.

A chance meeting with a Vogue Living editor lead to freelance work for the magazine and eventually full time work photographing audio-visuals with Martin Williams Films . His own business soon followed doing advertising and commercial work from the old Salvation Army hall in Paddington, Brisbane.

Eric Victor-Perdraut became an Australian Citizen in 1978 and is an AIPP Master of Photography. Eric has served the AIPP on both state and national levels, holding the positions of Queensland state president, national president, chair of the AIPP Board, and a member of the Institute's Honours and Ethics committee. During his time as National President Eric was instrumental in attracting major sponsorship for the Institute to strengthen the Institute and assure its position as Australia's premier association for professional photographers.

Eric was also an early adopter of digital technology and after addressing the APN News and Media board on the subject, the newspaper group decided to test it out in 1994. With the help of loan equipment from Kodak, Eric organised around thirty Institute photographers to shoot a special digital publication for the group called Dawn to Dusk in Toowoomba. The bid was successful and the paper predicted 'the domestic application of digital photographic technology will be widespread before the year 2000'.

Dr Les Walkling, FAIPP

Born in 1953, Les Walkling is an artist, educator and digital imaging consultant. In 1975 he studied science and philosophy at Monash University and in 1981 Les received an Australia Council Arts grant to study in the United States

Since then Les has exhibited widely, including the retrospective one-person show 'So to Live as to Dream' at the National Gallery of Victoria in 1990. His work is also represented in many public collections including The Center for Creative Photography, Arizona, The Metropolitan Museum of Art, New York, The National Gallery of Australia, Canberra, and The National Gallery of Victoria.

Les presented his first photography workshop in 1977 and has conducted regular digital photography courses since 1993 through the Centre for Contemporary Photography

His first university appointment was in 1983 as a lecturer in drawing, and subsequently in fine art photography and media arts history and theory. In 2011, Les took early retirement from RMIT in order to remove all administrative constraints from his research and practice.

In 2012 he was awarded the title Fellow of the Australian Institute of Professional Photography in recognition of his contribution to the worlds of professional photography and the help he gave photographers translating from film to pixels.

Michael Warshall, M.Photog. FAIPP

Russian born Michael Warshall graduated from the Royal Melbourne Institute of Technology during the 1970s. He aimed high and attained excellence and the goals he now teaches other to reach.

Michael is acknowledged both in Australia and overseas as an astute businessman and an excellent photographer and he is frequently requested as a speaker at local and international conventions.

At a young age he reached the status of Master of photography and has won numerous awards from both the USA and England. He has served on the Institute's Victorian Council and been an Awards judge.

Alan Waugh, Claude McCarthy Award

Alan Waugh has been a long serving member of the Tasmanian divisional council and was membership officer for more than two decades. As the proprietor of the film processing laboratory Photoforce, he provided processing services to Tasmanian photographers for 29 years before closing his lab in 2011. In recognition of his long term sponsorship of the Tasmanian division, Alan was presented with the Claude McCarthy Award in 2007.

Michael Wennrich, Hon.FAIPP

Michael Wennrich was a fashion and advertising photographer who became a lecturer at the Royal Melbourne Institute of Technology in 1972. In 1975, Michael became RMIT course coordinator and recognised his first challenge was to broaden the existing course from a purely photographic discipline to one in which his students as visual communicators used photography as a base discipline. Michael was also a photographic educator who managed to continue his former profession and thus lead his students by example.

James White, Hon.FAIPP

New Zealander James White got his first camera when he was 21. He went into business, photographing weddings, celebrations and dances and gained experience in all aspects of photography.

He served as president of the New Zealand Institute of Professional Photography and as chairman of its Honours Committee.

He represented New Zealand in the development of the relationship between the New Zealand and Australian Institutes and James became the first member of the New Zealand Institute of Professional Photography to become a Fellow of the Australian Institute of

Professional Photography. James is now deceased.

Richard White, M.Photog. FAIPP

Richard White has won more than forty awards in Victorian and national judgings , including the AIPP Victorian Landscape Photographer of the Year in 2003.

Richard exhibits regularly in Victorian galleries and in 2009 he presented an exhibition of his landscape photographs at the Wilderness Gallery at Cradle Mountain in Tasmania.

Richard White has actively championed photography as an art form, engaging the community through his many inspirational exhibitions and through his High Country calendars. He has shared his knowledge and philosophy over the past 15 years through regular articles in Better Photography, SilverShotz and other magazines. He is a frequent presenter and keynote speaker, he holds photography workshops at his home studio and darkroom in Mansfield, Victoria and leads tours around the country and overseas. Richard is a past president of the Victorian division, a Master of Photography, and he continues to contribute to the AIPP as an APPA judge and panel chair.

John Whitfield-King, FAIPP

A staunch advocate of black and white photography, John Whitfield-King was based in Western Australia, but his well printed prize winning photojournalistic work won him Australia wide recognition for his creativity. Never afraid to push the boundaries, his ground-breaking techniques were an inspiration to many of his peers.

His tragically early death led to the West Australian division introducing a special John Whitfield-King Memorial Award.

Lyn Whitfield-King, GM.Photog. FAIPP

In 1986, Lyn won her first Silver Award and in 1987 became an Associate of the AIPP. Lyn's mentor was the late, legendary John Whitfield-King, one of the profession's most innovative photographers. However, far from becoming a clone of John, Lyn developed her own unique style.

In 1993 Lyn became the first female Master of Photography before going on to become the Institute's first Grand Master. Lyn has won the portrait, wedding and photo-journalistic categories in West Australia and was the first woman to win the Ilford Trophy for the highest scoring print in the National Awards and went on to become the Institute's first Grand Master.

Her photography has taken her to Singapore, New Zealand, Hong Kong, India, England and Italy. She has shared her knowledge through numerous presentations and has contributed to this Institute regularly as an Awards judge.

Peter Whyte, AAIPP Hon.FAIPP

Peter founded Churchill Colour Laboratories in Subiaco, Western Australia in 1977. With his wife Lyn at his side, Peter built up Churchill Colour Laboratories into one of Australia's leading E6 and Cibachrome labs.

Peter was always available to help wherever possible and his technical knowledge was keenly sort out by many. Peter's great photographic passion was aerial photography and he designed and built several special purpose aerial cameras.

Peter had a keen interest in the Institute and in 1980 became the first West Australian to be elected as federal president.

Peter once said, 'Photography is unique, for I know of no other profession that attenuates all the senses to such a degree'. Peter is now deceased.

Bevan Williams, Hon.LM

Based in Western Australia, Bevan's photography covers everything from portrait to commercial work.

For his contribution to the West Australian division of the Institute, Bevan was made an honorary life member.

Max Williams, Hon.FAIPP

Max Williams was one of the founders of the Institute joining the Institute of Victorian Photographers in the mid 1950s. In 1960 he became the Association's youngest president in its 46 year history. Max explained, 'I wanted to be educated. I wanted to move alongside the photographers I admired. I could talk to Athol Shmith or John Warlow or anybody. They showed there was no black magic about photography.' In 1962 Max began a thirty year association with the Institute's Professional Photography Magazine with the Portrait Column. This was a pot pourri of critiques of readers' photographs and discussions on items of interest to the portrait and wedding photographer. Later it more frequently contained equipment reviews written from the viewpoint of a working photographer rather than a PR copywriter.

His writing style was an honest, straight-from-the shoulder approach. For instance: 'The overall impression of these prints could be compared to the three 'D's of the local art world; Dargic, Dobel and Deplorable.' Those falling into the Dargie School were flatteringly honest and straightforward. Those in the Dobel class showed some creative ability. The Deplorable could be compared to the Melbourne Moomba Art Show: flat prints, fuzzy prints, outdated poses and some so heavily coloured in oils in an effort, I suspect, to cover up poor technical ability.'

In terms of his commercial business, Max reached a pinnacle in the late sixties and early seventies working foremost in fashion, but with some PR work, a little architecture, a number of industrial assignments and studio still-lifes. At the same time he was writing, talking and preaching the gospel of craft in photography while trying to persuade manufacturers to better their products, Max served for a record continuous 25 years on the Victorian divisional council from 1967 to 1992.

Richard Woldendorp, AM M.Photog. Hon.LM, FAIPP

In 1927, Richard Woldendorp was born, in Utrecht, Holland and migrated to Australia in 1950. He began photography in 1956, initially on various projects in Indonesia. He became a professional photographer in 1961 after winning two prizes in the Craven-A national photography competition.

His work has been prolific and extensively collected in art and photography galleries around Australia and overseas. He was named Australian Photographer of the Year for his landscape photography and now specialises in photographing the Australian landscape from the air which has led to extensive travels throughout the country. His photographs have been exhibited in Australia and overseas. He was made a State Living Treasure for his contribution to the Arts and was made a Fellow of the Australian Institute of Professional Photography in 1991 and an Honorary Life Member in 1997.

He has provided photographs for and produced over 15 books.

Mike Wood, Hon.LM

A successful photographer and an excellent all rounder in the commercial world Mike spent eight years behind the scenes of the Awards where his painstaking attention to detail and passion for statistics proved of enormous benefit.

Mike also served as a state councillor and federal delegate for many years and in recognition of his Institute support was made an Honorary Life Member

Milton Wordley, M. Photog. FAIPP

Milton Wordley's early career as a photographer was as a photojournalist. He worked on many newspapers, including the Adelaide News, The Australian, the London Daily Express, the Australian Womens Weekly and the Bulletin.

Milton established Southlight Photo Agency in the early 1980's as a cooperative for freelance photographers.

Now working as a corporate advertising photographer, Milton pays tribute to the institute saying that the workshops, council activities and friendships have all helped broaden his approach to photography.

He was instrumental in conceiving and running the famous Barossa Weekends for many years, and most recently was a member of the AIPP Commercial Group.

Marie Young, Hon.LM

Marie Young played a key part in the development of the New South Wales division of the Institute at a critical time.

For her pivotal role, hard work, determination and dedication, Marie was awarded an Honorary Life Membership.

Yervant Zanazanian, GM. Photog. FAIPP

Born in Ethiopia and of Armenian origin, Yervant studied in Venice Italy for a number of years before moving to Australia in the mid seventies. Yervant is one of the pioneers of digital imaging in the wedding and portrait area and has won numerous awards, including the WPPI Most Innovative Photographer of the Year.

Teaching workshops in Melbourne, around Australia and recently in the United States, Yervant believes that this new trend needs to be adopted and embraced to keep growing in business.

Not content just to enhance the Australian industry, he has written software to offer this opportunity to photographers worldwide, enabling them to also be a positive part of this technology boom.

Mark Zed, Claude McCarthy Award

In 2017 the Institute's Honours Committee took the unusual step of presenting the Claude McCarthy Award for an outstanding contribution to the Institute to not one, but two people at the same time. They were Melinda Comerford and Mark Zed.

Melinda and Mark were co-chairs of the newly formed Awards Committee at a time of a controversial change in direction by the board. The duo worked tirelessly to build bridges and keep the AP-PAs strong through a difficult period. Their commitment ensured the APPAs continued to be a strong force.

Roll Of Institute Presidents

The organisation was first founded in 1912 with various degrees of State inclusivity. It was not until 1963 that the organisation unified all the states at the same time. Until 1991 all terms were from January to December, then after incorporation in 1991 the terms were changed to be from July 1 to June 30.

1963, '64,'65 '66 & 1967	Claude McCarthy (QLD)
1968 & 1969	Geoff Cummings (NSW)
1970, '71, '72 & 1973	Val Foreman (VIC)
1974 & 1975	Max Farrell (SA)
1976 & 1977	David McCarthy (QLD)
1978 & 1979	Ian McKenzie (VIC)
1980	Peter Whyte (WA)
1981	Norman Danvers (NSW)
1982 & 1983	Peter Foeden (VIC)
1984 & 1985	Will Street (QLD)
1986 & 1987	Robert Gray (QLD)
Jan 1988 – June 1991	Kevin O'Daly (SA)
July 1991 – June 1993	Malcolm Mathieson (NSW)
July 1993 – June 1995	Richard Bennett (TAS)
July 1995 – June 1997	Mark Fitz-Gerald (SA)
July 1970 – June 1999	Greg Hocking (WA)
July 1999 – May 2000	Marc Fenning (ACT)
May 2000 – June 2002	Eric Victor (QLD)
July 2002 – June 2004	Ian Van der Wolde (VIC)
July 2004 – June 2006	Philip Kuruvita (TAS)
2006 – 2008	Jackie Dean (NSW)
2008 – 2010	Alice Bennett (TAS)
2010 – 2012	Robert Edwards (NSW)

2012 – 2014	Kylie Lyons (NSW)
2014-2016	Ross Eason (QLD)
2016 -2018	Vittorio Natoli (WA)
2018 -	John Swainston (NSW)

Roll of Print Awards Chair Persons

1977 – 1983	Peter Foeden M.Photog. Hon.FAIPP FAIPP
1984 – 1986	Val Foreman Hon.FAIPP FAIPP
1984 – 1990	Ian Hawthorne M.Photog. Hon. FAIPP FAIPP
1991 – 1998	Doug Spowart M.Photog. Hon.FAIFP FAIPP
1999 – 2005	Richard Bennett M.Photog IV, Hon. FAIPP, FAIPP
2006 – 2009	Peter Eastway GM.Photog. Hon.FAIPP Hon.FNZIPP FAIPP
2010 – 2012	David Paterson M. Photographer and Hon LM
2012-2014	Kylie Lyons
2010 - 2015	David Paterson
2016 -	Tony Hewitt, M. Photog. FAIPP, HON. FAIPP

Chapter Ten

Then and Now

Some successful entries from the first Awards judging. Some of these photographers are still competing at the Awards and it is interesting to note the changes from 1977 to this selection of category winners from the last two years.

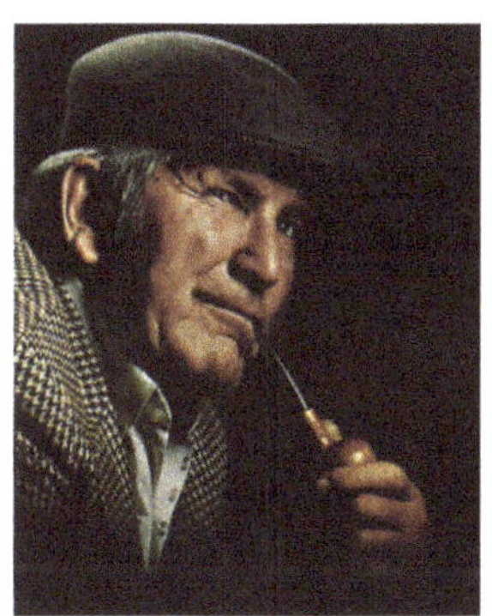

C.A. Lutz

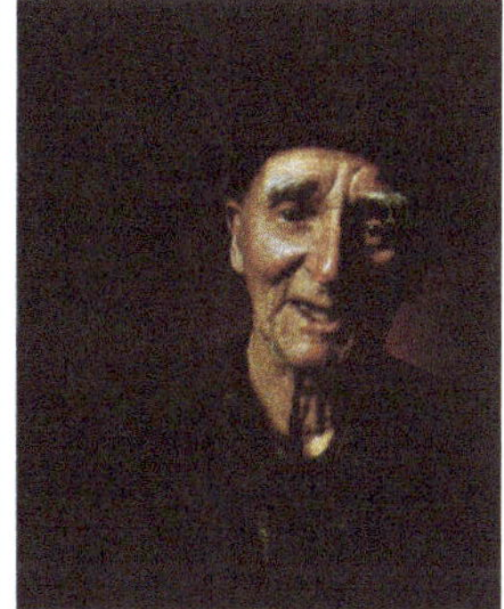

Robert Imhoff

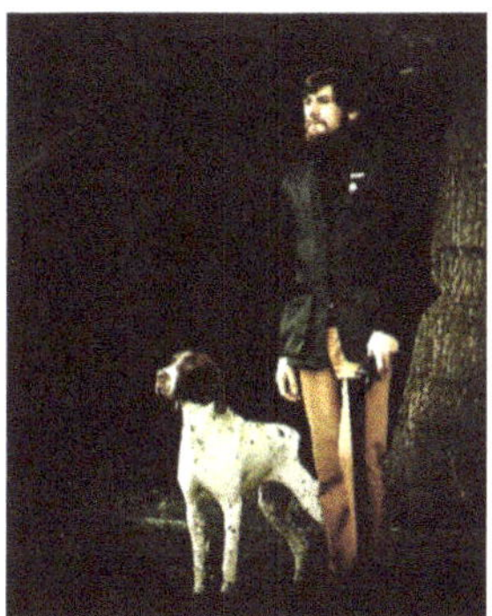

Richard Bennett

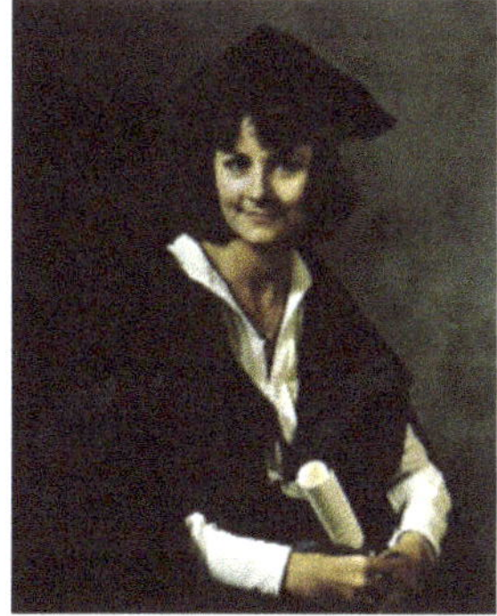

Jim Norton

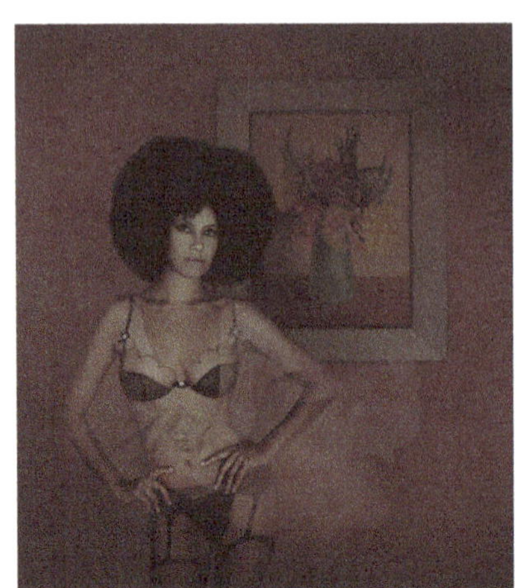

Sue Bryce

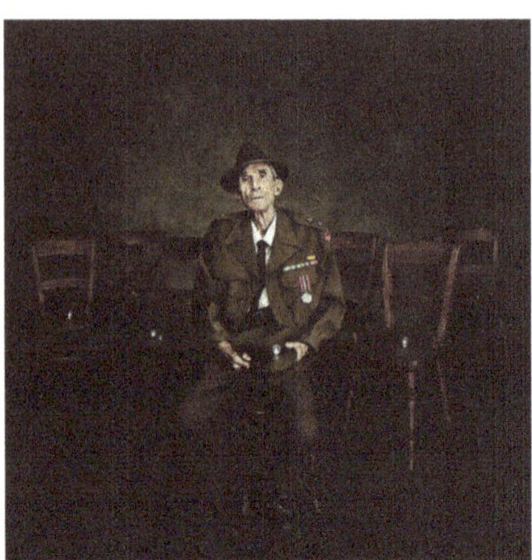

Peter Rossi

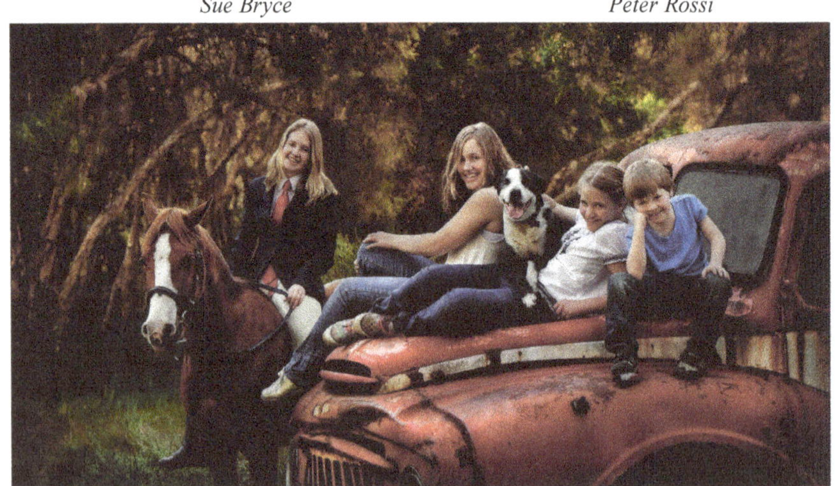

Jonelle Beveridge

Australia's Top Ten Iconic Photographs

After receiving nominations for Australia top ten iconic photographs from Institute and other photographers, the vote determined the following top ten presented here in date order:

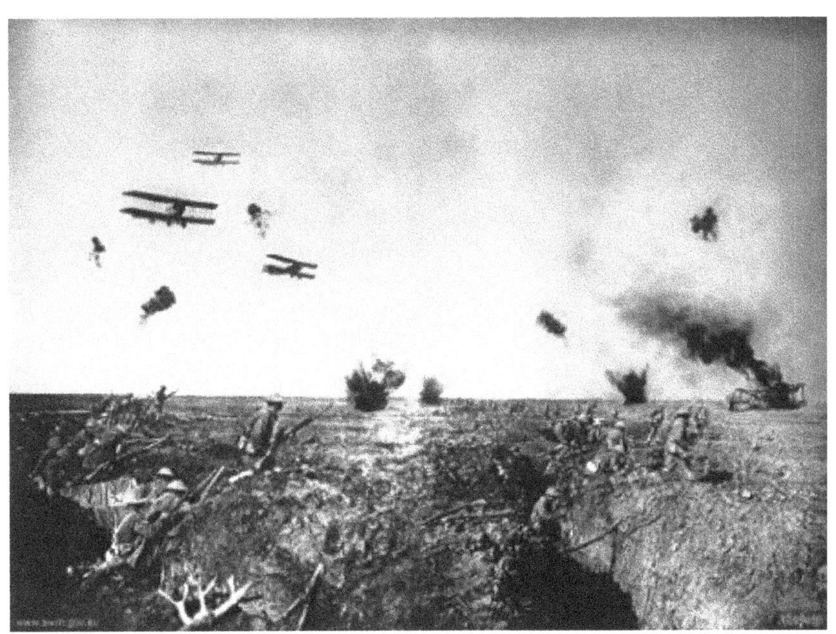

Frank Hurley Battle at Passchendaele 1917 (composite image)

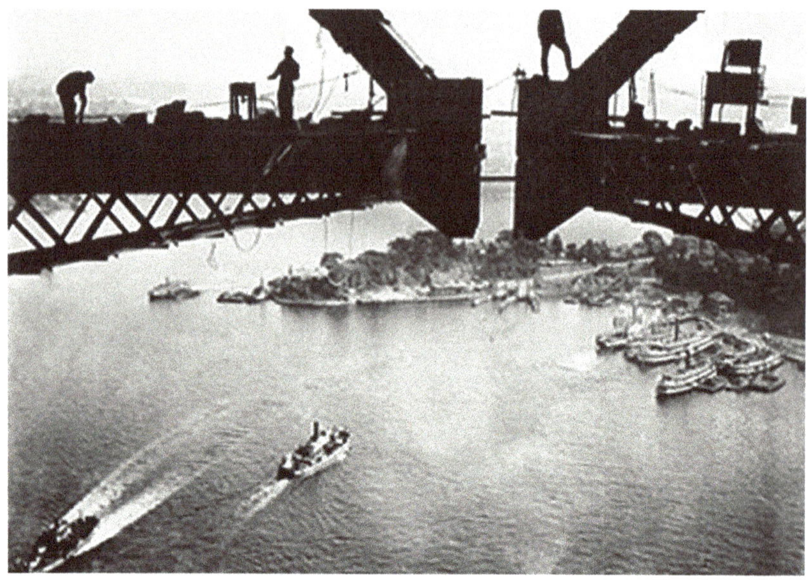

Henri Mallard Untitled Sydney Harbour Bridge (1932)

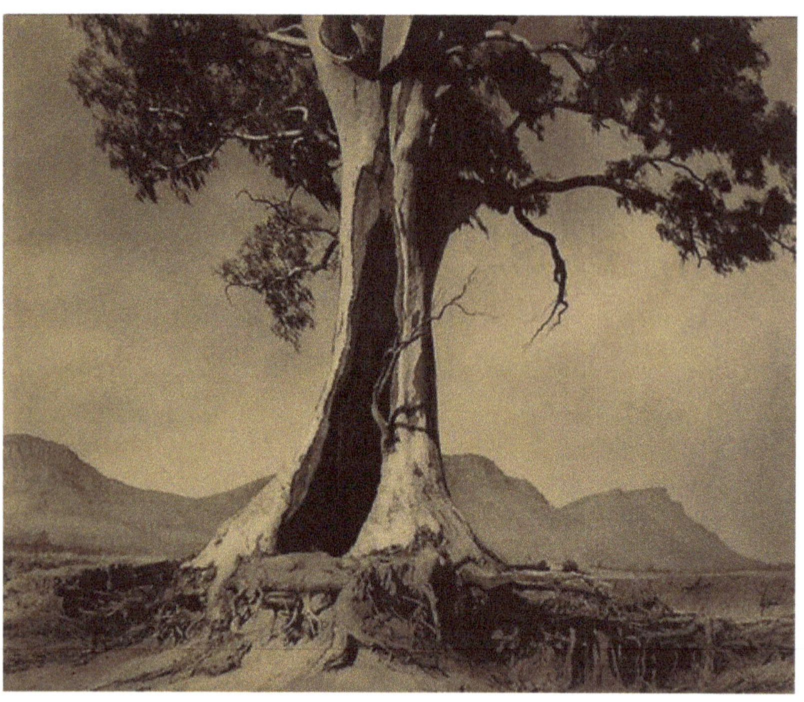

Harold Cazneaux Spirit of Endurance (1937)

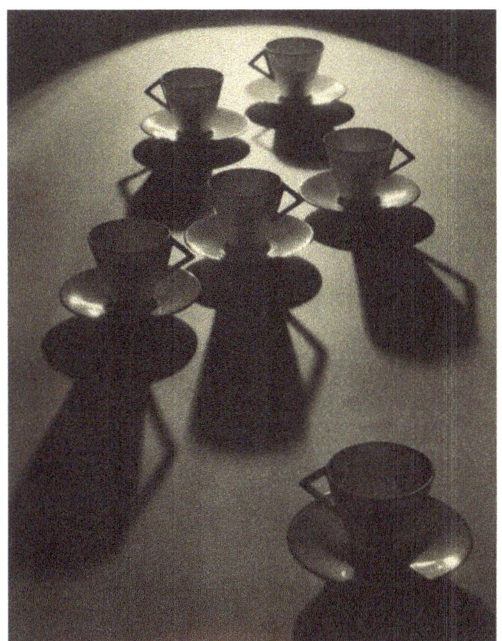

Olive Cotton Teacups Ballet (1935)

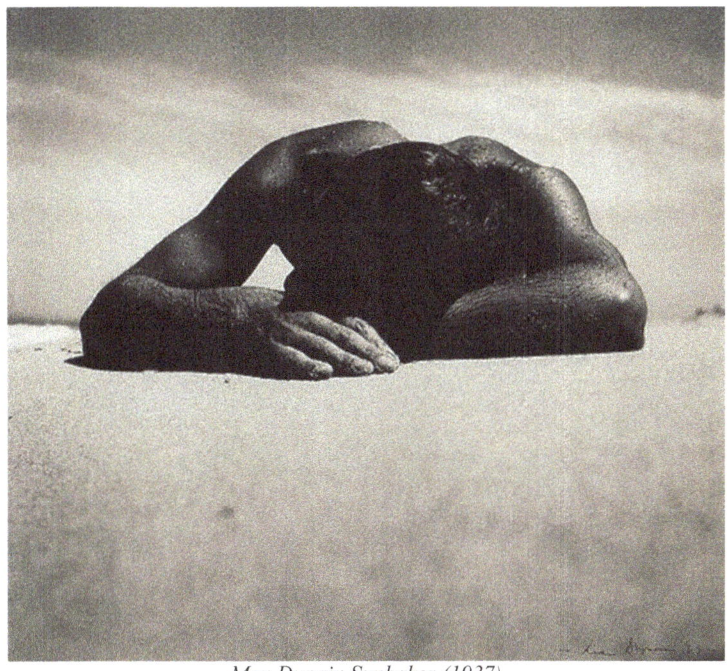

Max Dupain Sunbaker (1937)

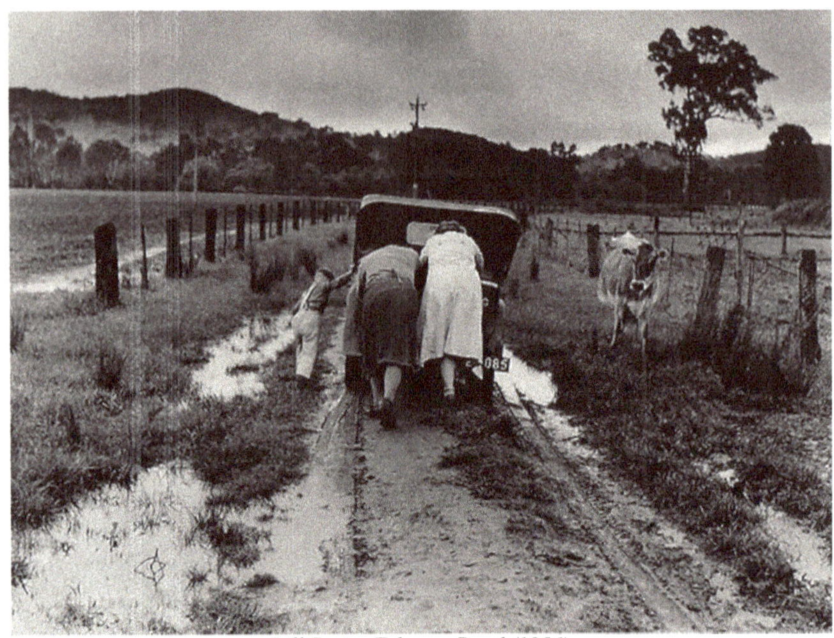

Jeff Carter Tobacco Road (1956)

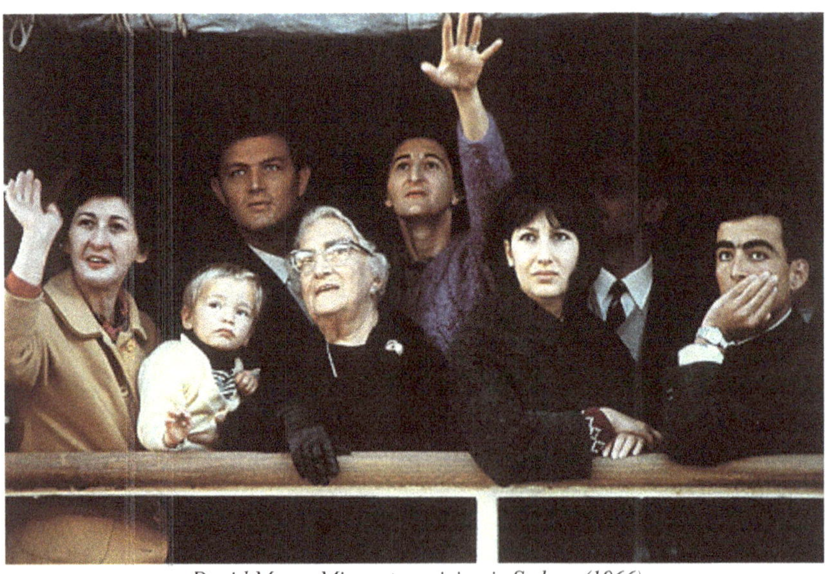

David Moore Migrants arriving in Sydney (1966)

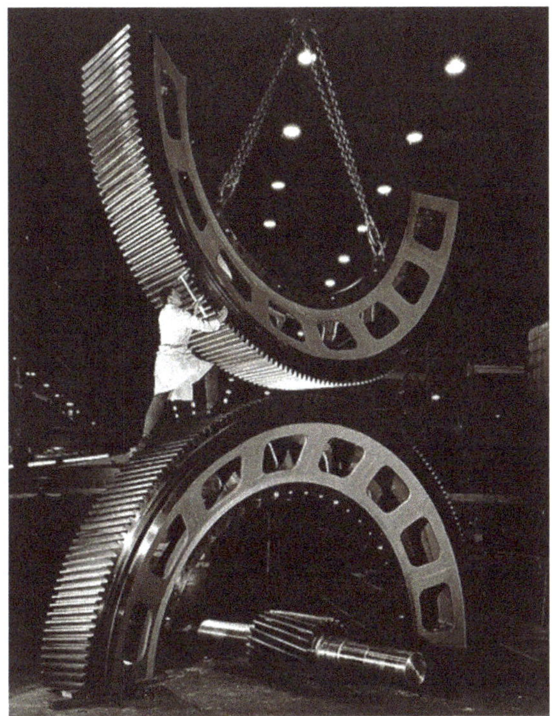

Wolfgang Sievers Gears for Mining Industry (1967)

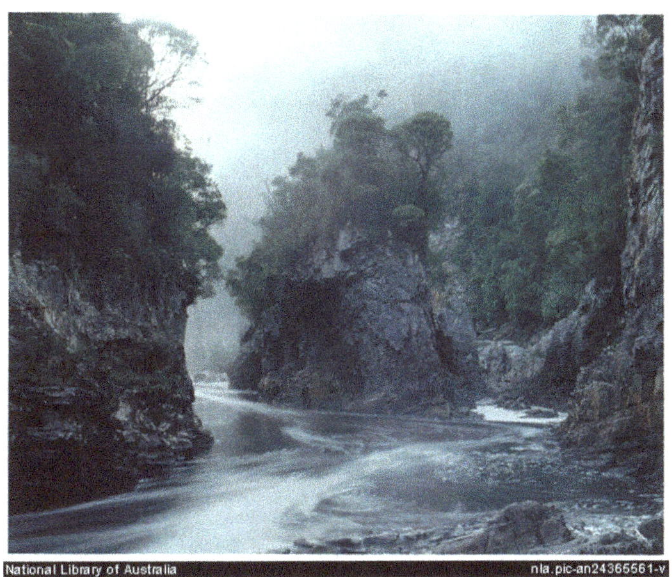

Peter Dombrovskis Morning Mist, Rock Island Bend (1979)

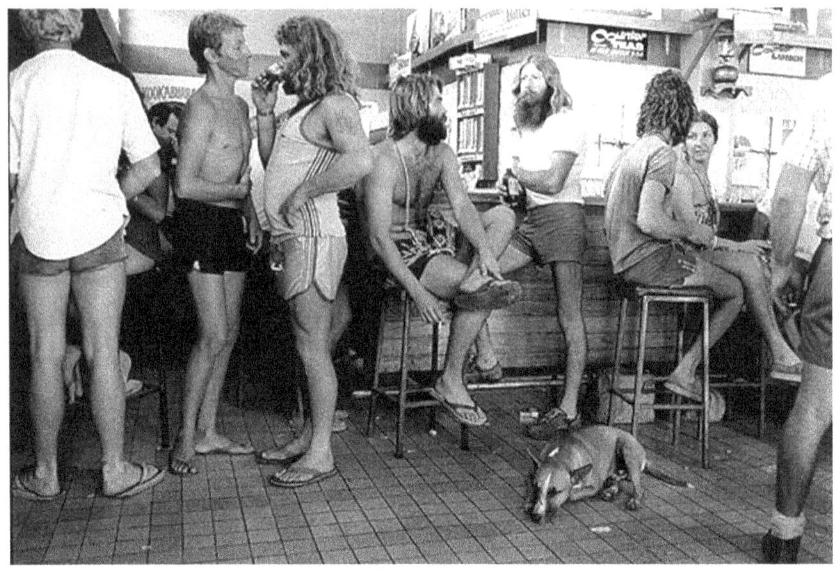

Rennie Ellis At the Pub 1982

Australia's Top Ten Iconic Photographs

The images reproduced here are as a result of our competition to find the top ten iconic photos and are intended only as a quick reminder of the original photographs. They in no way reflect the quality of the finished print. Max Dupain's Sunbaker reproductions can be purchased from the Art Gallery of New South Wales and for prints of the work of Rennie Eillis, visit www . rennieellis . com . au. The National Library of Australia and private galleries can also help with information on the other artists.

Acknowledgements

After Richard Bennett first approached me, filled me with red wine and got me to agree to writing this history, I began to wonder why me! In the end, I realised it was only because I've been around for a very long part of it! However, it would not have been possible to complete the project without the assistance of Ian McKenzie and David McCarthy. Their contribution has been outstanding.

Also helping as valuable fact checkers were Richard Bennett, Greg Hocking, Ian Van der Wolde, Eric Victor-Perdraut, Christine Chester, Jacqui Dean, Sandie Barrie, Peter Foeden, Rob Gray, Mark Fitz-Gerald, Kevin O'Daly, Robert Edwards and Kylie Lyons.

I also received valuable help from Peter Adams, Stephen Jones, Heide Smith, Rick Sherwin, Philip Kuruvita, Stan Kessanis, David O'Sullivan, Steve Packer, John Koens, Peter Rattray, John Swainston, Malcolm Mathieson, John de Rooy, Ian Poole and in particular, Margaret Curtis.

From the Institute's head office I received particular help from Randal Armstrong, Peta Maskell, and Peter Myers and of course, our very hard working design artist for this book, Kashifa De Antonis.

Much of the research material was drawn from the profession's publications and this book would have been in no way possible without the enormous assistance I received from Paul Burrows and Peter Eastway. I have freely borrowed from their writings, together with those of my former colleagues Neil Murray, Max Williams and Stuart Tomkins.

I have also been helped by the writings of Keith Shipton, Marc Gafen, Ian Hawthorne, David Paterson, Ian McKenzie and Jack Cato. Where I have used phraseology not my own, I have endeavoured to give credit. However, in some instance, such as in the Who's Who listing, the editing the format required has been so drastic that the original writer might be very keen to deny having any part of it!

So you would like to think that with these people helping me, I had got everything right! But any errors that have crept in are all my own work!

Compiling this history has been an interesting journey but also a bit of a nightmare! As I have mainly traced the happenings of the day through the records kept at the Institute's head office, the story is biased towards national presidents of the day and the board's outcomes rather than the forces at work by the various state representatives that served on these boards. This tends to give the impression that not much was happing in the States and this is certainly not the case. In fact each individual state is worthy of a book of its own. Then such stories as William Long's twenty years involvement in Queensland and Perth's Rob Baxter's return to his 30 year old career could be told.

Equally not included, but not forgotten is the tremendous support the Institute has received from various members of the trade suppliers. The role of trade support has been crucial to the success of the profession.

To all those that have contributed so much to the profession over the years but failed to get mentioned here, please accept my apologies for this book's format constraints. In these days of short run printing and possible e-book publication, second editions are relatively simple. Do not hesitate to email me if you have corrections or comments for any possible future edition. My email is paul@ paulcurtis.com.au

Paul Curtis
Sydney 2013

Where does inspiration come from?

The Impressionists, The Heidelberg School and The Brushmen of the Bush all discovered the secret was to get together, share experiences and inspire each other to new levels of creativity. And so it is with photographers.

The Australian Institute of Professional Photography is the creative hub that ensured the level of Australian artistry in photography is amongst the highest in the world.

Forget the claims of the camera manufacturers. No matter how smart cameras become, it takes skill and inspiration to create a masterpiece.

This book is the story of how professional photographers struggled with technology, boom and bust cycles and the politics of the day to push themselves to new heights.

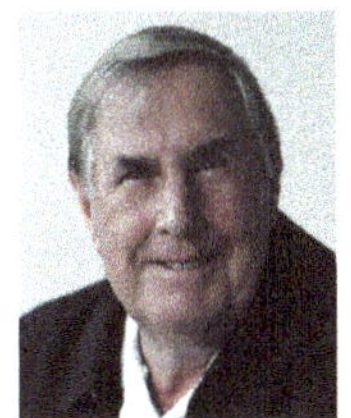

Paul Curtis
Photo: John de Rooy

Paul Curtis has been on the Australian photo scene as the long time organiser of the largest annual photo show in the Southern Hemisphere and as a photography and technology commentator in magazines, newspapers, radio and television for more than fifty years. He has a twisted sense of humour which makes this book both amusing and informative.